The Heart of
Christianity

Other Books by Marcus J. Borg:

The God We Never Knew
Jesus: A New Vision
The Meaning of Jesus (with N. T. Wright)
Meeting Jesus Again for the First Time
Reading the Bible Again for the First Time

The Heart of
Christianity

REDISCOVERING A LIFE OF FAITH

Marcus J. Borg

HarperOne
An Imprint of HarperCollins*Publishers*

HarperOne

THE HEART OF CHRISTIANITY: *Rediscovering a Life of Faith.* Copyright © 2003 by Marcus J. Borg. All rights reserved. Printed in the United States of America. No part of this book may be used or reproduced in any manner whatsoever without written permission except in the case of brief quotations embodied in critical articles and reviews. For information address HarperCollins Publishers, 10 East 53rd Street, New York, NY 10022.

HarperCollins books may be purchased for educational, business, or sales promotional use. For information please write: Special Markets Department, HarperCollins Publishers, 10 East 53rd Street, New York, NY 10022.

HarperCollins Web site: http://www.harpercollins.com

HarperCollins®, 📖 ®, and HarperOne™ are trademarks of HarperCollins Publishers.

FIRST HARPERCOLLINS PAPERBACK EDITION PUBLISHED IN 2004

Designed by Kris Tobiassen

Library of Congress Cataloging-in-Publication Data

Borg, Marcus J.
    The heart of Christianity : rediscovering a life of faith / Marcus J. Borg.—1st ed.
        p.   cm.
    Includes bibliographical references and index.
    ISBN: 978-0-06-073068-0
    1. Theology, Doctrinal—Popular works. I. Title.
BY77.B72   2003
230—dc21   2003050813

        14   15   16   RRD(C)   30   29   28   27

For Ike and Beechie Kampmann

of San Antonio and Houston, Texas,
and their commitment to progressive Christianity

"Do you still not perceive or understand? . . .
Do you have eyes, and fail to see? Do you
have ears, and fail to hear?" (Mark 8:17–18)

Contents

PREFACE What Does It Mean to Be Christian Today? xi

ONE The Heart of Christianity in a Time of Change 1

Part One: Seeing the Christian Tradition Again

TWO Faith The Way of the Heart 25

THREE The Bible The Heart of the Tradition 43

FOUR God The Heart of Reality 61

FIVE Jesus The Heart of God 80

Part Two: Seeing the Christian Life Again

SIX Born Again A New Heart 103

SEVEN The Kingdom of God The Heart of Justice 126

EIGHT Thin Places Opening the Heart 149

NINE Sin and Salvation Transforming the Heart 164

TEN The Heart of the Matter Practice 187

ELEVEN Heart and Home Being Christian in an
Age of Pluralism 207

Index 227

What Does It Mean to Be Christian Today?

What is the heart of Christianity? What does it mean to be Christian today? In this book, I describe two quite different answers to this question. The first is an earlier vision of Christianity; the second, an emerging vision. Both are present in the churches of North America today, deeply dividing Christians. We live in a time of conflict and change in the church.

I write with both conviction and passion. The conviction: Christianity makes sense. In my own life, this conviction took time to develop. For about twenty years, from my mid-teens to mid-thirties, Christianity did not make much sense to me. Largely for intellectual reasons, the form of Christianity that I learned in my childhood ceased to be persuasive.

For some time now I have been convinced that there are no serious intellectual obstacles to being Christian. There is a way of seeing Christianity that makes persuasive and compelling sense of life in the broadest sense—a way of seeing reality and our lives in relationship to what is real; a way of seeing God, our relationship to God, and the path of transformation. The sacrifice that Christianity asks of us is not ultimately a sacrifice of the intellect.

The passion: to communicate this way of seeing to those for whom an earlier understanding of Christianity makes little or no sense. They number in the millions. Some have left the church, becoming part of what Episcopal bishop John Shelby Spong aptly calls the "church alumni/ae association." Others remain within the church but struggle with the beliefs they learned in childhood—they either think they should believe them, or they reject them without having anything to put in their place. And some, especially many under forty, have never been very involved in the church and find little in Christianity that attracts them, but often are hungry for a source of meaning and values.

For the past few centuries, this earlier way of seeing Christianity, what I call an "earlier paradigm," has been shared in common by most Christians in Western culture. It remains a major voice within North American Christianity, perhaps still the majority voice. As I explain more fully in Chapter 1, this earlier way of being Christian views the Bible as the unique revelation of God, emphasizes its literal meaning, and sees the Christian life as centered in believing now for the sake of salvation later—believing in God, the Bible, and Jesus as the way to heaven. Typically, it has also seen Christianity as the only true religion.

The second way of seeing Christianity, the "emerging paradigm," has been developing for over a hundred years and has recently become a major grass-roots movement within mainline denominations. Positively, it is the product of Christianity's encounter with the modern and postmodern world, including science, historical scholarship, religious pluralism, and cultural diversity. Less positively, it is the product of our awareness of how Christianity has contributed to racism, sexism, nationalism, exclusivism, and other harmful ideologies.

This book seeks to describe this emerging way of seeing Christianity. It is written primarily for people for whom the earlier vision of Christianity no longer works. In this time of change and conflict within the church, what is the heart of Christianity? What is most central to an authentic Christianity and Christian life today?

This book is personal in more than one sense. On the one hand, it comes out of my own Christian journey. I have lived through the changes I describe, and over the years a persuasive and compelling vision of Christianity has emerged in my own life.

On the other hand, it comes out of my experience of lecturing to more than two hundred Christian groups throughout North America over the past decade. Initially, because I was known as a historical Jesus scholar, I was invited to lecture about Jesus. But, not surprisingly, my audiences were interested not only in what historians were saying about Jesus, but how this connected with larger questions of the Christian life: God, faith, the Bible, biblical authority, atonement, resurrection, the creed, prayer, ethics, Christianity and other religions, and so forth. Their interest in Jesus was part of a larger interest in the meaning of Christianity itself.

Learning from my audiences, I have increasingly over the years been addressing these larger questions. The experience has been both educational and encouraging. It has been educational in that I have learned which issues are most central in the struggle to move from an earlier and unpersuasive vision of Christianity to one that satisfies both head and heart. It has been encouraging as I have become aware of the large appetite for a different way of seeing Christianity, one that takes seriously both the Christian tradition and who we have become. I am also encouraged that the vision I describe strikes a responsive chord among many. If it did not, I would consider myself idiosyncratic and simply riding my own hobbyhorse.

Because in this book I describe a way of viewing Christianity "as a whole," its content overlaps topics I have treated in books about Jesus, God, and the Bible. Here I seek to integrate what I have said elsewhere with new material into a way of seeing the "heart" of Christianity—what is most central to Christianity and the Christian life. When I treat topics I have treated before, I have sought to do so in a fresh way, even though there is basic continuity with my fuller treatment in previous books.

And I have given myself permission to say, "This is how I see things." Of course, this is true of any book any of us might write. But I also mean that this book is the cumulative product of what I have thus far been able to formulate about the "heart of Christianity"—what Christianity and the Christian way of life are about.

It integrates scholarship, experience, and memory. Though it reflects my study of Christianity and religion over the years, it is equally based on my experience of life in general and of being Christian in particular. To state the obvious, how we see is to a large extent the product of what we have seen.

It is also based on my memory of things I have read or heard that have stayed with me, even though I was not "doing research" at the time. Thus at times I have not been able to specify the source of a statement and have needed to say, along with the author of the New Testament letter to the Hebrews, as "someone has testified somewhere" (Heb. 2:6a). Always nice to have a biblical precedent.

My hope is that this integration of study, experience, and memory may be helpful to people seeking to understand what is going on in the church in North America today and seeking to deepen their own understanding of Christianity and the Christian life. To use words I owe to my wife, Marianne, this is a book "for lovers of faith and those seeking a faith to love."

There are many people to thank for the process that has made this book possible, more than I can name. I have spoken about its themes in scores of church groups around the country, summer-school courses at Hartford Theological Seminary in Connecticut and the Graduate Theological Union in California, and at Ring Lake Ranch in Wyoming. I have learned from their responses and questions.

I also wish to thank my colleagues in the Philosophy Department at Oregon State University. They have been very supportive of my work of writing and lecturing beyond the university. In particular, I want to thank Dr. Judy Ringle, whose able assistance with my classes and correspondence creates for me additional amounts of that most valuable commodity, time.

And I wish to thank several people involved in the production of this book: my editor, John Loudon, and his assistant, Kris Ashley; my production editor, Lisa Zuniga; my designer, Kris Tobiassen, and my copyeditor, Ann Moru. Their efficiency, helpfulness, and good judgment are much appreciated.

Finally, this book is dedicated to Ike and Beechie Kampmann of San Antonio and Houston, Texas. Ike is a lawyer and churchman, and he and Beechie are committed to the spread of progressive Christianity in the church in North America in our time. I thank them for their support of my work.

The Heart of
Christianity

ONE

The Heart of Christianity in a Time of Change

What is the "heart" of Christianity? What is most central to Christianity and to being Christian?

The question arises in each new period of Christian history. It is especially important in our time. A new way of seeing Christianity and what it means to be Christian is emerging in the church in North America. Because this vision of Christianity is quite different from the dominant way of seeing Christianity over the past few hundred years, our time is also a time of conflict. In our context of change and conflict, what is Christianity's "heart"?

Like all good metaphors, *heart* has more than one nuance of meaning. To begin with, it suggests what is most central. What is the core of Christianity, the "heart of the matter"? What is the essence of Christianity and the Christian life?

If "core" and "essence" suggest something too abstract, too lifeless, *heart* is also an organic metaphor, suggesting something alive, pulsating, the source of life. What is the heart, the animating source or driving force, of Christianity without which it would cease to live?

Furthermore, as in the phrase "head and heart," *heart* suggests something deeper than the intellect and the world of ideas. What is it about Christianity that is deeper than any particular set of Christian ideas and beliefs? And what is it about Christianity that reaches us at our "heart" level—at a level of ourselves deeper than the intellect? The heart, this deeper level of the self, is the "place" of transformation. What is it about Christianity that gives it power to transform people at the "heart" level?

A Time of Change and Conflict

Christians in North America today are deeply divided about the heart of Christianity. We live in a time of major conflict in the church. Millions of Christians are embracing an emerging way of seeing Christianity's heart. Millions of other Christians continue to embrace an earlier vision of Christianity, often insistently defending it as "traditional" Christianity and as the only legitimate way of being Christian.

I have struggled with what to call these two ways of being Christian and have settled on the "earlier" and "emerging" ways of being Christian. What I mean by these terms will become clear in this chapter.

The familiar labels of "conservative" and "liberal" do not work very well, because both are imprecise. "Conservative" covers a spectrum ranging from Jerry Falwell and Pat Robertson to C. S. Lewis to (perhaps) Karl Barth.[1] The latter two would find the first two to be strange bedfellows. "Liberal" can be applied to a range of Christians from those with a strong sense of the reality of God and a deep commitment to the Christian tradition to advocates of a nontheistic Christianity for whom "tradition" is a negative term. Thus "conservative" and "liberal" don't tell us very much.

Moreover, there is much about the emerging way of being Christian that is conservative and traditional: it conserves the tradition by recovering it and envisioning it afresh. And there is much about the earlier way of being Christian that is innovative: its most distinctive features are largely the product of the last few hundred years. Indeed, both are modern products, as we shall see later in this chapter. Neither can claim to be *the* Christian tradition. Both are ways of seeing the tradition.

The differences between the earlier and emerging ways of seeing Christianity and being Christian involve specific conflicts as well as more foundational issues. These include how to see the Bible, God, Jesus, faith, and the Christian life.

To begin with, examples of specific issues that divide the contemporary church:

- **Ordination of women:** The earlier way of being Christian did not ordain women, and in many circles still does not. The emerging way does. Within mainline Protestant churches, the number of women clergy (including bishops) is rapidly increasing. Indeed, in many mainline seminaries, half or more of the students are women.

- **Gays and lesbians:** The earlier form of Christianity continues to regard homosexual behavior as sinful. Within it, the only options for homosexual Christians are celibacy or conversion to heterosexuality. For the emerging form of Christianity, the question of whether sexually active gays and lesbians can be Christians is mostly settled. The debate now is whether gays and lesbians in committed relationships can be married (or the equivalent) and whether they can be ordained as clergy, a debate virtually unimaginable a few decades ago.

- **Christian exclusivism:** Is there only one true religion, one path to salvation? Or are there several true religions, several paths to salvation? The earlier way of being Christian was (and is) confident that Christianity is the "only way." Now that is beginning to change. In a poll taken in 2002 in the United States, only 17 percent of the respondents affirmed the statement, "My religion is the only true religion." Most of these are in churches that affirm the earlier way of being Christian. But 78 percent did not, and this is typical of the emerging form of Christianity.[2]

Beneath these specific differences is conflict about more foundational matters, including especially how to see the Bible and its authority. For the earlier way of being Christian, the Bible is seen as the revealed will of God, as "God's truth," and thus as absolute and unchangeable. The changes listed above challenge passages in the Bible that (1) teach the subordination of women and forbid them to have authority over men, (2) declare homosexual behavior to be sinful, and (3) proclaim Jesus as the only way to salvation. To regard these passages as not expressing God's will for all time implies a very different understanding of the Bible's authority and interpretation.

Here too there is statistical evidence of significant change. In a Gallup Poll taken in the United States in 1963, almost two-thirds (65 percent) agreed with a statement affirming biblical literalism: "The Bible is the actual word of God and is to be taken literally, word for word." Some forty years later, in 2001, this figure had dropped to 27 percent.[3] To state the obvious, biblical literalism is declining among Christians in North America. The emerging way of being Christian welcomes this development, whereas the earlier way of being Christian views it as an abandonment of traditional Christianity.

So significant is this time of change and conflict in North American Christianity that some observers speak of a "new reformation" in our time comparable in importance to the Protestant Reformation of the sixteenth century. Though it is an overstatement, even overstatements can contain truth: we are living in a time of major change.

A Time of Paradigm Change

The name of this kind of change is *paradigm* change, to introduce a term central to understanding what is happening in the church today. A paradigm is *a comprehensive way of seeing,* a way of seeing a *"whole."*

Sometimes called a *gestalt,* a paradigm is a large interpretive framework that shapes how everything is seen, a way of constellating particulars into a whole. Our time of conflict is about more than specifics, for it concerns a change in how the Christian tradition and the Christian life are viewed *as a whole*.[4]

The history of astronomy provides an illuminating illustration of what is involved in a paradigm change. The sixteenth and seventeenth centuries saw a change from a Ptolemaic paradigm to a Copernican paradigm, each a way of picturing the solar system as a whole and the earth's place in it. The Ptolemaic paradigm (named after Ptolemy, an ancient Greek astronomer) was dominant in Western science for about fifteen hundred years. A geocentric, or earth-centered, paradigm, it sought to understand the motion of the planets and stars in relationship to a stationary earth at the center. The Copernican paradigm is named after Nicholas Copernicus, a Polish monk and mathematician. In a book published in 1543, Copernicus argued for a heliocentric view of the solar system: the sun, not the earth, is at the center. It transformed the way the movement of the planets was seen, even as it also transformed our sense of our "place" in the universe.

Significantly, the change from a Ptolemaic to Copernican paradigm was not about a detail or two; it affected how the "whole" was seen. Both paradigms are ways of looking at the same phenomena (in this case, the solar system), *but the phenomena are seen differently*. The shift in how the "whole" was seen affected how all the details were seen.

So also in contemporary Christianity. The paradigm change is about how the "whole" of Christianity is viewed. The same "phenomena" are in view (God, the Bible, Jesus, the creeds, faith, and so forth), but *they are seen differently*. The analogy to what is happening in Christianity is not perfect, of course. Science proceeds by different rules than religion, and one may speak of the Copernican paradigm as "verified" and the Ptolemaic paradigm as "wrong." Such verification and falsification are not so readily possible in religion.

But the analogy does work in this way. Christians in North America are living in a time of paradigm change and conflict. The conflict is not about a few items of Christian theology or behavior, but between two comprehensive ways of seeing Christianity as a whole.

A Tale of Two Paradigms

Seeing the "heart of Christianity" as a whole involves two major elements. First, how is the *Christian tradition* seen? "Christian tradition" includes the Bible plus whatever elements in postbiblical tradition are considered normative—for most Christians, the creeds, and for many Christians, doctrinal statements from their own denominations. Second, how is the *Christian life* seen? What is most central to it? What is it about? Is it, for example, about believing and doing what we need in order to be saved? Or is it about something else?

The earlier paradigm's view of Christianity is very familiar. Most of us over age forty (and many younger) grew up with it. It has been the most common form of Christianity for the past few hundred years. Today, it is affirmed by fundamentalist, most conservative-evangelical, and many Pentecostal Christians. And because it dominates Christian television and radio, it is the most publicly visible vision of Christianity and the Christian life.

The emerging paradigm has been visible for well over a hundred years. In the last twenty to thirty years, it has become a major grassroots movement among both laity and clergy in "mainline" or "old mainline" Protestant denominations. These include the United Church of Christ, the Episcopal Church, the United Methodist Church, the Christian Church (Disciples of Christ), the Presbyterian Church USA, the American Baptist Convention, and the Evangelical Lutheran Church in America. The emerging paradigm is also present in the Catholic church.

Yet earlier-paradigm Christians are also found within mainline denominations. Some are insistent advocates of the earlier vision of Christianity and protest the movement of their denominations away from it. Others are not as insistent, but affirm the earlier paradigm because they grew up with it and it still makes sense to them, so they see no good reason to change. Still others remain within the earlier way of being Christian because they aren't aware of an alternative.

In some mainline denominations, emerging-paradigm Christians are in the majority. Others are about equally divided between these two ways of being Christian. The conflict thus exists within mainline denominations themselves. As already suggested, the difference is not simply about specific issues, but about much larger matters. The two paradigms are quite different visions of what it means to be Christian.

As I now describe these two ways of being Christian, I recognize that any short description will inevitably leave out much that matters. Yet there is value in seeking to understand what is common to each way of being Christian, a skeletal understanding, a bare-bones account of its structure and shape. Within each paradigm, the structure is fleshed out and comes alive in a myriad of ways. What I seek to describe here is the "meta-theology" of each paradigm, the framework that shapes its vision of Christianity and the Christian life.

The Earlier Paradigm:
Its Vision of the Christian Tradition

The earlier paradigm sees Christianity as grounded in divine authority. For most Protestants, divine authority resides in the Bible. For Catholics, it resides not only in the Bible but also in the teaching authority of the church, expressed especially clearly in the notion of papal infallibility.

Because of the importance of the Bible to both Protestants and Catholics, I will focus on the earlier paradigm's way of seeing and interpreting the Bible. As I do, I seek to describe something very familiar to most of us. Until recently, this was the impression created by growing up in the church, whether explicitly affirmed or implicitly conveyed.

The earlier paradigm sees the Bible as a divine product. For this paradigm, the Bible comes from God as no other book does. It is the unique revelation of God. This is the natural impression created by traditional Christian language about the Bible: it is the "Word of God" and "inspired by God." This is why the Bible is "sacred scripture": it comes from God. And this is why it has authority: as a divine product, it has a divine guarantee. Thus both its status as sacred scripture and its authority are grounded in its origin in God.

Viewing the Bible as a divine product with a divine guarantee exists in both harder and softer forms. The hard form leads to claims of biblical infallibility or inerrancy: everything in the Bible is the direct result of God's inspiration. Whatever it says—about the origin and early history of the earth, about God, about Jesus, about ethics and behavior—is "God's truth." The Bible tells us how God sees things. In effect, the hard form of infallibility understands the Christian claim "The Bible is the *Word* of God" to mean "The Bible is the *words* of God." In British scholar Karen Armstrong's memorable comment, it sees the Bible as a kind of holy encyclopedia in which one may look up information about God.[5]

The softer form of seeing the Bible as a divine product does not claim that every statement in the Bible is inerrant. Rather, it affirms that the Spirit of God guided the writers of scripture in such a way to prevent them from making any serious errors, namely, about anything that matters for our salvation. The softer form can thus allow for statements in the Bible that reflect an ancient worldview, including premodern "science" and archaic laws. But harder and softer forms agree that the Bible is true *because* it comes from God.[6] Origin and truth go together.

The earlier paradigm interprets the Bible literally. It emphasizes the literal-factual interpretation of the Bible. I use the combined word *literal-factual* because the earlier paradigm's literalism is to a large extent concerned with the factuality of the Bible.

Biblical infallibility and biblical literalism typically go together, but they are not intrinsically related. There is no necessary connection. God could speak infallibly in the language of poetry, metaphor, and myth. We have no reason to think that God must be a literalist. But for the last few hundred years, they have been linked. Like the notion of infallibility, biblical literalism in the modern world exists in both harder and softer forms. The hard form insists upon the literal-factual interpretation of the whole of the Bible, including, for example, the Genesis account of creation and biblical stories that report spectacular events.

Softer forms of literalism are willing to grant that not all of the biblical stories are to be understood in a literal-factual way. For example, the six days of creation might be understood metaphorically, perhaps as geological epochs; and the story of Jonah spending three days in the belly of a big fish may be a parable rather than factual history.

But soft literalism affirms that the really important events in the Bible happened more or less as they are described. For example, the sea really did part in two to permit the Hebrew slaves to escape the Egyptians in the time of the exodus, Jesus really was born of a virgin, and he really did walk on water, multiply loaves, and so forth. The stories of "the spectacular" matter to both hard and soft literalism. Indeed, Christian literalism is to a large extent a literalism of the spectacular. For the earlier paradigm, "the miraculous" is central to the truth of Christianity.

Biblical literalism also typically affirms the absolute character of biblical teachings, both doctrinal and ethical. The Bible as the revealed will of God is the ultimate authority for both faith and morals. As such, it tells us what God wants us to believe and how God wants us to live. From this point of view, considering the teachings of the Bible as anything other than absolute leads to a "cafeteria" way of being Christian, in which we "pick and choose" the beliefs and ethical teachings we like.

For earlier-paradigm Christians in denominations that give a central place to the creeds, this way of seeing the Bible typically applies to the creeds as well. The creeds are understood as summaries of essential Christian doctrine. And, despite their manifestly metaphorical language, they are often understood literally, by both those who can say them and those who can't. For the earlier paradigm, to be Christian means to be able to say the creeds without crossing one's fingers or becoming silent during any of the phrases. To be Christian is to believe all of the statements of the creed to be factually true.

The Earlier Paradigm: Its Vision of the Christian Life

The earlier paradigm's vision of the Bible and the Christian tradition, whether in harder or softer forms, goes with a way of seeing the Christian life. Three features are particularly important.

Faith as believing is central. The reason is obvious: the earlier paradigm's way of seeing the Bible and the tradition is hard to believe, and that's why it takes faith. Of course, faith has always been central to Christianity, but, as I shall explain in Chapter 2, an emphasis upon faith as believing difficult things to be true is modern, the product of the last few hundred years. For the earlier paradigm, the Christian life is about more than believing, of course. It includes living in accord with those beliefs. But believing is its foundation.

The afterlife is central. For the earlier paradigm, the afterlife is central as both promise and motive. Ultimately, it is why one should be a Christian. In the form of the earlier paradigm that I had learned by the end of childhood, the promise of heaven and the specter of hell loomed large. Indeed, if you had been able to convince me at age twelve that there was no afterlife, I would have had no idea why I should be a Christian. That's how central it was. The earlier paradigm can also speak of transformation in this life, especially the importance of becoming more loving. But ultimately the really important question is: Where will you spend eternity?

The Christian life is about requirements and rewards. For the earlier paradigm, at the heart of Christianity is the dynamic of requirements and rewards. The main reward, of course, is a blessed afterlife. The notion of requirements flows directly out of this emphasis on the afterlife.

The logic is simple and to some people compelling. If there is a blessed afterlife, a heaven, it doesn't seem fair that everybody gets to go there regardless of what they have believed and how they have lived. So there must be something that differentiates those who do get to go to heaven from those who don't. For those unwilling to affirm a teaching known as double predestination (the belief that God predestines some to heaven and some to hell), the "something" that differentiates those who go to heaven from those who don't must be something that we believe or do. This commonsense conclusion turns Christianity into a religion of requirements and rewards.

For Christians living within the earlier paradigm, the minimum requirement is that one be a Christian. The Bible says "Jesus is the only way," and so they are skeptical that non-Christians can be saved. And for most, what it means to be a Christian must mean more than simply being baptized. Surely a mere ritual can't save you.

So one must be a "good" Christian. What that means is variously understood. Often within the earlier paradigm, it means believing central claims about Jesus: that he was the Son of God, born of a virgin; that he died for our sins and that God raised him physically and bodily from the dead; and that he will come again some day. And it means seeking to live in accord with the moral teachings of the Bible and seeking forgiveness when we fail. It means repentance and being right with God.

Of course, the earlier paradigm uses the language of God's grace and compassion and love, but its own internal logic turns being Christian into a life of requirement and rewards, thereby compromising the notion of grace. Indeed, it nullifies grace, for grace that has conditions attached is no longer grace.

In very compact form, the vision of the Bible and the Christian life that I have just described is the "meta-theology" that shapes the earlier paradigm. The elements are intertwined. Put most simply, it sees the Christian life as believing in Christianity now for the sake of salvation later. It sees the Bible as God's message of salvation (meaning a blessed afterlife), and sees the Christian life as believing in the message and seeking to live accordingly. And believing is the central requirement: it is *believing* that will save you.

A *Modern Product*: Modernity has deeply affected Christianity. By modernity, I mean Western cultural history since the Enlightenment of the seventeenth century, marked above all by the birth of modern science and scientific ways of knowing. With the Enlightenment as its foundation, modernity called into question both the divine origin and the literal-factual truth of many parts of the Bible.

Significantly, modernity has not only affected the forms of Christianity that have accepted it and sought to integrate it, but also the forms of Christianity that have strongly rejected it. In particular, the earlier paradigm is very much a product of modernity. Though it sounds like traditional Christianity to many people, including those who embrace it as well as those who reject it, it is important to realize that its central features are the product of the last few hundred years. To be specific:

- The notions of biblical infallibility and inerrancy first appeared in the 1600s, and became insistently affirmed by some Protestants only in the nineteenth and twentieth centuries. Papal infallibility was affirmed only in 1870.

- An emphasis upon the literal-factual interpretation of the Bible is also modern, a reaction to the Enlightenment. Prior to the Enlightenment, it was not the literal meaning of the Bible that mattered most for Christians, but its "more-than-literal" meaning, about which I shall soon say more. But the Enlightenment largely identified truth with factuality. In our time, if somebody asks, "Is that story true?" we are likely to assume that they're asking, "Is it factual? Did it happen?" Truth and factuality go hand in hand. And so for the earlier paradigm, defending the truth of the Bible meant defending its literal-factual truth.

- The notion that Christian faith means "belief" is modern, a theme to which I return in Chapter 2.

Thus the earlier paradigm is not "the Christian tradition," but a particular and relatively recent way of seeing the tradition, shaped by the conflict with modernity over the past few hundred years. No less than the emerging paradigm, it is a modern product.

Because it is no secret that I find the earlier paradigm less than compelling, I want to emphasize that it nourished the lives of millions of Christians for centuries. The Spirit of God has worked through it and continues to work through it. It has not only been a comfort to many, but has produced lives of love and compassion. I will say more about this later in this chapter. For now, I simply note that, for many in our time, its vision has ceased to be compelling.

The Emerging Paradigm: Its Vision of the
Christian Tradition and the Christian Life

The emerging paradigm has been visible for well over a century. Like the earlier paradigm, its central features are a response to the Enlightenment. Though the description is mine, the vision is not. This way of seeing Christianity is widely shared among theological and biblical scholars and increasingly among laity and clergy within mainline denominations. I seek to describe something that already exists, a development well under way.

Because the rest of this book is about the emerging paradigm, I here provide only a compact preview of its vision of the Bible and the Christian life, using five adjectives put into two phrases. The first three adjectives describe *a way of seeing the Bible* (and the Christian tradition as a whole): historical, metaphorical, and sacramental. The last two adjectives describe *a way of seeing the Christian life*: relational and transformational.

In Chapter 3 in particular, I explain more fully what I mean by the first three adjectives. To anticipate that briefly, a historical, metaphorical, and sacramental way of *seeing the Bible* (and the tradition as a whole) means the following:

- **Historical:** For the emerging paradigm, the Bible is the historical product of two ancient communities, ancient Israel and the early Christian movement. The Bible was not written to us or for us, but for the ancient communities that produced it. A historical approach emphasizes the illuminating power of interpreting these ancient documents in their ancient historical contexts.

- **Metaphorical:** The emerging paradigm sees the Bible metaphorically, by which I mean its "more-than-literal," "more-than-factual," meaning. It is not very much concerned with the historical factuality of the Bible's stories, but much more with their meanings. It is not bothered by the possibility that the stories of Jesus' birth and resurrection are metaphorical rather than literally factual accounts. It asks, "Whether it happened this way or not, what is this story saying? What meanings does it have for us?"

■ **Sacramental:** The emerging paradigm sees the Bible sacramentally, by which I mean the Bible's ability to mediate the sacred. A sacrament is something visible and physical whereby the Spirit becomes present to us. A sacrament is a means of grace, a vehicle or vessel for the Spirit.

Like the earlier paradigm, the emerging paradigm sees the Bible as sacred scripture, but *not* because it is a divine product. It is sacred in its *status* and *function*, but *not* in its *origin*. The point is not to believe in the Bible and the Christian tradition, but to live within them as a metaphor and sacrament of the sacred, as a means whereby the Spirit continues to speak to us today.

The emerging paradigm *sees the Christian life* as a life of relationship and transformation. Being Christian is not about meeting requirements for a future reward in an afterlife, and not very much about believing. Rather, the Christian life is about a relationship with God that transforms life in the present. To be Christian does not mean believing in Christianity, but a relationship with God lived within the Christian tradition as a metaphor and sacrament of the sacred.

To preview one more feature of the emerging paradigm: it affirms religious pluralism. In this paradigm Christianity is one of the world's great enduring religions, the response to the experience of God in our particular cultural stream. Yet the particularity of Christianity is not lost. It is important, as I will argue throughout and especially in the final chapter, to affirm the great value of the distinctiveness of the Christian tradition.

Summarizing the Differences Between the Paradigms

So different are these two views of Christianity that they almost produce two different religions, both using the same Bible and language. Our time of two paradigms is virtually a tale of two Christianities. To summarize the differences:

	Earlier Paradigm	Emerging Paradigm
The Bible's origin	A divine product with divine authority	A human response to God
Biblical interpretation	Literal-factual	Historical and metaphorical
The Bible's function	Revelation of doctrine and morals	Metaphorical and sacramental
Christian life emphasis	An afterlife and what to believe or do to be saved	Transformation in this life through relationship with God

The two ways of being Christian are often suspicious of, even hostile toward, each other. From the earlier paradigm's point of view, the emerging paradigm looks like a reduction of Christianity, a subtraction. Letting go of the notion that the Bible is a divine product seems to call its authority into question. Being relatively indifferent to whether the virgin birth and empty tomb are historical facts seems to call the divinity of Jesus and the wonder-working power of God into question. Letting go of the utter uniqueness of Jesus and the necessity of believing in him as the only way of salvation seems to call Christianity itself into question. Can one let go of any or all of this and still be Christian?

From the emerging paradigm's point of view, the earlier paradigm seems anti-intellectual and rigidly (but selectively) moralistic.

Its insistence on biblical literalism makes little sense, as does its rejection of science whenever it conflicts with literalism. Advocates of the emerging paradigm are particularly perplexed and often impatient with the earlier paradigm's subordination of women, its negative attitude toward gays and lesbians, and its preoccupation with conservative political issues rather than issues of justice. It seems to emphasize personal righteousness more than compassion and justice. And its exclusivism, its rejection of other religions as inadequate or worse, is unacceptable. How can it be that God is known in only one religion—and then perhaps only in the "right" form of that religion?[7]

Bridging the Differences

It is unfortunate that this division exists. These differences about the heart of Christianity are sharp, and they will be with us throughout the book. And because I often contrast these two ways of being Christian, it is important to emphasize potential ways of bridging the gap.

Christian Diversity: One element in a potential bridge is the recognition of Christian diversity. Historically and culturally, there are many ways of being Christian, many ways of interpreting Christianity and living the Christian life. The notion that there is one right way of being Christian is made impossible by thinking about the diverse configurations there have been in Christian history.

There are diverse forms and styles of Christian worship. They vary from Pentecostal enthusiasm at one end of the spectrum to Quaker silence at the other. In the middle are sacramental and liturgical forms of worship. To state the obvious, it's not that one of these forms of worship is right and the others wrong. They are simply different.

We can also perceive Christian diversity in the various cultural forms that Christianity has taken. To illustrate without seeking to be comprehensive: there is a second-century Syrian way of being Christian, an eighth-century Irish way, a twelfth-century Eastern Orthodox way, a fifteenth-century Chinese way, and a nineteenth-century Scandinavian Lutheran peasant way (to name my own heritage).

There is theological diversity as well. Without explaining the differences, there were, from the early days of Christianity, Arian and Athanasian Christians, Monophysite and non-Monophysite Christians, predestination and non-predestination Christians, infant-baptism and adult-baptism Christians. Christians have believed a wide variety of things. Being Christian therefore can't be about getting our beliefs "right," even though we have often acted that way.

The point is, there is no single right way of understanding Christianity and no single right way of being Christian. Of course, there are some wrong ways of being Christian, as when Christian language is used to legitimate hatred, the most obvious examples of which would be groups like the Ku Klux Klan and the White Aryan Nation. But there are many different and legitimate ways of seeing Christianity and being Christian.

This is the context in which to think about our time of conflict between an earlier paradigm and an emerging paradigm. It's not that one of these paradigms is right and the other wrong. Both are ways of being Christian.

What the Paradigms Share in Common: Despite their differences, the two paradigms share central convictions in common. The emerging paradigm, as I describe it, strongly affirms the reality of God, the centrality of the Bible, the centrality of Jesus, the importance of a relationship with God as known in Jesus, and our need (and the world's need) for transformation. To state the obvious, all of these matter to the earlier paradigm as well.

To underline one element of their commonality: both emphasize a relational vision of the Christian life. Though the earlier paradigm emphasizes believing, its devotees typically emphasize the importance of a personal relationship with God and Jesus. Of course, beliefs remain important to them: it's because they believe that the relationship matters. For many of them, believing has been the point of entry into the Christian life. But it seems clear that what energizes and nourishes their lives is the relationship with God mediated by the beliefs. The earlier paradigm "works" because of the relationship to which it leads.

The earlier paradigm has nourished and continues to nourish lives of deep devotion, faith, and love. The Spirit of God can and does work through it. It has for centuries and still does. When it leads to a strong sense of the reality and grace of God, to following Jesus, and to lives filled with compassion and a passion for justice, as it sometimes does, all one can say is, "Praise the Lord."

Yet for many, the beliefs that matter to the earlier paradigm create a lot of static. For millions, especially in North America and Europe, the earlier paradigm has become an obstacle. Thus it is important to realize that its vision of the Bible and the Christian life is but one way of seeing Christianity, and a modern one at that. A deepening relationship with God can be nourished by a different way of understanding the Bible and the Christian tradition.

So the issue isn't that one of these visions of Christianity is right and the other wrong. Rather, the issue is functionality, whether a paradigm "works" or "gets in the way." For millions, the earlier paradigm still works. And if it works for you—if it hasn't become an obstacle and if it genuinely nourishes your life with God and produces growth in compassion within you—there's no reason for you to change. Being Christian isn't about getting our beliefs (or our paradigm) "right."

But for millions of others, the earlier paradigm no longer works. Unpersuasive to them, it has become a stumbling block. What is the Christian message, the Christian gospel, for people who can't be literalists or exclusivists? What do we have to say to them? In an important sense, this is an issue of evangelism. For these millions, the emerging paradigm provides a way of taking Christianity and the Christian life seriously.

Conclusion:
An Unending Conversation

Articulating the heart of Christianity involves a "given" and a context. The "given" is the Christian tradition itself: the Bible, God, Jesus, the creeds, rituals, and so forth. We receive this from the past. The context is a cultural context—namely, the time and place in which we live and who we have become because of our context. The task of Christian theology is to interpret a "given," a received tradition, in a present cultural context. It has always been so.

Of course, the "given" cannot simply be conformed to the present; it must be allowed its own voice. But the "given" must from time to time be reformulated to speak to a changed cultural context. This has happened many times in Christianity's history. God may or may not be the same yesterday, today, and tomorrow, but the cultural context in which we speak about God does change.

To a large extent, the Christian tradition is constituted by language, by words. Of course, it also includes rituals and practices, but these also are a kind of language. The key question is: How are we to understand this language that comes to us from the past?

Discerning the heart of Christianity thus involves us in an "unending conversation." I owe the metaphor to Kenneth Burke, an American intellectual whose life spanned most of the twentieth century. Burke wrote primarily about language and culture and the relationship between the two—about the way in which culture is created by language. And history—what Burke calls the "drama of history"—is about the creation and re-creation of culture and communities through language. History is the product of what he calls the "unending conversation."

Where does the drama of history get its material? From the "unending conversation" that is going on at the point in history when we are born. Imagine that you enter a parlor. You come late. When you arrive, others have long preceded you, and they are engaged in a heated discussion, a discussion too heated for them to pause and tell you exactly what it is about. In fact, the discussion had already begun long before any of them got there, so that no one present is qualified to retrace for you all the steps that had gone before. You listen for a while; then you put in your oar. Someone answers; you answer him; another comes to your defense; another aligns himself against you, to either the embarrassment or gratification of your opponent, depending upon the quality of your ally's assistance. However, the discussion is interminable. The hour grows late, you must depart. And you do depart, with the discussion still vigorously in progress.[8]

So also being Christian involves us in an unending conversation—with the Bible, the Christian tradition, and each other.

Of course, being Christian is about more than "conversation." Other traditions sometimes joke about us poor "talky" Christians—always trying to get our "doctrines" right. Being Christian involves not just "talk," but the transformation of our lives. But it also involves discerning the heart of Christianity, and such discernment involves us in an unending conversation. Much of the conversation in our time is between the earlier paradigm and the emerging paradigm. The task is the ongoing construction of what it means to be Christian.

---

1. Karl Barth (1886–1968), one of the two most important Protestant theologians of the twentieth century, is associated with a movement known as neoorthodoxy. His books are brilliant and comprehensive; his multi-volume *Church Dogmatics* is about ten thousand pages long.

2. The poll was commissioned jointly by PBS's *Religion and Ethics Newsweekly* and *U.S. News and World Report,* and reported in *The Christian Century* (May 8–15, 2002): 16. It included 2002 adults.

3. For figures for 1963, see George Gallup Jr. and Jim Castelli, *The People's Religion* (New York: Macmillan, 1989), p. 61; and George Gallup Jr. and D. Michael Lindsay, *Surveying the Religious Landscape* (Harrisburg, PA: Morehouse, 1999), pp. 34–36. Figures for 2001 were reported in a news story in June 2001.

4. For the use of the notion of "paradigm" in recent theology, see especially Nancey Murphy, *Beyond Liberalism and Fundamentalism* (Harrisburg, PA: Trinity Press International, 1996); Hans Küng, *Theology for the Third Millennium,* trans. Peter Heinegg (New York: Doubleday, 1988); Garrett Green, *Imagining God* (San Francisco: Harper and Row, 1989). For a novel about a conservative-evangelical pastor moving from the earlier paradigm to a form of the emerging paradigm, see Brian McLaren, *A New Kind of Christian* (San Francisco: Jossey-Bass, 2001).

5. Karen Armstrong, in a lecture at Trinity Episcopal Cathedral in Portland, Oregon, in February 2002.

6. Catholics also understand papal infallibility in hard and soft forms. The hard form tends to see all papal pronouncements as "infallible." The soft form (which is actually the correct understanding) restricts papal infallibility to statements made *ex cathedra*, that is, statements in which the pope explicitly invokes infallibility. Since the doctrine of papal infallibility was affirmed in 1870 (it's very recent), there has been only one such pronouncement: the direct assumption of Mary into heaven, proclaimed in 1950. More broadly, the soft form of infallibility affirms that the church, in spite of its errors and checkered history, has been preserved from making fundamental mistakes that would threaten our salvation.

7. Those of my university students who have grown up outside of the church (about half of them) have a very negative stereotypical view of Christianity. When I ask them to write a short essay on their impression of Christianity, they consistently use five adjectives: Christians are literalistic, anti-intellectual, self-righteous, judgmental, and bigoted. The reason for their perception: they are familiar primarily with the most publicly visible form of Christianity in the United States, namely, the kind that one encounters in much of Christian radio and television, the kind they hear about from classmates who are trying to convert them to a conservative form of college Christianity, and the kind they see in Christian participation in the political Right. In short, what they are encountering is the earlier paradigm in its more extreme forms.

8. Kenneth Burke, *The Philosophy of Literary Form*, 3d ed. (Berkeley: University of California Press, 1973; originally published in 1941), pp. 110–11. I owe my acquaintance with Burke to one of my graduate students, Josh Beach.

Part One

Seeing the Christian Tradition Again

TWO

Faith
The Way of the Heart

On a recent plane trip, the woman sitting next to me said, "I'm much more interested in Buddhism and Sufism than I am in Christianity." When I asked why, she said, "Because they're about a way of life, and Christianity is all about believing." She continued, "I don't think beliefs matter nearly as much as having a spiritual path and following a way."

I understood her comment, even as I silently disagreed with part of it. To begin with the disagreement, Christianity *is* about a way of life, a path, and it has been from its very beginning. At the center of Jesus' own teaching is the notion of a "way" or a "path," and the first name of the early Christian movement was "the Way." Indeed, seeing Christianity as a "way" is one of the central features of the emerging paradigm.

Yet her statement reflects the most common understanding of the word "faith" in modern Western Christianity: that faith means holding a certain set of "beliefs," "believing" a set of statements to be true, whether cast as biblical teachings or doctrines or dogma. Indeed, this understanding of faith is central to the earlier paradigm. Most people today, in the church and outside of it, take it for granted that Christian faith means believing a set of Christian beliefs to be true.

There is more than one reason for this widespread understanding of faith as "belief." For now I simply want to underline how common the vocabulary of believing and belief is in contemporary Christianity. Christian faith means believing that there is a God, believing that the Bible is the revelation of God, and believing that Jesus is the Son of God and that he died for our sins.

For some Christians, the list would be longer: believing that the Bible is the inerrant Word of God, believing in Genesis rather than evolution; believing that Jesus was born of a virgin, that he walked on water and raised the dead, that he himself was raised from the dead in a physical bodily form, and that he will come again someday. Sometimes the beliefs become very specific: believing in infant baptism instead of adult baptism (or vice versa), believing in the "rapture," or believing (or not believing) in purgatory. Affirming the "right" set of beliefs matters to a good number of Christians.

But whether the list is short or long, the notion that Christian faith is about believing a set of claims to be true is very widespread. Indeed, in England, the word "believer" is a synonym for "Christian." "Are you a believer?" means "Are you a Christian?"

This preoccupation with "believing" and "beliefs" has a crucially important effect: it turns Christian faith into a "head matter." Faith becomes primarily a matter of *the beliefs in your head*—of whether you believe the right set of claims to be true.

Yet the twin notions that being Christian is about "believing" in Christianity and that faith is about "belief" are a modern development of the last few hundred years, as we shall soon see. Prior to the modern period, the most common Christian meanings of the word "faith" were not matters of the head, but matters of the heart. In the Bible and the Christian tradition, the "heart" is a metaphor for a deep level of the self, a level below our thinking, feeling, and willing, our intellect, emotions, and volition. The heart is thus deeper than our "head," deeper than our conscious self and the ideas we have in heads.[1] Faith concerns this deeper level of the self. Faith is the way of the heart, not the way of the head.

The virtual identification of faith with believing a set of statements is thus a serious impoverishment of the word "faith." The word has several rich meanings that we will explore in this chapter. To see faith as "belief" not only obscures the other meanings, but also distorts the notion of faith itself. Seeing the heart of Christianity requires recovering the rich meanings of faith, a recovery that leads to a relational understanding of faith and to an understanding of Christianity as a "way"—as the way of the heart.

The Centrality of Faith

Faith is at the heart of Christianity. Its centrality goes back to the New Testament. All but two of its twenty-seven books use the noun "faith" or the verb "believe."[2]

Moreover, the New Testament gives it crucial significance. Jesus spoke of it often, making statements such as "Your faith has made you well." For Paul, we are "justified"—that is, made right with God—"by grace through faith." In the eleventh chapter of Hebrews, the Jewish Bible becomes a story of faith. The author of Hebrews extols its heroes as having lived by faith: "By faith our ancestors received approval." Then follows a litany beginning with Abel: "By faith, Abel . . . By faith, Enoch . . . By faith, Noah . . . By faith, Abraham . . ." through Moses and unnamed people, climaxing with Jesus, "the pioneer and perfecter of our faith."

Probably the most widely known Bible verse emphasizes the importance of believing. To quote John 3:16 in the noninclusive language of the King James Bible that I learned as a child, "For God so loved the world that he gave his only begotten son, *that whosoever believeth in him* should not perish, but have everlasting life." And in the church of my childhood, every Sunday the absolution (the pronouncement of forgiveness) concluded with, "He *who believes* and is baptized shall be saved."

Though faith is important for all Christians, it is especially so for Protestants because of the centrality of "faith" in the Protestant

Reformation of the sixteenth century. Drawing upon Paul, the Reformation emphasized "justification by grace through faith," often shortened to "justification by faith." The same notion was expressed by "We are saved by faith, not works." Faith is what will save us.

Four Meanings of Faith

Thus faith is utterly central to the Christian life. But what does the word mean? In the history of Christianity, it has four primary meanings. The first of these is closest to faith as a "matter of the head." The remaining three all understand faith as a "matter of the heart." As I describe these four meanings, I name each with a Latin term in order to show its antiquity, even as I also name each in English. I then explain each relatively concisely, and also speak about the opposite of each, for seeing the opposite of a word is often illuminating.

Faith as *Assensus*

The meaning of the Latin word *assensus* is suggested by its closest English equivalent: "assent." This is faith as belief—that is, as giving one's mental assent to a proposition, as believing that a claim or statement is true. Sometimes called a propositional understanding of faith, it is the dominant meaning today, both within the church and outside it.

But this notion—that Christian faith is primarily about *assensus*, about belief, about a "head" matter—is recent, as I have briefly mentioned. It is illuminating to see how this happened. Two developments account for its dominance in modern Western Christianity.

The first is the Protestant Reformation, which not only emphasized faith, but also produced a number of new denominations. Each defined itself by distinguishing itself from other Protestants by what they "believed," that is, by their distinctive doctrines or confessions. Lutherans believed x, Presbyterians believed y, Baptists believed z, and so forth. Roman Catholics followed suit, distinguishing themselves by what they believed compared to what Protestants believed. Christian faith thus became believing the right things, having "right" beliefs instead of "wrong" beliefs.

This development changed the meaning of the word "orthodoxy." Before the sixteenth and seventeenth centuries, orthodoxy referred to "right worship" or "correct worship." If you did the liturgy right, the practice right, you were orthodox. Then, in the aftermath of the Reformation, orthodoxy began to mean "right belief" or "correct belief." And faith began to mean "believing the right things."[3]

The second development was the birth of modern science and scientific ways of knowing in the Enlightenment of the seventeenth century. The Enlightenment has pervasively shaped modern Western culture. Two of its effects are most important in our immediate context. On the one hand, as mentioned in Chapter 1, the Enlightenment identified truth with factuality: truth is that which can be verified as factual. Modern Western culture is the only culture in human history that has made this identification. On the other hand, the Enlightenment called into question the factuality of parts of the Bible and of many traditional Christian teachings

The effect on the meaning of "faith" and "believe" has been extraordinary. For many, Christian faith began to mean believing questionable things to be true—as assenting to the truth of claims that have become "iffy." According to a modern American dictionary, this is the most widespread contemporary understanding of "belief." Its first definition of "belief" is "an opinion or conviction." And then, as an example, it provides a mistaken belief, "the belief that the earth is flat."[4] Belief is about believing a notion contrary to evidence, contrary to what reasonable people know.

I find this understanding among my students. I ask them, "What do you understand the word 'believing' to mean? When do you use the word 'believe'"? Their most frequent response: "When you're not sure, or when you don't know." There are some things you know, and other things you're not sure about, and so you can only believe. Believing and knowing are contrasted. Faith is what you turn to when knowledge runs out. Even more strongly, faith is what you need when beliefs and knowledge conflict.

Thus, for many modern people, faith as *assensus* has become primary precisely because the central claims of Christianity have become

questionable. For many today, faith means believing in spite of difficulties, believing even when you have reasons to think otherwise. It
means believing "iffy" things to be true.

This is very different from what faith as *assensus* meant prior to
the modern period. Imagine for a moment what *assensus* meant in
Christian Europe in the Middle Ages. Most people took the truth of
Christianity and the Bible for granted. It was the conventional wisdom of the time. There was no conflict between Christianity and science. In that setting, faith as *assensus* was effortless, and the emphasis
was thus on the other meanings of faith, which we will soon consider.
Indeed, in the most common modern sense of the word "faith,"
accepting the Christian vision of the way things are didn't take faith.
But now, faith as *assensus* has become effortful.

The opposite of faith as *assensus* has both milder and stronger
forms. The milder form is doubt; the stronger form is disbelief. If
you have doubts, you don't have much faith. And disbelief is the
absence of faith. And if one thinks that "belief" is what God wants
from us, then doubt and disbelief are experienced as sinful. So it
was for me as an adolescent. I experienced my doubts and burgeon-
ing disbelief as sins and I prayed for forgiveness. Most often, I
ended my prayers with words from the gospel of Mark: "I believe;
help thou my unbelief."

This understanding of faith is very widespread, so pervasive that
for many it's hard to see that faith could mean anything else. But it
puts the emphasis in the wrong place and thus distorts the meaning
of Christian faith.

That Christian faith is about belief is a rather odd notion, when
you think about it. It suggests that what God really cares about is the
beliefs in our heads—as if "believing the right things" is what God is
most looking for, as if having "correct beliefs" is what will save us. And
if you have "incorrect beliefs," you may be in trouble. It's remarkable
to think that God cares so much about "beliefs."

Moreover, when you think about it, faith as belief is relatively
impotent, relatively powerless. You can believe all the right things
and still be in bondage. You can believe all the right things and still be

miserable. You can believe all the right things and still be relatively unchanged. Believing a set of claims to be true has very little transforming power.

There is more to be said about faith as *assensus,* and near the end of this chapter I will return to it and its role in the Christian life. Now I turn to the meanings of faith that have more to do with the "heart." These meanings are relational. They see faith as not very much about believing. Instead, faith is about the relationship of the self at its deepest level to God.

Faith as *Fiducia*

There is no close English word for faith as *fiducia.* The closest is "fiduciary," which doesn't get us very far. So I move to the best English translation: *fiducia* is faith as "trust," as radical trust in God. Significantly, it does not mean trusting in the truth of a set of statements about God; that would simply be *assensus* under a different name. Rather, it means trusting in God.

Faith as trust is like floating in a deep ocean. I owe the metaphor to Søren Kierkegaard, a radical Christian and one of the philosophical giants of the nineteenth century: faith is like floating in seventy thousand fathoms of water. If you struggle, if you tense up and thrash about, you will eventually sink. But if you relax and trust, you will float. It's like Matthew's story of Peter walking on the water with Jesus—when he began to be afraid, he began to sink.

To help an adult class see this meaning of faith, my wife asked them, "How many of you have taught a small child to swim?" Many had. When asked to describe the experience, all said that the biggest hurdle was getting the child to relax in the water. Their consistent refrain was, "It's okay, just relax. You'll float, it's okay."[5] Faith as trust is trusting in the buoyancy of God. Faith is trusting in the sea of being in which we live and move and have our being.

To move from a sea metaphor to other biblical metaphors, this is faith as trusting in God as our rock and fortress. The point is the same: we trust in God as the one upon whom we rely, as our support and foundation and ground, as our safe place.

We can also see this meaning of faith by turning to its opposite. The opposite of trust is not doubt or disbelief, but mistrust. More interestingly and provocatively, its opposite is "anxiety" or "worry." We see this meaning in familiar words attributed to Jesus. He invites his hearers to see reality as marked by a cosmic generosity:

> Consider the birds of the air; they neither sow nor reap nor gather into barns, and yet God feeds them. . . . Consider the lilies of the field, how they grow; they neither toil nor spin, yet I tell you, even Solomon in all his glory was not clothed like one of these.

Four times in the extended passage in which these familiar lines appear, Jesus says to his hearers: "Do not worry," in other words, "Do not be anxious"—and then adds, "You of little faith."[6] Little faith and anxiety go together. If you are anxious, you have little faith.

Thus we can measure our degree of faith as trust by the amount of anxiety in our lives. I mention this not to provide yet one more failing for which to chastise ourselves, but because of the good news implicit in this realization. Growth in faith as trust casts out anxiety. Who of us would not want a life with less anxiety, to say nothing of an anxiety-free life? If we were not anxious, can you imagine how free we would be, how immediately present we would be able to be, how well we would be able to love? Faith as radical trust has great transforming power.

Faith as *Fidelitas*

As with *assensus*, the meaning of the Latin term is suggested by its closest English equivalent: faith as "fidelity." This is faith as "faithfulness." Faith is faithfulness to our relationship with God. It means what faithfulness does in a committed human relationship: we are faithful (or not) to our spouses or partners. Faith as fidelity means loyalty, allegiance, the commitment of the self at its deepest level, the commitment of the "heart."

Faith as *fidelitas* does not mean faithfulness to *statements* about God, whether biblical, credal, or doctrinal. Rather, it means faithfulness to the God to whom the Bible and creeds and doctrines point. *Fidelitas* refers to a radical centering in God.

Its opposite is not doubt or disbelief. Rather, as in a human relationship, its opposite is infidelity, being unfaithful to our relationship with God. To use a striking biblical metaphor, the opposite of this meaning of faith is *adultery*. When the Bible speaks about adultery, most often it is not speaking about human sexual relationships. Sometimes it is, as in the Ten Commandments and in some other passages. But when the prophets indict Israel as adulterous or Jesus speaks of "an evil and adulterous generation," they are not saying that there is a lot of spouse swapping going on. Rather, they are referring to unfaithfulness to God and God's covenant.

Another vivid biblical term for infidelity to God is *idolatry*. Though the command to avoid idolatry includes not worshiping graven images, its central meaning is giving one's ultimate loyalty or allegiance to something other than God. Idolatry is centering in something finite rather than the sacred, who is infinite and beyond all images. As the opposite of idolatry, faith means being loyal to God and not to the many would-be gods that present themselves to us. Christian faith means loyalty to Jesus as Lord, and not to the seductive would-be lords of our lives, whether the nation, or affluence, or achievement, or family, or desire.

In the Hebrew Bible, faith as fidelity is the meaning of the first of the Ten Commandments: "You shall have no other gods before me."[7] In the New Testament, it is the meaning of the Great Commandment: "You shall love the Lord your God with all your heart, and with all your life force, and with all your mind, and with all your strength." It is followed immediately by a second "like it": "You shall love your neighbor as yourself."[8] *Fidelitas* means loving God and loving your neighbor and being faithful, above all, to these two great relationships.

And how are we faithful to God? Though challenging, faith's ways are also simple. It means paying attention to our relationship with God—just as faithfulness in a human relationship means not only "not straying," but being attentive to the relationship. We are attentive through the simple means of worship, prayer, practice, and a life of compassion and justice. To be faithful to God means not only to love God, but to love that which God loves—namely, the neighbor, and indeed the whole of creation. Faith as *fidelitas* thus includes an ethical imperative.

Faith as *Visio*

As the closest English word, "vision," suggests, this is faith as *a way of seeing*. In particular, this is faith as a way of seeing *the whole*, a way of seeing "what is." I owe the germ of this understanding to the mid-twentieth-century theologian H. Richard Niebuhr in his book *The Responsible Self*.[9] In it, he speaks of the central importance of how we see the whole of what is, for how we see the whole will affect how we respond to life. Hence in the title of his book, the *responsible* self refers not to the especially dutiful or conscientious self, but to the *responding* self.

There are three ways we can see the whole, and each goes with a particular way of responding to life. First, we can see reality as hostile and threatening. The clinical form of this is paranoia, of course, but you don't have to be paranoid to see reality this way. The bottom line is that none of us gets out of here alive. And this is the fate of not just me and us, but of everybody we love, including our children and grandchildren. Death will get us all. Moreover, astrophysicists tell us, even the earth and the solar system will one day be destroyed as the sun explodes in its dying gasp. On a more finite level, life is filled with threats to our existence: accidents, disease, violence, unemployment, poverty. Life easily looks threatening.

If we do see reality this way, how will we respond to life? In a word, defensively. We will seek to build systems of security and self-protection to fend off the hostile powers as long as possible. The attempt to secure ourselves in the face of a threatening reality takes many forms, secular and material as well as religious.

Indeed, many forms of popular Christianity throughout the centuries have viewed reality this way. God is the one who is going to get us—unless we offer the right sacrifices, behave the right way, or believe the right things. This is the "threat" of the earlier paradigm:

God will judge us and punish those who didn't "get it right." But if we do "get it right," then perhaps the consuming fire that will otherwise devour everybody and everything will spare us.

In the second way of seeing the whole, it is perceived as indifferent. Not as paranoid as the first, this view doesn't assume reality is "out to get us." Rather, "what is" is simply indifferent to human purposes and ends. This is the most common modern secular viewpoint. The universe is made up of swirling force fields of matter and energy, but is neither hostile to nor supportive of our lives and dreams. Though it may be perceived as elegant and even magnificent, it is ultimately indifferent to human meanings.

If we see reality this way, our response to life will be less anxious and paranoid than that of the first way, but we are still likely to be defensive and precautionary. We respond by building up what security we can in the midst of an indifferent universe. There can be a rich aesthetic to this life. We may seek to enjoy its beauty while we are here, we may even seek to take care of the world as well as we can, but ultimately we are likely to be concerned primarily for ourselves and those who are most important to us.

The third way we can see "what is" is to view it as life-giving and nourishing. It has brought us and everything that is into existence. It sustains our lives. It is filled with wonder and beauty, even if sometimes a terrible beauty. To use a traditional theological term, this is seeing reality as gracious. It is the way of seeing spoken of by Jesus in his words about the birds and the lilies. God feeds them, clothes them, and, to echo another saying of Jesus, God sends rain upon the just and unjust. God is generous.

This way of seeing the whole makes possible a different response to life. It leads to radical trust. It frees us from the anxiety, self-preoccupation, and concern to protect the self with systems of security that mark the first two viewpoints. It leads to the "self-forgetfulness of faith" and thus to the ability to love and to be present to the moment.[10] It generates a "willingness to spend and be spent" for the sake of a vision that goes beyond ourselves.[11] Both the active and passive voice in the phrase are significant: to spend ourselves and to allow ourselves to be spent. It leads to the kind of life that we see in Jesus and in the saints, known and unknown. Or, to use words from Paul, it leads to a life marked by freedom, joy, peace, and love.

To some, this way of seeing may seem naively optimistic. But Niebuhr was no Pollyanna. He knew about the Holocaust and all the terrible things that we are capable of doing to each other. The point is not that reality is simply "nice," or that one can *demonstrate* that it is gracious. Rather, the point is that *how we see reality matters*, for how we see "what is" profoundly affects how we experience and live our lives.

Thus faith as *visio* is seeing reality as gracious. Its opposite—"un-faith"—is seeing reality as hostile and threatening or as indifferent. This meaning of faith is closely related to faith as *fiducia*, as trust. What it adds, though, is that how we see reality and our ability to trust are connected to each other. Trust and *visio* go together; trust in God and how we see God go together.

As a way of seeing, faith as *visio* connects to the emerging para-digm's emphasis upon metaphor. Metaphor has to do with "how we see." For the emerging paradigm, the Bible and the Christian tradi-tion are understood as a giant metaphor through which we see God. Christian faith is about living within the Christian tradition as a metaphor of God.

Significantly, the last three understandings of faith are all rela-tional. Faith as *visio* is a way of seeing the whole that shapes our rela-tionship to "what is," that is, to God. Faith as *fidelitas* is faithfulness to our relationship with God. And faith as *fiducia* is deepening trust in God, flowing out of a deepening relationship with God.

The last three understandings are also the most important ones. The experience of Martin Luther, one of the church's heroes of faith and the spiritual mentor of my childhood, exemplifies this. Perhaps more than any other person in the last five hundred years, Luther is responsible for "faith" being so central to the Christian vocabulary.

But for Luther faith was not primarily *assensus*. After his decision to enter a monastery in a moment of terror during a lightning storm, Luther went through a decade of agonized torment and ascetic self-denial, seeking to be righteous enough for God. During these years, he had *assensus* aplenty—and it terrified him. Precisely because he believed "all of it," he was filled with fear and anxiety. His transformation occurred through an experience of radical grace that transformed how he saw *(visio)*, led him to see that faith was about trusting God *(fiducia)*, and led him to a life of faithfulness *(fidelitas)* to God. For Luther, saving faith was not *assensus*. It was about *visio, fiducia,* and *fidelitas.*[12]

Faith in these three senses enables us to live our lives and to face our deaths in a new way. In this life, a radical centering in God leads to a deepening trust that transforms the way we see and live our lives. Seeing, living, trusting, and centering are all related in complex ways. They are all matters of the heart, and not primarily of the head. And in our deaths, dying means trusting in the buoyancy of God, that the one who has carried us in this life is the one into whom we die.

Returning to Faith as *Assensus*

I return to faith as *assensus*, in part because I was very hard on it earlier in this chapter, arguing that emphasizing it distorts the meaning of faith and the Christian life. Now I return to it because it does matter—it does play a role. There are *affirmations* that are central to Christian faith.

In particular, three affirmations are foundational: the reality of God, the centrality of Jesus, and the centrality of the Bible. These will be the topics of the next three chapters. Here I provide a very compact summary:

- **Being Christian means affirming the reality of God.** God is real. There is a "More," to use language I will also use in Chapter 4. The Bible, and all of the enduring religions of the world, unambiguously affirm that there is a stupendous, magnificent, wondrous "More." Christian faith includes affirming this.

- **Christian faith means affirming the utter centrality of Jesus.** It means seeing Jesus as the decisive disclosure of

God and of what a life full of God looks like. It means affirming Jesus as the Word of God, the wisdom of God, the light of the world, the way, and more, all known in a person. And as Christians, we can say that's who Jesus is for us, without needing to say that he's the only such disclosure or the only adequate one among the religions of the world. Affirming the centrality of Jesus for Christians need not lead to Christian exclusivism.[13]

■ **Christian faith means affirming the centrality of the Bible.** Just as Jesus is for us the Word of God disclosed in a person, so the Bible is the Word of God disclosed in a book. Being Christian means a commitment to the Bible as our foundational document and identity document. The Bible is our story. It is to shape our vision of life—our vision of God, of ourselves, and of God's dream for the earth.

Christian faith as *assensus* means to affirm all of the above deeply but loosely. Deeply: faith involves our loyalty and trust and seeing at the deepest level of the self. Loosely: we need to avoid the human tendency toward excessive precision and certitude. Christian theology has often been bedeviled by both—by the desire to know too much and to know it too precisely. The history of Christian doctrinal disputes often leaves one wondering how people could ever have thought that they could know matters about God with precision and certitude. For example, whether one can know about internal relationships within the Godhead—about whether the Spirit proceeds "from the Father" or "from the Father and the Son," to name a conflict that was the theological reason for the division between Western and Eastern Christianity a thousand years ago.

A deep but humble (and therefore imprecise) understanding of Christian faith as *assensus*, as involving affirmation of the centrality of God as known in the Bible and Jesus, is very close to faith as *visio*. It is a way of seeing reality. Ideally, it is assent as something we freely give, as something drawn forth from us because we have been captivated by a persuasive and compelling vision, and not assent as the effortful fulfilling of a requirement, as in, "You must believe *x*, *y*, and *z* in order to be saved." When assent is understood that way, faith becomes a work.

There is yet one more thing to be said about faith as *assensus* and its role. I realize that I have spent a very large part of my life working on faith as *assensus*—namely, on coming up with a way of seeing Christianity that does make persuasive and compelling sense to me. From this realization, I draw the generalization that we cannot easily give our heart to something that our mind rejects.

Returning to Faith as Believing

Earlier in this chapter I emphasized that for many in the modern world, faith means primarily "believing," with believing understood to mean accepting uncertain claims to be true. As I conclude this chapter, I want to emphasize that the premodern meanings of the English words "believe" and "believing" and the Latin word *credo* are very different from what believing has come to mean in our time. By recovering these premodern meanings, we will see that faith *is* believing. Here I am greatly indebted to the Harvard historian of religion and theologian Wilfrid Cantwell Smith.[14]

I begin with the meaning of the Latin word *credo*. It is the root of the word "creed" as well as the first word of the Nicene Creed and the Apostles' Creed. Both are seen as definitive statements of Christian faith.

We commonly translate *credo* as "I believe." And because most modern people understand "I believe" as "I give my assent to," many Christians have difficulty with the creeds. Indeed, if I were to make a list of the ten questions I am most frequently asked when I talk to Christian groups, on that list would be, "What are we going to do with the creeds?" The reason: they think saying "I believe" means giving one's mental assent to the literal truth of each statement in the creed. *Assensus* and literalism are often combined in the modern world, by believers and unbelievers alike.

But *credo* does not mean "I hereby agree to the literal-factual truth of the following statements." Rather, its Latin roots combine to mean "I give my heart to." As mentioned earlier in this chapter, the heart is the self at its deepest level, a level below the intellect. As the giving of one's heart, *credo* means "I commit my loyalty to," "I commit my allegiance to."

Thus, when we say *credo* at the beginning of the creed, we are saying, "I give my heart to God." And who is that? Who is the God to whom we commit our loyalty and allegiance? The rest of the creed tells the story of the one to whom we give our hearts: God as the maker of heaven and earth, God as known in Jesus, God as present in the Spirit.

Just as *credo* involves a level of the self deeper than the intellect, so do the premodern meanings of the word "believe." Prior to the seventeenth century, the word "believe" did not mean believing in the truth of statements or propositions, whether problematic or not. Grammatically, the object of believing was not statements, but a person. Moreover, the contexts in which it is used in premodern English make it clear that it meant: to hold dear; to prize; to give one's loyalty to; to give one's self to; to commit oneself. It meant what *fidelitas* and *fiducia* mean: faithfulness, allegiance, loyalty, commitment, and trust.

Most simply, "to believe" meant "to love." Indeed, the English words "believe" and "belove" are related. What we believe is what we belove. Faith is about beloving God.

To relate this to the four meanings of faith, originally the word "believing" covered all of these meanings. But in the modern period, we have suffered an extraordinary reduction in the meaning of "believing." We have reduced it and turned it into "propositional believing"—believing a particular set of statements or claims to be true. But originally, believing included all of the dimensions of faith that I have described.

The premodern meanings of "faith" generate a relational understanding of the Christian life. I return to the words of Jesus as he spoke about the greatest commandment, and as I do so, I substitute the word "relationship." It is exegetically defensible and expresses the meaning well. At the center of the Christian life are two relationships that are ultimately one. The first relationship is "You shall love the Lord your God with all your heart, life force, mind, and strength." The second relationship, "like it," is "You shall love your neighbor as yourself."

And the passage concludes with "Upon these two relationships hang all the law and the prophets."[15] In the time of Jesus, the law and the prophets, the first two parts of the Hebrew Bible, were all that had been canonized. Thus Jesus declares that the whole of scripture hangs on these two relationships. The Christian life is as simple and challenging as this: to love God and to love that which God loves.

This is the central meaning of faith. Given the premodern meaning of "believe," to believe in God is to belove God. Faith is about beloving God and all that God beloves. The Christian life is about beloving God and all that God beloves. Faith is our love for God. Faith is the way of the heart.

---

1. For a much fuller treatment of the metaphor of the "heart," see Chapter 8.

2. The exceptions are 2 and 3 John, two of its shortest books.

3. Aidan Kavanaugh, *On Liturgical Theology* (New York: Pueblo, 1984), pp. 81–95.

4. The 1966 edition of the *Random House Dictionary*, cited by Wilfrid Cantwell Smith, *Belief and History* (Charlottesville, VA: University Press of Virginia, 1977), p. 65. I am indebted to this book and his masterful *Faith and Belief: The Difference Between Them* (Oxford: Oneworld, 1998; first published in 1979).

5. My wife's question is indebted to remarks made by Craig Dykstra of the Lilly Endowment at a clergy gathering sponsored by the Louisville Institute.

6. Matt. 6:25–33 = Luke 12:22–31. It is thus Q material and very early.

7. Exod. 20:3.

8. Mark 12:30–31. See also Matt. 22:37–39 and Luke 10:27. I have changed the NRSV's "soul" to "life force" because it better expresses the underlying Hebrew and Greek meaning.

9. H. Richard Niebuhr, *The Responsible Self* (San Francisco: Harper and Row, 1963), esp. pp. 139–45. See also pp. 115–21. Niebuhr in turn attributes the germ of

his development to A. N. Whitehead, *Religion in the Making* (New York: Macmillan, 1926). See also Niebuhr, *Radical Monotheism and Western Culture* (New York: Harper and Brothers, 1960), pp. 16–23, 116–26.

10. Robin Scroggs, *Paul for a New Day* (Philadelphia: Fortress, 1977), p. 59.

11. I owe the phrase to James Fowler, whose many books on faith development are important and insightful. See esp. *Stages of Faith* (San Francisco: Harper and Row, 1981); *Becoming Adult, Becoming Christian,* rev. ed. (San Francisco: Jossey-Bass, 2000); and, with Sam Keen, *Life-Maps: Conversations on the Journey of Faith* (Waco, TX: Word Books, 1978).

12. Similarly for John Calvin, the other most important voice of the Reformation: faith is primarily about trusting in God's goodwill toward us. In *The Institutes of the Christian Religion,* Calvin defines faith as "a firm and certain knowledge of *God's benevolence toward us,* founded upon the truth of the freely given promise in Christ, both revealed to our minds and sealed upon our hearts through the Holy Spirit." For a wise and insightful treatment of faith that draws heavily on Luther, see Grace Adolphsen Brame, *Faith, The Yes of the Heart* (Minneapolis: Augsberg, 1999).

13. See Chapter 5, pp. 88–89.

14. Smith, *Belief and History,* pp. 36–69.

15. Matt. 22:40.

THREE

The Bible

The Heart of the Tradition

Christianity is centered in the Bible. Of course, it is ultimately centered in God, but it is the God of whom the Bible speaks and to whom it points. God is also known in other ways and other religions, I am convinced, but to be Christian is to be centered in the God of the Bible. This is a mark not of Christian exclusion, but of Christian identity. The Bible is for us as Christians our sacred scripture, our sacred story.

Yet the Bible has become a stumbling block for many. In the last half century, probably more Christians have left the church because of the Bible than for any other single reason. More precisely, they left because the earlier paradigm's way of seeing the Bible ceased to make sense to them. Contemporary biblical literalism—with its emphasis on biblical infallibility, historical factuality, and moral and doctrinal absolutes—is an obstacle for millions of people.

An illustrative list of the kinds of claims that people find difficult when understood literally:

That the earth (and universe as a whole) was created in six days,
    and not very long ago (Gen. 1–3).

That Adam and Eve were real people, and that "the fall" brought
death into the world (Gen. 2–3).

That God sent a worldwide flood that destroyed all life, except
for Noah, his family, and reproductive pairs of all animals
who were saved in an ark (Gen. 6–7).

That all people initially spoke the same language and only later
were divided into different language groups (Gen. 11).

That God ordered the slaughter of the Amalekites, men, women,
children, and infants (1 Sam. 15:3).

That God regulated (and therefore legitimated) slavery (found in
both Testaments).

That God cares (or has ever cared) about whether we wear
garments made of two kinds of cloth (Lev. 19:19).

That God ordered the subordination of women.

That Jesus is the only way of salvation, and that people can be
saved only by believing that he literally died for our sins.

That unbelieving Jews are children of the devil (John 8:44).

That the second coming of Jesus will involve the destruction of
most of humankind.

All of these (and many more) are in the Bible. Because of these,
many simply cannot believe the premise of the earlier paradigm: that
the Bible is a divine product and thus, in harder or softer forms, the
infallible and inerrant Word of God. It is not because of what they
don't know about the Bible that they have difficulty with infallibility
and literalism. It's because of what they do know.

The emerging paradigm provides an alternative to biblical literalism. To use the three adjectives with which I describe it: a *historical,*
metaphorical, and *sacramental* understanding of the Bible. With these
words, I attempt to describe a view that is broadly shared by mainline
biblical scholars who are involved in the life of the church and by laity
and clergy shaped by modern study of the Bible. And though I here
emphasize and illustrate its approach to the Bible, I think it applies to
the creeds and other normative Christian teachings as well.

The Bible as a Historical Product

Because I have recently written at length about the Bible as a historical product,[1] I here present the central points in summary form:

- The Bible is the product of two historical communities, ancient Israel and the early Christian movement.

- As such, it is a human product, not a divine product. This claim in no way denies the reality of God. Rather, it sees the Bible as the response of these two ancient communities to God.

- As their response to God, the Bible tells us how they saw things. Above all, it tells us how they saw their life with God. It contains their stories about God's involvement in their lives, their laws and ethical teachings, their prayers and praises, their wisdom about how to live, and their hopes and dreams. It is not God's witness to God (not a divine product), but their witness to God.

- As a human product, the Bible is not "absolute truth" or "God's revealed truth," but relative and culturally conditioned. To many, "relative" and "culturally conditioned" mean something inferior, even negative. But "relative" means "related": the Bible is related to their time and place. So also "culturally conditioned" means that the Bible uses the language and concepts of the cultures in which it took shape. To use a nonbiblical example, the Nicene Creed uses the language of fourth-century Hellenistic philosophy to express the convictions that mattered most to the Christians who framed it. It is not a set of absolute truths, but tells us how they saw things. So also the Bible tells us how our spiritual ancestors saw things—not how God sees things.

■ When the Bible is approached in this way, many of the problems that people have with the Bible largely disappear.[2] The conflict between the Genesis creation stories and science vanishes. The laws of the Bible need not be understood as God's laws for all time, but as the laws and ethical teachings of these communities. The stories of God destroying Israel's enemies are Israel's way of telling its story, just as a violent destruction of the enemies of Christ is what some early Christians hoped for. Of course, this realization doesn't make these "good stories"; but at least the problem of thinking of them as expressing the will of God disappears. In general, the literal and absolute reading of the Bible as infallible words of God disappears and is replaced by a historical and metaphorical reading, which I will soon describe.

Just as this view of the Bible does not deny the reality of God, it does not deny that the Bible is "inspired by God." But it understands inspiration differently. In recent centuries, some Christians have understood it to mean "plenary inspiration": that every word is inspired by God, and thus has the truth and authority of God standing behind it. For them, inspiration effectively means that the Bible is a divine product.

Within the emerging paradigm, inspiration refers to the movement of the Spirit in the lives of the people who produced the Bible. The emphasis is not upon *words* inspired by God, but on *people* moved by their experience of the Spirit, namely, these ancient communities and the individuals who wrote for them.

Viewing the Bible this way also has implications for how we see religious pluralism. It enables us to affirm the Bible as the response to God in our particular cultural stream, even as it enables us to recognize the sacred texts of the other enduring religious traditions as the response to the sacred in their particular cultural streams.

The Bible as Sacred Scripture

Like the earlier paradigm, the emerging paradigm sees the Bible as sacred scripture. But unlike the earlier paradigm, the emerging paradigm sees the Bible's status as sacred, as "Holy Bible," as the result of a historical process, not as the consequence of its divine origin. The process is known as *canonization*. The documents that now make up the Bible were not sacred when they were written, but over time were declared to be sacred by ancient Israel and early Christianity. The process took about five centuries for the Hebrew Bible and about three centuries for the Christian Testament. By declaring these writings to be sacred, our spiritual ancestors declared them to be the most important documents they knew.

To call the Bible sacred scripture refers to both its status and its function. The two go together. Its sacred status for Christians means that it continues to be the most important collection of documents we know. As sacred scripture, it functions as:

- **Our foundation document:** the foundation upon which Christianity is built, without which the structure will fall into ruins.

- **Our identity document:** its stories and vision are to shape our sense of who we are and of what our life with God is about.

- **Our "wisdom tradition":** in its comprehensive sense, "wisdom" concerns the two most central questions of life: What is real? And how shall we live?

To be Christian means to be in a primary continuing conversation with the Bible as foundational for our identity and vision. If this conversation ceases or becomes haphazard, then we cease to be Christian, for the Bible is at the heart of Christianity.

The Bible is thus both sacred scripture and a human product. It is important to affirm both. To use stereotypical labels, both conservatives and liberals within the church have sometimes been reluctant to do so. Conservative Christians resist affirming that the Bible is a human product, fearing that doing so means it will lose its status as divine authority and divine revelation. Liberal Christians are sometimes wary of affirming that the Bible is sacred scripture, fearing that doing so opens the door to notions of infallibility, literalism, and absolutizing. But a clear vision of the Bible and its role in the Christian life requires seeing it as both sacred scripture and human product. It is human in origin, and sacred in status and function.

The Illuminating Power of Historical Context

Rather than a literal-factual interpretation, the emerging paradigm employs a historical-metaphorical interpretation of the Bible. Both adjectives are important, and I begin with the first.

A historical approach takes seriously that the Bible comes to us from the distant past. It was not written to us or for us, but for the people who lived then. It thus *emphasizes the importance of historical context*: the illuminating power of setting a biblical text in its ancient context. It helps us to see what these words meant for the communities that produced them. Indeed, this is the defining characteristic of a historical approach. The historical context of a text includes:

- Its ancient context in the life of the community. For example, it is greatly illuminating to hear the words of the second half of Isaiah in the context of the Jewish people's exile in Babylon. The words come alive in that context.

- Its ancient literary context in the document in which it is found—the relationship between a text and other texts in the same book.

■ Its ancient canonical context—that is, its relationship to other parts of the Bible. For example, the gospel stories of Jesus feeding the multitude in the wilderness echo the stories of Israel being fed in the wilderness.

An important clarification: the historical approach *can* ask about the history behind a text. Did the reported event really happen? But the question is not always important and is seldom ultimately important. Indeed, its importance has often been overemphasized in the modern period. It is not always or ultimately important because much of the language of the Bible is metaphorical, which leads to the second adjective.

The Truth of Metaphor

As I use the word, "metaphor" is a large umbrella category. It has both a negative and positive meaning. Negatively, it means *nonliteral*. Positively, it means the *more-than-literal meaning* of language. Thus metaphorical meaning is not inferior to literal meaning, but is more than literal meaning.[3]

There is more than one justification for using a metaphorical approach to the Bible. One reason is that much of its language is obviously metaphorical. The Bible regularly speaks of God as having hands and feet and ears and eyes, but of course God doesn't.

Another reason is that the Bible contains both history and metaphor. It combines historical memory and metaphorical narrative. Some of the events it speaks about really happened, and the community preserved the memory. But even when a text contains historical memory, its more-than-literal meaning matters most. For example, the exile in Babylon in the sixth century BCE really happened, but the way the story is told gives it a more-than-historical meaning. It became a metaphorical narrative of exile and return, abiding images of the human condition and its remedy.

In other cases, there may be little or no historical factuality behind the stories. For example, the Genesis stories of creation, the Garden of Eden, the expulsion of Adam and Eve, Cain's murder of Abel, Noah and the flood, and the Tower of Babel are what might be called "purely metaphorical narratives." They are not reporting the early history of the earth and humankind; they are not history remembered. Yet as metaphorical narratives, they can be profoundly true, even though not literally factual.

This claim—that metaphorical language can be true—needs to be emphasized in our time. We in modern Western culture tend to identify truth with factuality and hence devalue metaphorical language. To a large extent, we have become tone-deaf to metaphor, often viewing it as "pretty" language for something that could be said more directly.

For example, when people ask, "Is that story true?" they often mean, "Did it happen?" Another example: my students sometimes respond to the suggestion that a story is metaphorical or symbolic with the question, "You mean it's *only* a metaphor, *only* a symbol?" In their minds, metaphorical and symbolic language is less important, less truthful than factual language.

Even well-trained scholars sometimes say this. A reviewer of my book on the Bible wrote that "a metaphor is always a lie" and decried my view of the Bible as containing "metaphorical fictions." The notion that all metaphors are lies is remarkable, as is the combination of metaphor and fiction.

However, I do not speak of metaphorical fictions, but of metaphorical truths. Because of the importance of this point, I make it in several ways:

I have been told that the German novelist Thomas Mann defined a myth (a particular kind of metaphorical narrative) as "a story about the way things never were, but always are." So, is a myth true? Literally true, no. Really true, yes.

To quote a Swedish proverb and then to modify it: "Theology is poetry plus, not science minus."[4] The proverb affirms that theological language is more like poetic language than factual language, even as it is more than poetry in that it makes a truth claim. As such, it is not "science minus," not inferior to the language of factuality. Thus *biblical* metaphor is poetry plus, not inferior to factual language.

A Catholic priest once said in a sermon, "The Bible is true, and some of it happened." To make his point obvious: the truth of the Bible is not dependent on its historical factuality.

The same point is made by a Native American storyteller as he begins telling his tribe's story of creation: "Now I don't know if it happened this way or not, but I know this story is true."

I sometimes ask my audiences how many of them listen to "The News from Lake Wobegon" on Garrison Keillor's radio show, *Prairie Home Companion*. Typically, more than half do. I then ask them, "Are these true stories?" They get the point immediately. We all know that Keillor is making them up, and yet we hear truth in these stories. We find them not only entertaining, humorous, and often moving, but often recognize ourselves and people we know in them.

Of course, the analogy to the Bible is not exact. "The News from Lake Wobegon" is the product of one contemporary creative mind, whereas the Bible is the product of a thousand years of community experience. Moreover, there is history in the Bible; it is not simply creative fiction. But the point remains: stories can be true, can be revelatory, can be epiphanies, even if they are not factual reports.

I now illustrate what it means to speak of the "truth of metaphor" with some familiar biblical stories. I begin with the Genesis stories of creation, from the creation of the universe in six days through the expulsion of Adam and Eve from the Garden of Eden. For the past two centuries, some Christians have strongly defended the literal factuality of these stories. Conflicts raged over Genesis versus evolution, God versus science. Though their numbers are decreasing, we still hear advocates of creation science speak of a "young earth" and of Christians engaged in school-board battles over the teaching of evolution. The reason for their passion is that they have identified truth with factuality; thus, in their minds, if the stories aren't factual, they aren't true. And if these stories aren't true, the Bible isn't true. What is at stake is their view of the Bible.

A metaphorical approach leads to a very different result. The Genesis stories of creation are seen as Israel's stories of creation, not as God's stories of creation. They therefore have no more of a divine guarantee to be true in a literal-factual sense than do the creation stories of other cultures. When they are seen as metaphorical narratives, not factual accounts, they are "myths" in Thomas Mann's sense of the word: stories about the way things never were, but always are. They are thus really true, even though not literally true.

And what truth claims are they making? To summarize them in a series of statements is virtually to violate the stories themselves, which are rich with detail and nuance, insight and elegance. Nevertheless, for reasons of economy I do so:

> God is the creator of all that is.
> The creation is good, indeed very good.
> We are created in the image of God.
> We live our lives east of Eden: something has gone wrong.
> And we yearn to return.

These are among the metaphorical meanings of these stories. Are they true? They cannot be demonstrated, but they can be seen as the way things are. There is little or no conflict with other things we think we know. Thus they can indeed be true, and these stories express these truths. But even more, as metaphorical narratives these stories invite us into these truths. Metaphorical language is an invitation to see in a particular way. These stories invite us to see both reality and our lives in this way.

The stories of Jesus' birth in Matthew and Luke provide a second illustration of the truth of metaphor. Like the Genesis stories of creation, they have been a source of conflict among Christians. Some Christians insist that they are and must be seen as factual narratives: that Jesus really was born of a virgin, that there really were wise men who were led by a special star to Bethlehem, that angels really sang to

the shepherds in the night sky. Often they see this as a test of orthodoxy. Other Christians see these stories as metaphor and not as historical reports, in part because they see symbolic motifs in them and
in part because they wonder if God ever intervenes in this way.

What does a metaphorical reading yield? The stories are so rich
that I can only suggest some of the major meanings:

> The story of Jesus being conceived by the Spirit of God affirms
> that what happened in Jesus was of God.

> The special star and the glory of the Lord filling the night sky
> suggest that this is the story of light in our darkness, that, in the
> language of the gospel of John, Jesus is the "light of the world,"
> the "true light that enlightens every person."

> The story of Gentile wise men coming to the birthplace affirms
> that Jesus is the light not only for Israel but for all nations, for
> everybody, Jew and Gentile.

> The story of shepherds as the first to be told of the birth affirms
> that the good news—the gospel—is especially for the
> marginalized.

> The song of the angels declares that Jesus is Lord and Savior (and
> thus Caesar, who also used these titles for himself, is not).

> The story of King Herod ordering the slaughter of male babies
> echoes the story of Pharaoh issuing a similar order in the time of
> Moses. It suggests that Jesus is like a new Moses, that a new
> exodus is about to happen, and that the Pharaohs and Herods of
> this world always try to destroy the bearer of God's liberating
> word. But they do not have the final word.

Read metaphorically, the stories mean all of this—and more. And they
mean it independently of their historical factuality.

Moreover, emphasizing the historical factuality of the stories can
distract from their meaning. When their factuality is emphasized, the
miraculous elements are emphasized so that "believing" these stories

means believing that all these spectacular events happened. This emphasis often produces a sterile debate between those who think they are factual and those who think they aren't, an endless back-and-forth: "It happened this way," "No, it didn't," "Yes, it did." When this happens, the rich, more-than-literal meanings are most often lost.

When this debate breaks out in my classroom, I say to my students, "Believe whatever you want about whether it happened this way; now let's talk about what the story means." The statement applies to the Genesis stories of creation, the gospel birth stories, and the stories of the Bible generally: a preoccupation with factuality can obscure the metaphorical meanings and the truth of the stories as metaphor.

As my third illustration of the truth of metaphor and metaphorical narratives, I turn from the birth stories to the Easter stories. To state my understanding of the truth of the Easter stories without arguing it, I see their truth, most broadly speaking, as twofold:

Jesus is a figure of the present and not simply of the past. He continued to be experienced by his first followers after his death and continues to be experienced to this day. It's not just that his memory lived on or that his spirit lived on, as we sometimes speak of the spirit of Lincoln living on. Rather, he was and is experienced as a figure of the present. In short, Jesus lives.

Not only does Jesus live, but "Jesus is Lord." In the New Testament, this is the foundational affirmation about Jesus, and it is grounded in the Easter experience. To say that Jesus is Lord is to say more than simply that Jesus lives. It means that he has been raised to God's right hand, where he is one with God. And to affirm that he is Lord is to deny all other lords.

Because I see the meaning of the Easter stories this way, I can be indifferent to the factual questions surrounding the stories. For example, was the tomb really empty? Was his corpse transformed? Did the risen Jesus really eat a fish? Did he appear to his disciples in such a visible, physical way that we could have videotaped him if we had been there?

For me, the truth of the Easter stories is not at stake in these questions. For example, the story of the empty tomb may be a metaphor of the resurrection rather than a historical report. As metaphor, it means: you won't find Jesus in the land of the dead. As the angel in the story puts it, "Why do you look for the living among the dead?" The truth of the Easter stories is grounded in the ongoing experience of Jesus as a figure of the present who is one with God and therefore "Lord."

For some Christians, the historical factuality of the Easter stories matters greatly. As a result, I am sometimes involved in public dialogues about whether the tomb was really empty, whether the resurrection involved the physical body of Jesus, and so forth. In a recent dialogue, a conservative scholar completed his case for affirming the literal and factual truth of the Easter stories by saying, "In addition to all these historical arguments for being confident that Jesus rose physically and bodily from the dead, there is one more reason I know these stories are true—and that's because I walk with Jesus every day."

At the conclusion of my response, I returned to his closing point and said, "I accept completely the truth of your statement that you walk with Jesus every day. Now, if I were to follow you around with a camera, would there be a time during the day when I could get a picture of the two of you?" I continued, "Of course, that's silly. But my point is, I think your statement is really true, even though I don't for a moment imagine that it's literally true."[5]

So also I would say that the story of the empty tomb is really true, even though it may not be literally true; the story of the Emmaus road is really true, even though it may not be literally true, and so on. Stories can be true without being literally and factually true.

Indeed, I wonder if the emphasis of some Christians on the Bible being *literally* true is because they are concerned to say it's *really* true. There is a colloquial use of the word "literally" today in an emphatic sense. We have all heard someone say about an angry person, "He literally blew his top" or "He literally exploded." Does this mean his body came apart? Well, of course not. But we all understand what is meant: the person got very angry. Interestingly, "literally" is here used in a nonliteral sense to mean "really." So also, when people say, "I believe the Bible is *literally* true," I want to ask, "Are you saying that you believe the Bible is *really* true? If so, I agree with you."

Metaphor as Bridge

A metaphorical approach to the Bible has the potential to be a bridge between the earlier and emerging paradigms. In Christian history, the more-than-literal meaning of biblical texts has always been most important. Only in the last few centuries has their literal factuality been emphasized as crucial.

Moreover, much of conservative Christian preaching today emphasizes the more-than-literal, the more-than-historical meaning of biblical texts. From my recent experience, I provide two brief examples.

The first was in a Pentecostal church. The preacher's text was the story of Jesus healing a paralyzed man in the second chapter of Mark's gospel. The "punch line" of the text and his sermon was, "Jesus said to the paralytic, 'Rise, take up your bed and walk.'" The preacher told several brief and moving stories of people paralyzed, immobilized in their lives, by addictions of various kinds, by long-term unemployment and giving up on ever finding a job, by abuse that prevented intimate relationships, and so forth. And after each story, he paused dramatically and then said emphatically, "And to that person Jesus says, 'Rise, take up your bed and walk!'" It occurred to me that he was preaching the text *as metaphor*; that is, he was preaching the more-than-literal, the more-than-historical meaning of the text.

The second was an Easter sermon in a conservative Baptist church. The pastor's sermon repeated one sentence over and over again, with great emphasis on the last four words: "They went to the tomb, but *the tomb was empty!*" In between the repetitions, he told stories of people who had encountered what felt like the "end" of their lives and hopes: bitter disappointments, devastating griefs, tragic betrayals, children killed in accidents or imprisoned, financial catastrophes—the whole terrain of human trouble. And after each, often with his eyes getting big, his voice lowering to a hushed but loud whisper filled with amazement, he said, "And they went to the tomb—but *the tomb was empty*." His point was clear: what they had feared was the place of endings and death was the place of beginnings and new life. It was enormously effective.

Like the Pentecostal preacher, he was preaching the text as metaphor. Of course, if I had asked them, "Do you think this story really happened?" they no doubt would have said, "Certainly." But that's not what they were preaching. Their point was not that because Jesus had healing powers he must have been the Son of God, or that because Jesus was really raised physically and bodily from the dead, this proves that Christianity is true. Their point was that these words still speak to us today and speak powerfully to the circumstances of our lives.

So perhaps metaphor can be a bridge between conflicting understandings of the Bible among Christians today. It would mean declaring a moratorium on the question of literal factuality, or at least agreeing to disagree on that issue. To repeat language I used earlier: believe whatever you want about whether the story happened this way; but now let's talk about what the story means.

One final comment about a metaphorical approach: metaphor means "to see as." Metaphorical language is *a way of seeing*. To apply this to the Bible: the Bible not only includes metaphorical language and metaphorical narratives, but may itself be thought of as a "giant" metaphor. The Bible as metaphor is a way of seeing the whole: a way of seeing God, ourselves, the divine-human relationship, and the divine-world relationship. And the point is not to "believe" in a metaphor—but to "see" with it. Thus the point is not to believe in the Bible—but to see our lives with God through it.

The Bible as Sacrament

By a sacramental approach, I mean seeing the Bible as sacrament. Indeed, this is one of its primary functions as sacred scripture. A sacrament is a finite, physical, visible mediator of the sacred, a means whereby the sacred becomes present to us. A sacrament is a vehicle or vessel of the sacred.

In Christian language, a sacrament is an "outward and visible sign" that functions as "a means of grace." Sacraments are "doors to the sacred"[6] as well as bridges to the sacred. Something finite, something of this world, becomes a means whereby the sacred becomes present to us.

To use the Eucharist (Communion, the Lord's Supper, the Mass) as an example, the visible, physical, and human products of bread and wine are the means whereby Christ becomes present to us. Christians have differed about the explanation of the process—whether the bread and wine are changed into Christ's body and blood, or whether the body and blood of Christ are present "in, with, and under" the bread and wine, or whether the meal is a "remembering."[7] But even the "softest" of these understandings, a remembering, involves bringing Christ into the present. The human products of bread and wine become a means of grace, earthen vessels whereby the sacred becomes present to us.

So also the Bible is sacrament, a human product whereby God becomes present to us. Its words become a means whereby the Spirit speaks to us in the present. The Bible's function as sacrament is familiar to many Christians in its private devotional use. This common Christian practice involves spending time with a passage from the Bible and lingering over it. The passage is not read rapidly or for information, but space is left around it in the hope that a phrase or sentence will become the means for the Spirit to speak to us as individuals in the particularity of our lives, in the dailiness of our lives.

The Bible also functions sacramentally in collective Christian settings. *Lectio divina* is an ancient Christian contemplative practice that involves the repetitive reading of a passage from the Bible with periods of silence between each reading. So also in Christian worship services, the reading of biblical texts can become sacramental. The words—human products—become vessels for the Word of God.

And thus after the reading of the Bible in the services of many denominations, the reader says, "The Word of the Lord." Even more clearly, in the New Zealand version of the Anglican *Book of Common Prayer,* the reader says, "Hear what the Spirit is saying to the church." In these examples, the Bible functions sacramentally through speaking and hearing: we hear the Spirit speaking to us through these ancient words.

The sacramental function of the Bible is also suggested by language of eating, feeding upon, and digesting it. In the Bible itself, Jeremiah, Ezekiel, and the author of Revelation all speak of "eating" God's words. One of the traditional prayers of the church says about the words of the Bible, "Grant us so to hear them, read, mark, learn, and *inwardly digest* them."[8] The Bible becomes nourishment, God's Word becomes daily bread. Like Jesus, the Bible is both the "Word of God" and the "bread of life."

Christians regularly speak of two primary means of grace: Word *and* sacrament. Such language is appropriate. I suggest that we also think of Word *as* sacrament; namely, in the experience of Christians, the words of the Bible become a mediator of the reality of which they speak. When the Spirit speaks through its words, they become sacrament, the Word of God in earthen vessels.

The Bible and the Christian Life

The emerging paradigm for seeing the Bible—a historical, metaphorical, and sacramental approach—leads to a vision of the Bible and the Christian life quite different from that of the earlier paradigm. The earlier paradigm emphasized believing—believing in the Bible and in the theological teachings derived from it. In the modern period, this has often meant believing that the Bible is infallibly, literally, and factually true, an approach that is often extended to the creeds and central theological doctrines.

For the emerging paradigm, the Bible—human in origin, sacred in status and function—is both metaphor and sacrament. As metaphor, it is a way of seeing—a way of seeing God and our life with God. As sacrament, it is a way that God speaks to us and comes to us. This view of the Bible's function can be extended to the Christian tradition as a whole. Not only the Bible, but Christian creeds, worship, rituals, practices, and doctrines can be seen as metaphor and sacrament.

Within this framework, being Christian is not primarily about believing, in the modern sense of believing certain propositions to be true. Instead, the emerging paradigm emphasizes the relational meanings of faith and leads to a relational and transformational vision of the Christian life. To be Christian means a relationship with God, lived within the Christian tradition, including especially the Bible as the foundation of the tradition, as both metaphor and sacrament. The Christian life is about a relationship with the one whom the Bible both points to and mediates—namely, a relationship with God as disclosed through the Bible as metaphor and sacrament. To be Christian is to live within this tradition and let it do its transforming work among us.

---

1. *Reading the Bible Again for the First Time* (San Francisco: HarperSan-Francisco, 2001), chap. 2.

2. For additional examples, see *Reading the Bible Again*, pp. 23–26.

3. See also *Reading the Bible Again*, chap. 3.

4. The proverb is attributed to Krister Stendahl by Wilfrid Cantwell Smith in his book *What Is Scripture?* (Minneapolis: Fortress, 1993), p. 277, n. 2.

5. Because some readers may be aware that I have had several public dialogues with N. T. Wright, I mention that this dialogue was not with him.

6. From the title of a book on the Christian sacraments by Joseph Martos, cited by John Macquarrie, *A Guide to the Sacraments* (New York: Continuum, 1999), p. 5.

7. The three views, in order, are transubstantiation, consubstantiation, and *anamnesis* (remembering). The first is commonly associated with Catholics, the second with Lutherans and Anglicans, and the third with most other Protestants.

8. Ezek. 2:9–3:3, Jer. 15:16, Rev. 10:9–10. The words of the prayer are from the Collect for the Sunday closest to Nov. 16.

FOUR

God
The Heart of Reality

At the heart of Christianity is God. Without a robust affirmation of the reality of God, Christianity makes no sense. And just as important, how we "see" God—how we think of God, God's relationship to the world, and God's character—matters greatly.

In North American Christianity today, there are two very different ways of thinking about God, two very different understandings of God. To a large extent, they correspond to the earlier paradigm and the emerging paradigm.

The Reality of God

To use William James's generic term for God or the sacred, "Is there a 'More'?"[1] Is God "real"? This is the central religious question in modern Western culture.

In the United States, one might not think so. The Gallup Poll has consistently reported for about fifty years that about 95 percent of Americans say they believe in God. But it's hard to know what to make of this figure. It seems clear to me that God is not the central passion of 95 percent of our population. This is not a judgment, but an observation: saying that you believe in God without being passionate about God may not mean much.

In England, this figure is about 35 percent. In several of the countries of northern Europe, it is even lower. What accounts for this decline in the importance of God in much of Western culture?

The Significance of Our Worldview

Central to understanding the question of God in the modern world is the notion of "worldview." Our worldview is our *image of reality*—our image or picture or understanding of *what is real* and *what is possible*. Colloquially, our worldview is our "big picture" of the way things are. Philosophically, it is our metaphysics or ontology.

We all have a worldview, whether we've ever thought about it or not. We acquire one simply through the process of growing up. Socialization involves among other things internalizing our community's way of seeing things. If we do not internalize this, we will be somewhere on the spectrum that has unconventionality and eccentricity at one end and madness and pathological behavior at the other.

When I speak of internalizing a community's way of seeing things, I am using "community" in a comprehensive sense to mean "culture"— the broad culture in which people live, as well as the subcultures that exist in many cultures. For example, most of us were socialized into modern Western culture, even as we were also socialized into more particular communities, including religious communities. Thus, for most of us, our worldview is a mixture of elements internalized from our culture's worldview and from the worldview of a religious tradition. Unlike people in most premodern societies, we often have conflicts in our worldview.

Our worldview is not only our image of reality, but also a lens through which we see reality. The internalization of a worldview domesticates reality by imposing a map or a grid upon it, thus making it familiar. Moreover, we will entertain and accept (or not entertain and accept) extraordinary notions and reports of extraordinary events to the extent that they fit into our worldview. Our worldview shapes our sense of what is real.

Two Kinds of Worldviews

Of course, there are many worldviews, as many as there are cultures and subcultures. But at a very foundational level, there are two primary kinds: religious worldviews and nonreligious worldviews.

In a *religious worldview,* there is, to use William James's term again, a "More." In addition to the visible world of our ordinary experience and as disclosed by science, there is a "More," a nonmaterial layer or level of reality, an extra dimension of reality.

This view is shared by all the enduring religions of the world. To echo language from the contemporary historian of religion Huston Smith, this conviction was until recently the "human unanimity."[2] "The More" has been named in various ways: God, Spirit, the sacred, Yahweh, the Tao, Allah, Brahman, Atman, and so forth.

In a *nonreligious worldview,* there is no "More." There is only "this"—the space-time world of matter and energy and whatever other natural forces lie behind or beyond it. Born in the Enlightenment of the seventeenth century, it is sometimes called a secular or naturalistic or material worldview. It is the familiar image of the universe as a giant system made up of tiny particles of stuff plus mysterious force fields, all operating in accord with natural laws, which we are discerning more and more. And because this is the dominant worldview in modern Western culture, it is often called the modern worldview or the world-view of modernity.

In the last three centuries, these two worldviews have collided in Western culture—and that's why the central religious issue of our time is the reality of God. The modern worldview has no foundational place for God. It thus makes the reality of God problematic. For some, it leads to rejecting the reality of God, or at least to serious doubts about God, and thus to atheism or agnosticism.

And for those who continue to believe in God, it changes how God is thought of. Many Christians basically accept the modern world-view's image of reality and then add God onto it. God is the one who created the space-time world of matter and energy as a self-contained system, set it in motion, and perhaps sometimes intervenes in it. God becomes a supernatural being "out there" who created a universe from which God is normally absent. This is, as we shall see, a serious distortion of the meaning of the word "God."

To return to a religious worldview: there is "more" than the space-time world of matter and energy. And the most common term in Western culture to refer to this "More" is the word or name "God." And so the question "Is God real?" is really the question "Is there a 'More'?" My own answer is an emphatic "yes."

Of course, I cannot demonstrate or prove the reality of God. But I will briefly cite the kinds of data to which I would appeal. I use the word "data" rather than "evidence," simply because "evidence" may suggest "proof," which is impossible. But the data are suggestive.

First, there is the collective witness and wisdom of the world's religions, which I have mentioned briefly. Of course, the fact that most people and cultures prior to modernity affirmed the reality of God does not prove anything. But it is reasonable to take seriously the possibility that their affirmation was grounded in what they did know, not in what they didn't know.

Second, the data of religious experience is highly suggestive, especially in its more dramatic forms of mystical, shamanic, and visionary experiences. People throughout history and across cultures have had experiences that seem overwhelmingly to them to be experiences of the sacred. There also are "quieter" forms of religious experiences in the dailiness of our lives. The experiential base of religion is very strong, and for me is ultimately its most persuasive ground.[3]

Third, there are the provocative affirmations of postmodern science, especially postmodern physics. In his recent book *Why Religion Matters,* Huston Smith refers to two contemporary physicists who have said that the most fundamental processes of the universe occur outside of space and time. The statement stretches, indeed shatters, the modern worldview, which affirms only the space-time world of matter and energy.[4]

Of course, such statements do not prove the reality of God. But they do call into question the ultimacy and adequacy of the modern worldview. Indeed, the vision of reality emerging in postmodern physics is compatible with a religious worldview. The conflict between religion and science that marked the last two centuries is subsiding in many parts of the church. Religion and postmodern science alike both point to a stupendous "More."

Two Concepts of God

How are we to think of "the More"? Concepts of God concern what we think the word "God" refers to as well as how we think of the relationship between God and the world, the "God-world relationship." Is God "out there"? Or "right here"? Or both?

In the history of Christianity, there are two primary ways of thinking about God and the God-world relationship. In common with many others, I call these two concepts of God "supernatural theism" and "panentheism."[5]

One of the central themes of Karen Armstrong's impressive bestselling book A *History of God* is that these two concepts of God run side by side throughout the history of the Abrahamic religions, Judaism, Christianity, and Islam. Both are ancient, going back to the beginnings of each.

Supernatural theism imagines God as *a personlike being.* To be sure, God is an exceedingly superlative personlike being, is indeed the supreme being. A long time ago, this personlike being created the world as something separate from God. Thus God and the world are sharply distinguished: God is "up in heaven," "out there," beyond the universe.

It follows from this image of God that the God-world relationship is seen in interventionist terms; namely, from "out there" God occasionally intervenes in this world. For supernatural theism in Christian form, these interventions include the spectacular events reported in the Bible, especially those associated with Jesus: his birth, miracles, death, and resurrection. Moreover, supernatural theists generally affirm that God continues to intervene to this day, especially in response to prayer.

Panentheism, the second way of thinking about God, imagines God and the God-world relationship differently. Though the word "panentheism" is only about two hundred years old, the notion is very ancient. Rather than imagining God as a personlike being "out there," this concept imagines God as *the encompassing Spirit* in whom everything that is, is. The universe is not separate from God, but *in* God. Indeed, this is the meaning of the Greek roots of the word "panentheism": *pan* means "everything," *en* means "in," and *theism* comes from the Greek word for "God," *theos.*

Like the language of supernatural theism, this notion is also found in the Bible. Its clearest compact expression is attributed to Paul in the book of Acts: God is the one in whom "we live and move and have our being."[6] Notice how the language works. Where are we in relation to God? We are in God; we live in God, move in God, have our being in God. God is not "out there," but "right here," all around us.

Significantly, this concept of God does not reduce God to the universe or identify God with the universe. As the encompassing Spirit, God is more than everything, even as everything is in God. Thus, God is not only "right here," but also "more than right here."

Though the word "panentheism" is unfamiliar to many Christians, the notion really shouldn't be. Most of us who grew up in the church heard God being spoken of both as "up in heaven" and as "everywhere," that is, as omnipresent. The traditional terms for these two dimensions of God are transcendence and immanence: the "moreness" and the "presence" of God. Combining these two affirmations produces the central claim of panentheism: God is "the More" who is "right here." Panentheism is not a modern invention, but an ancient and traditional concept of God.

Thinking of God as the encompassing Spirit leads to a different way of thinking about the God-world relationship. The notion of "intervention" disappears in the precise sense in which I define it: intervention presupposes that God is "out there," somewhere else and not here; thus God must intervene in order to act here. But thinking of God as "right here" (as well as "more than right here"), as present as well as transcendent, leads to a different model of the God-world relationship. Rather than speaking of divine intervention, panentheism speaks of divine intention and divine interaction. Or, to use sacramental language, it sees the presence of God "in, with, and under" every-thing—not as the direct cause of events, but as a presence beneath and within our everyday lives.

Because panentheism does not speak of divine intervention, people often wonder what happens to prayer in this context. This is another of the ten most frequently asked questions in my life as a lec-turer. If we don't affirm divine intervention, what happens to peti-tionary and intercessory prayer, our prayers for "help" for ourselves and others?

Panentheism does not deny the efficacy of such prayer. Its frame-work allows for prayers to have effects, including prayers for healing. It does not rule out extraordinary events. But it refuses to see effica-cious prayer or extraordinary events as the result of divine interven-tion. It does so for more than one reason. Intervention counters its notion of God: it does not see God as absent, but present. Moreover, it sees the notion of divine intervention as having an insuperable diffi-culty: if God sometimes intervenes, how does one account for the noninterventions? Given all of the horrible things that happen, does the notion that God ever intervenes make any sense?

If God could have intervened to stop the Holocaust but chose not to, what kind of sense does that make? Does it make sense to think that God could intervene to stop terrorist attacks, but (at least some-times) chooses not to? That God could choose to keep a plane from crashing or a tornado from striking? If so, why some and not others? And then there are all the tragedies that don't make the news: acci-dents, disfigurements, abuse, premature deaths from illness, and on and on. To suppose that God intervenes implies that God does so for some, but not for others.

And so panentheism rejects the language of "divine intervention." From its point of view, interventionism not only has insurmountable difficulties, but claims to know too much; namely, it claims to know that "intervention" is the explanatory mechanism for God's relation to the world. Except in the very general sense of "divine intentional-ity" and "divine interactivity," panentheism does not claim to have an explanation of the God-world relation. It is content not to know.[7]

As already mentioned, both supernatural theism and panenthe-ism are deeply rooted in the Christian tradition, but for the last few hundred years supernatural theism has become dominant in Western Christianity. The primary reason is once again the Enlightenment. Beginning in the seventeenth century, the universe was increasingly thought of as a natural system separate from God. God was thus removed from nature, creating a thorough "disenchantment of nature."[8] Separated from the universe, God came increasingly to be thought of as only "out there."

The dominance of supernatural theism in modern Western Christianity has had serious consequences. When "out there" is emphasized and separated from "right here," God's relation to the world is distorted, and the notion of God becomes harder and harder to accept. "Out there" means something different for us than it meant when our premodern ancestors used this language. For them, "up there" or "out there" was not very far away. They thought of the universe as small with the earth at its center; the sun, moon, planets, and stars were mounted on a dome not very far above the earth. It is diffi-cult to know how literally they took this language, but the basic notion of a small universe was shared by all.

In that context, thinking of God as "our Father who art in heaven" did not make God very far away. But for us, "up there" or "out there" is very far away. If God is only "out there," as supernatural theism sug-gests, then God is very distant, not intimately close. God becomes remote, absent. And the difference between a remote and absent God and "no God" is slender.

So common is supernatural theism in our time that many people think its concept of God is the only meaning the word "God" can have. For them, believing in God means believing in a personlike being "out there." Not believing this means not believing in God.

I encounter this in my university students. Every term one or more of them says to me after class, "This is all very interesting, but I have a problem every time you use the word 'God,' because, you see"—here there's usually a pause and a deep breath—"I really don't believe in God." I always respond the same way: "Tell me about the God you don't believe in." Invariably, it is the God of supernatural theism. I then tell them that I don't believe in that God either. They are surprised, for they know that I believe in God. They're simply not aware that there is an option other than supernatural theism.

That option, of course, is panentheism. Significantly, it is a form of theism. Thus I do not speak of the "end of theism," as a few religious thinkers in our time do. I understand them to mean the "end of supernatural theism"; namely, that for many people supernatural theism is no longer compelling and persuasive. With this, I agree. But I think it is confusing to call this the "end of theism." To many people, this sounds like rejection of the very idea of God; in their minds, not surprisingly, the alternative to theism is atheism.

But a panentheistic way of thinking about God is an alternative form of theism. It is just as biblical as supernatural theism. Indeed, in an important respect, it is more biblical and more orthodox than supernatural theism, for it emphasizes both the transcendence and presence of God, whereas supernatural theism in its modern form emphasizes only the transcendence of God.

As I end this section on concepts of God, there are two more considerations. The first concerns the meaning of the word "God" itself. To echo a comment made a half century ago by Paul Tillich, one of the twentieth century's two most important Protestant theologians: if, when you think of the word "God," you are thinking of a reality that may or may not exist, you are not thinking of God. Tillich's point is that the word "God" does not refer to a particular existing being (that's the God of supernatural theism). Rather, the word "God" is the most common Western name for "what is," for "ultimate reality," for "the ground of being," for "Being itself," for "isness."

Very important, God is not simply a name for "what is" as defined by the modern worldview, not simply a poetic name for the space-time universe of matter and energy. Rather, to use a phrase from Thomas Keating, a contemporary Benedictine teacher of contemplative prayer, God is the name we use for "isness without limitations," "isness" without limits.[9] To ask what seems like a silly question, is "isness"? Of course. And so the question of God is not the question

"Is there another being, a supreme being, in addition to the universe?" It is the question of how you are going to name, how you are going to see, "isness."

The second consideration concerns our language about God. The religions of the world often emphasize that God or the sacred is beyond all words, beyond all language. The semitechnical word for this is "ineffable." Lao Tzu, a sixth-century BCE Chinese religious figure, spoke of the sacred as the "Tao" (pronounced "dow"). The opening line of the *Tao te Ching*, the collection of sayings attributed to him, says, "The Tao that can be named is not the eternal Tao." If you name the sacred, you are distinguishing it from the rest of reality and thus you are no longer talking about it. The sacred, the Tao, is beyond all our words.

Belden Lane, a contemporary Christian theologian, makes the same point about language about God:

> We must speak, yet we cannot speak without stammering. . . . [Language about God] stalks the borderland of the limits of language, using speech to confound speech, speaking in riddles, calling us to humble silence in the presence of mystery.[10]

God is the name we use for the nonmaterial stupendous, wondrous "More" that includes the universe even as God transcends the universe. This is God as the "encompassing Spirit," the one in whom "we live and move and have our being," the one who is all around us and within us. God is the one in whom the universe is, even as God is more than the universe; the Mystery who is beyond all names, even as we name the sacred Mystery in our various ways.

God as Personal

In the Christian tradition, as in most religions, God is often spoken of as "personal"—as a personlike being with personal characteristics. But is God personal? Supernatural theism unambiguously affirms this, whereas panentheism seems to some people to be disappointingly impersonal. So, is God personal? If so, in what sense?

In the rich concluding chapter of *The Varieties of Religious Experience,* William James makes passing reference to a God who does "wholesale business" and a God who does "retail business."[11] I will refer to these as the "wholesale God" and the "retail God," and I will develop these notions in a way that James does not, but a way I think he might approve of.

The "wholesale God" is God abstracted from the language of any particular religious tradition. This is the God of philosophical theology—to use language I just used, this is God as "ultimate reality," as "Being itself," as "isness without limitation," or, from William James himself, as "the More." The "wholesale God" is what we talk about when we talk about what the word "God" means, what it points to.

The "retail God" is the sacred named the way it is done in the various religions. This is God (or the gods) as the central character(s) in the sacred texts and stories of the world's religions. To continue the analogy, this is the god of the retail outlets, the local distributors. Typically (though not always), the "retail God" is personified—God spoken of as having personal characteristics, as if God were a personlike being. Such personification is the natural language of what we might call "retail religion." It is the natural language of devotion and worship.

I have no problem with the "retail God," that is, with the use of personal language for God. I use such language all the time. I use it when I join in the worship of my church and in my private devotional life. I have no problem personifying God and addressing God as if God were a person.

Problems arise only when we literalize or semiliteralize these personifications. This happens in both hard and soft ways. Hard literalization is when we take our personifications of God quite literally—that, for example, the phrase "the right hand of God" means that God really has hands.

Few Christians are literalists to this extent, though some are. For example, a couple of years ago, a group of Baptists separated themselves from the Texas Baptist Convention on the grounds that they believe that God is a gendered being, and specifically that God is a male being (of course).[12] One wonders what this could mean. Does it mean that God has male sex organs? That God has to shave? Well, of course, that's silly.

But there is a softer literalization of personal language for God that is much more common—not that God has feet or hands or arms, and so forth, but that *God is a personlike being.* God is a personal being separate from the universe and from other beings, personal in the sense of being somewhat like us, even though to a superlative degree. In short, the literalization of our personifications of God, whether in hard or soft form, leads to supernatural theism and to the problems associated with it.

I intend no value judgment between the "wholesale God" and the "retail God." Both are legitimate ways of speaking about God. But I add that there are many people in our time who need to hear about the "wholesale God" in order to be able to take the "retail God" seriously. Like many, I cannot myself think of God as personal in the sense of being a personlike being, even though I am very comfortable using personal language to refer to God.

So, what meaning or content can we give to personal language for God? Thus far I have been able to see three dimensions of meaning:

Whatever God is ultimately like, *our relationship to God is personal.* This relationship engages us as persons at our deepest and most passionate level.

I am persuaded that *God has more the quality of a "presence"* than of a nonpersonal "energy" or "force." To use language Martin Buber used, I am persuaded that God has more the quality of a "you" than of an "it," more the quality of a person than the quality of an impersonal "source."[13] I see this sense of God as a presence, as a "you," as grounded in experience. I also see it reflected in the centrality of the notion of *covenant* in the Jewish and Christian traditions. We are in a covenantal relationship with "what is," and covenant is an intrinsically relational model of reality.

Moreover, I think God *"speaks" to us*. I don't mean oral or aural revelation or divine dictation. But I think God "speaks" to us— sometimes dramatically in visions, less dramatically in some of our dreams, in internal "proddings" or "leadings," through people, and through the devotional practices and scriptures of our tradition. We sometimes have a sense—I sometimes have a sense—of being *addressed*.

The contemporary author Frederick Buechner writes powerfully about the way God speaks to us in the events of our lives:

> Listen to your life. Listen to what happens to you because it is through what happens to you that God speaks. . . . It's in language that's not always easy to decipher, but it's there powerfully, memorably, unforgettably.[14]

It is important not to misunderstand this passage. Buechner does not mean that everything that happens to us is the direct will of God. Rather, in, with, and under the events of our lives, we are addressed by God "in language that's not always easy to decipher, but [is] there powerfully, memorably, unforgettably."

So, is God personal? At the ontological level, I don't know, even as I am convinced that God is not a personlike being. Some theologians speak of God as transpersonal. Such language is useful, for we often think that the only alternative to "personal" is "impersonal." But transpersonal is another option: it means "more than personal," not "less than personal." I like the language, although I don't know if "transpersonal" is still "personal" in some reasonably normal sense of the word. But I do think that personal language for God is appropriate. Indeed, I think it is more appropriate than impersonal language, for I am persuaded that God is not *less* than personal.

The Character of God

Thus far we have been considering the *being* of God: how we might think of God and the God-world relationship. We turn now to the important question of how we think of the *character* of God.

By the character of God, I mean what is sometimes spoken of as the nature of God or even as the will of God, but I see character as deeper than will. To explain with a human analogy, our will is the product of something deeper within us; namely, it is the product of our character. We "will," we decide, in accord with our character. So too, God's character is deeper than God's will. Thus, by the character of God I mean, "What is your God most basically like?"

So, what is the character of your God?[15] I illustrate the importance of this question with a series of questions. Is your God:

- Primarily concerned about personal virtue?

- Primarily a lawgiver and judge, somebody you need to measure up to?

- A God of requirements and rewards?

- Primarily a God of heaven and hell?

- Primarily a national God?

- Mostly "nice"?

- Mostly indifferent?

- A God of compassion?

- A God of social justice?

The point: it makes a difference how we see the character of God, for how we see the character of God shapes our sense of what faithfulness to God means and thus what the Christian life is about.

The various ways of seeing the character of God suggested by these questions crystallize into two primary ways. Whether these two ways are complete contrasts or whether they can be combined, I leave unaddressed. I know the contrasts are pedagogically useful for our own thinking and clarity. Both are found in the Bible and in the continuing Christian tradition, and in many and perhaps most religious traditions.

In the first way of imaging God's character, God is a *God of requirements and rewards*. Like an ancient king, God is the lawgiver and judge who has requirements that must be met. It is what I and others have called "the monarchical model of God."[16] Our relationship to God is expressed in legal language. We have been disobedient to God's laws and deserve punishment, but God has provided a way of dealing with sin through sacrifice and repentance, with the death of Jesus understood as the sacrifice that makes our forgiveness and salvation possible. Believing this to be true is the requirement, the means of salvation.

In extreme form, this is the God of the best-selling "left behind" novels—the God of the "rapture" and the second coming who will rescue and save some people, but destroy most of humankind. In less extreme form, it has been the most common and widespread way of imaging God's character in popular Christianity through the centuries. Those who believe that Jesus died for our sins will be saved. Those who do not, will not. When God's character is thought of this way, then the Christian life is about meeting God's requirements, be they many or few.

The second way of imaging God's character sees God as a *God of love and justice*. This is a frequent emphasis in the Bible. The prophets of the Hebrew Bible use the language of love to speak of God's relation to Israel. God is the lover, Israel is the beloved. In God's name and personifying Israel as a woman, Hosea says, "I will now allure her, and bring her into the wilderness, and speak tenderly to her. . . . There she shall respond [to me] as in the days of her youth." Shifting to addressing Israel with the language of "you," Hosea continues: "On that day, you will call me 'My husband,' . . . and I will take you for my wife forever."[17] To the Jewish people in exile, Isaiah in God's name says, "You are precious in my sight, and honored, and I love you."[18]

From ancient times, the erotic love poetry of the Song of Songs (also known as the Song of Solomon and Canticles) has been understood as an allegory or parable of the God-Israel relationship, the divine-human relationship, or the Christ-church relationship. Who are we in relationship to God? We are the beloved of God. So also in the New Testament. To remind you of just one very familiar example, the opening words of John 3:16: "For God so loved the world . . ."

The God of love is also the God of justice. The two are related, for in the Bible justice is the social form of love. Thus the God of love is not simply "nice," but has an edge, a passion for justice. God loves everybody and everything, including the nonhuman world—not just me, and not just me and you, and not just us. To take the God of love and justice seriously means to take justice seriously and to be aware that prolonged injustice has consequences.

The image of the Christian life that goes with this view of God's character is quite different from the requirements-and-rewards emphasis of the first way. The Christian life is about a relationship with God that transforms us into more compassionate beings. The God of love and justice is the God of relationship and transformation.

Another way of putting this same contrast is the God of law versus the God of grace. A classic Lutheran contrast, it is also widespread among other Protestants. Very important, despite a common Christian stereotype, this contrast does not correspond to the difference between the Hebrew Bible and the New Testament or to the difference between Judaism and Christianity. Both ways of imaging God's character are found in both Testaments and in both religions.

God as the lawgiver and judge is the God of "works" that Paul and Luther and the Protestant Reformation in general rejected. Instead, they affirmed radical grace: God's acceptance of us is unconditional, not dependent upon something we believe or do. But radical grace has most often been too radical for most Christians. We most often put conditions on God's grace: God accepts you *if* . . . And whenever an "if" clause is added, grace becomes conditional and ceases to be grace.

An important clarification: unconditional grace is not about how we get to heaven or who goes to heaven. The notion that salvation is primarily about "going to heaven" is a distortion; and when it is seen as primary, the notion of unconditional grace leads to the notion that everybody gets to go to heaven, regardless of their life and faith. However, unconditional grace is not about the afterlife, but the basis for our relationship with God in this life. Is the basis for our life with God law or grace, requirements and rewards or relationship and transformation? Grace affirms the latter.

Taking the God of love and justice and the God of grace seriously has immediate implications for the Christian message. It becomes: God loves us already and has from our very beginning. The Christian life is not about believing or doing what we need to believe or do so that we can be saved. Rather, it's about seeing what is already true— that God loves us already—and then beginning to live in this relationship. It is about becoming conscious of and intentional about a deepening relationship with God.

These two ways of imaging the character of God lead to two very different versions of the Christian message. It can be heard as "bad news" or "good news." The "bad news" version is that there will be a last judgment, either at the end of our lives or at the end of history, and you better be ready or you'll be in deep trouble. This is Christianity as a religion of threat, anxiety, and self-preservation.

The "good news" version is the invitation into a new life here and now, one that transforms us personally and seeks to transform life in this world. The "bad news" version is the saving of some from the devouring fire that will consume the rest. The "good news" version is a vision of transformed people and a transformed earth filled with the glory of God.

What's at stake in the question of God's character is our image of the Christian life. Is Christianity about requirements? Here's what you must do to be saved. Or is Christianity about relationship and transformation? Here's the path: follow it. Both involve imperatives, but one is a threat, the other an invitation.

1. The term "More" is used frequently in William James's *The Varieties of Religious Experience,* published in 1902. In a survey of intellectuals taken in 1999 in the United States, it was named the second most important nonfiction book of the twentieth century originally published in English.

2. Huston Smith, *Forgotten Truth* (San Francisco: HarperSanFrancisco, 1976, 1992), pp. x, 5, 18. The first edition was subtitled *The Primordial Tradition.*

3. See also my *The God We Never Knew* (San Francisco: HarperSanFrancisco, 1997), pp. 37–44.

4. The physicists are Henry Stapp and Geoffrey Chew from the University of California, Berkeley. Smith quotes Stapp: "Everything we [now] know about nature is in accord with the idea that the fundamental process of nature lies outside space-time, but generates events that can be located within space-time." Huston Smith, *Why Religion Matters* (San Francisco: HarperSanFrancisco, 2001), p. 176.

5. For my development of this contrast at greater length, see my *The God We Never Knew,* chaps. 1 and 2.

6. Acts 17:28. See also Ps. 139. For more, see *The God We Never Knew,* pp. 34–37.

7. For more on petitionary and intercessory prayer, see Chapter 9, pp. 196–98.

8. See the use of this phrase from Max Weber by Harvey Cox, *The Secular City* (New York: Macmillan, 1965), pp. 21–24.

9. Remark made by Keating in a lecture at Trinity Episcopal Cathedral in Portland, Oregon, January 2002. For further reference to Keating and "centering prayer," the kind of contemplative prayer he teaches, see Chapter 10, pp. 198–99 and note 11.

10. Belden Lane, *The Solace of Fierce Landscapes* (New York: Oxford University Press, 1998), p. 69.

11. William James, *The Varieties of Religious Experience* (New York: Simon and Schuster, 1997), pp. 383–84.

12. Reported in *The Christian Century* (Summer 2001).

13. Martin Buber, *I and Thou* (New York: Charles Scribner's Sons, 1970); this edition and translation by Walter Kaufmann is better than the first English translation. An important, brilliant, and difficult book, it needs to be savored, and it richly repays patience. The book cannot be read for "information"; what it seeks to convey is another way of seeing.

14. From an interview in *The Christian Century* (September 11–24, 2002): 26–33. This is also a theme of the introduction to his book *The Sacred Journey* (San Francisco: Harper & Row, 1982).

15. I owe this phrasing to John Dominic Crossan, *The Birth of Christianity* (San Francisco: HarperSanFrancisco, 1998), pp. 575–86.

16. See *The God We Never Knew*, pp. 61–71.

17. Hos. 2:14–16, 19.

18. Isa. 43:4.

FIVE

Jesus
The Heart of God

The third affirmation at the heart of Christianity is the utter centrality of Jesus. Jesus is third merely in order of exposition, for Jesus is as
important as the Bible and God. The significance of Jesus, God, and
the Bible are all interwoven. We know about the God of Israel and
the figure of Jesus primarily through the Bible. And we know about
God—about God's character and passion—most decisively through
Jesus.[1]

Indeed, one of the defining characteristics of Christianity is that
we find the revelation of God primarily *in a person*, an affirmation
unique among the major religions of the world. For Judaism and
Islam, though Moses and Muhammad are receivers of revelation, God
is not revealed in them as persons, but in the words of the Torah and
Qur'an. So also in Buddhism: the Buddha as a person is not the revelation of God; rather, the Buddha's teachings disclose the path to
enlightenment and compassion.

But Christianity finds the primary revelation of God in a person.
This does not make Christianity superior, but does make it different.
For Christians, to use language from John's gospel, in Jesus "the Word
became flesh and lived among us." This is the central meaning of
incarnation: Jesus is what can be seen of God embodied in a human

life. He is the revelation, the incarnation, of God's character and passion—of what God is like and of what God is most passionate about. He shows us the heart of God.

And because Christians find the ultimate disclosure of God in a person and not in a book, Jesus is more central than the Bible. Jesus trumps the Bible; when they disagree, Jesus wins. Yet, of course, we know about him primarily through the Bible, and in particular through the New Testament. The interweaving of God, Jesus, and the Bible is at the heart of the Christian vision of life.

The emerging paradigm affirms the decisive centrality of Jesus, even as it sees Jesus quite differently than the earlier paradigm does. Its historical, metaphorical, and sacramental approach leads to "seeing Jesus again," just as it leads to seeing the Bible and God again. As I turn to the emerging paradigm's view of Jesus, I emphasize five major reasons why "seeing Jesus again" matters.

An Earlier Image of Jesus Unpersuasive

The first reason a historical-metaphorical approach matters is that an earlier image of Jesus and the image of the Christian life that goes with it have become unpersuasive to millions of people in the last century. The earlier image is quite familiar. Within the earlier paradigm of hard or soft literalism, the gospels are read literally or semiliterally as if they were straightforward historical documents.

When this is done, the following image of Jesus results. It emphasizes his identity: that he was the Son of God, the "light of the world," the "bread of life," the promised messiah who will come again, and so forth, and that he knew and taught this about himself. It emphasizes the saving significance of his death and sees it as the purpose of his life: he died for our sins. It emphasizes the miraculous, especially the virgin birth and physical bodily resurrection. It also emphasizes that Jesus is the only way of salvation, and that Christianity is therefore the only true religion.

The image of the Christian life that goes with this image of Jesus emphasizes believing all of this to be true: that Jesus is the only Son of God, born of a virgin; that he died for our sins; that he rose physically from the dead; that he will come again; and so forth. This image of Jesus no longer works for millions of people, both within and outside the church. For these millions, its literalism and exclusivity are not only unpersuasive, but a barrier to being Christian.

There are, of course, also millions of Christians who still see Jesus this way. But for people who can't accept the older image, the historical-metaphorical approach to Jesus and Christian origins provides a way to take Jesus seriously.

The Pre-Easter and Post-Easter Jesus

Second, a historical-metaphorical approach matters because of the important distinction between the pre-Easter Jesus and the post-Easter Jesus.[2] The pre-Easter Jesus is *Jesus before his death:* a Galilean Jew born around the year 4 BCE and executed by the Romans around the year 30 CE. The pre-Easter Jesus is dead and gone; he's nowhere anymore. This statement does not deny Easter in any way, but simply recognizes that the corpuscular Jesus, the flesh-and-blood Jesus, is a figure of the past.

To define the second phrase most concisely, the post-Easter Jesus is *what Jesus became after his death.* More fully, the post-Easter Jesus is the Jesus of Christian experience and tradition. Both nouns are important. By the post-Easter Jesus of Christian *experience,* I mean that Jesus continued to be experienced by his followers after his death as a divine reality of the present, and that such experiences continue to happen today; some Christians, but not all, have such experiences. The post-Easter Jesus is thus an experiential reality.[3] By the post-Easter Jesus of Christian *tradition,* I mean the Jesus we encounter in the developing traditions of the early Christian movement—in the gospels and the New Testament as a whole, as well as in the creeds.

Why is the distinction between Jesus before and after Easter so important? The primary reason: when we don't make it, we risk losing both the pre-Easter and post-Easter Jesus. To make the point autobiographically, when I was a child growing up in the church, I didn't know about this distinction. As a result, I took it for granted that Jesus was everything that I heard about him, whether from the New Testament, the creeds, sermons, or hymns. Thus I thought of him as a divine figure: that even as a historical person, he was the only-begotten Son of God, God in human flesh, the second person of the Trinity, and so forth, and that he knew this about himself. I thought of him as having divine knowledge and power. That's how he could know the future, speak with authority, and perform spectacular deeds like changing water into wine and raising Lazarus from the dead.

But notice what happened: Jesus ceased to be a credible human being. Anybody who has the mind and power of God is not one of us, no matter how much he may look like us. Moreover, whenever we emphasize the divinity of Jesus at the expense of his humanity, we lose track of the utterly remarkable human being that he was. If we think that his wisdom, compassion, courage, and healing powers were the result of his divinity, then they are in a sense "not much." Even the most spectacular events attributed to him—walking on water, stilling a storm, feeding a multitude, raising the dead—are not much more than parlor tricks for someone who has the power of God. Albert Nolan, a South African gospel and Jesus scholar, makes the point in language I've grown fond of: "Jesus is a much underrated man. To deprive him of his humanity is to deprive him of his greatness."[4]

When we don't make the distinction between the pre-Easter Jesus and the post-Easter Jesus, we not only lose the former; we also in a sense lose the latter. Jesus becomes a divine figure *of the past*. For thirty-five years, more or less, he was here. But after Easter, he ascended into heaven. He will come again someday, but in the meantime he's not here. And thus we lose the living Jesus as a figure of the present who is still here, still an experiential reality today. But when we do make the distinction, we get both—and both matter.

The Nature of the Gospels

Third, a historical-metaphorical approach matters because it helps us to see the nature of the gospels and thus to understand them better. Two claims are central for the emerging paradigm's way of seeing the gospels.

First, the gospels are the product of a developing tradition. The four gospels of the New Testament were all written several decades after Jesus' life. Mark, the earliest, was written around the year 70, some forty years after Easter; John is probably the latest, most likely written in the 90s. In the decades between Easter and the writing of the gospels, the traditions about Jesus developed; that is, they grew. In part, this was because of the community's continuing experience of the post-Easter Jesus, which affected the way they remembered the pre-Easter Jesus. In part, it was because of adapting the traditions about Jesus to the changing situation of the early Christian movement as the first century unfolded. The gospels were written in and spoke to Christian communities in the last third of the first century.

To use an archeological metaphor, the gospels as a developing tradition thus contain earlier and later layers. Some go back to the time of Jesus, and some are the product of the community at a later date. To shift to a voice metaphor, the gospels contain two voices: the voice of Jesus and the voice of the community. Both layers and voices are important. The former tell us about the pre-Easter Jesus; the latter are the witness and testimony of the community to what Jesus had become in their experience in the decades after Easter.[5]

Second, the gospels are not only a developing tradition, but they also combine memory and metaphor. Like the Bible in general, they are a mixture of historical memory and metaphorical narrative. Metaphor and metaphorical narratives, as I emphasized in my chapter on the Bible, can be profoundly true even though not literally factual.

In our time, many need to hear about the distinction between history and metaphor because there are many parts of the gospels that they can't take literally. When literalized, the story of Jesus becomes literally incredible. But it's not meant to be incredible; as good news, it is meant to be compelling.

Moreover, recognizing metaphor in the gospels matters because it helps us to see rich meanings in the texts that we would otherwise miss. A literal reading can flatten the text. The story of Jesus changing water into wine at the wedding in Cana in the second chapter of John's gospel illustrates the point. A literal reading emphasizes the spectacular deed: if Jesus could change 120 to 150 gallons of water into wine, he must really have been somebody—he must have had the power of God. The story becomes "evidence" of Jesus' identity, "proof" that he was who he said he was.

A historical-metaphorical reading of this story yields a very different meaning. It notes its literary context: in John's gospel, the wedding at Cana is the opening scene of the public activity of Jesus. As such, it is John's way of saying, "This is what the story of Jesus is about" (just as the inaugural scene of Jesus' public activity in the other gospels is an epiphany of what their stories of Jesus are about). The story begins in a highly evocative way: "On the third day, there was a wedding . . ." The story of Jesus is about a wedding, and the phrase "on the third day" evokes the Easter story at the very beginning of Jesus' story.

Wedding and marriage have rich metaphorical associations in the biblical and Christian traditions. There is the mystical imagery of the marriage of heaven and earth, of God as lover and us as the beloved of God. The story of Jesus is about this. It is also earthy: a wedding banquet was the most festive occasion in Jewish peasant life. A celebration lasting seven days, it involved dancing and copious amounts of food and wine, in sharp contrast to the basic peasant diet of grains, vegetables, fruit, and an occasional fish.

So, what is the story of Jesus about? According to John's inaugural story of Jesus' public activity, it is about a wedding. More: it is about a wedding banquet. More: it is about a wedding banquet at which the wine never runs out. More: it is about a wedding banquet at which the wine never runs out, and the best is saved for last. The story of the wedding at Cana invites us to see that the story of Jesus is about *this*.

A literal reading can miss all of that. Instead, it generates a factual question that is a distraction and can be a stumbling block: Do you believe this really happened? By not focusing on this question, a metaphorical reading enables us to see the rich meanings of the text. Rather than being inferior to a literal reading, a metaphorical reading is richer.

The Meaning of Our Christological Language

Fourth, a historical-metaphorical approach matters because it helps us to see the meaning of our christological language, by which I mean the exalted "titles" used to refer to Jesus' identity and significance in the New Testament. These include Son of God, Lord, Messiah, Word of God, Wisdom of God, Great High Priest and Sacrifice, Lamb of God, Light of the World, Bread of Life, True Vine, and so forth.

Though not all of this language is in sayings attributed to Jesus, some of it is (especially in John), so that he is presented as making these claims about himself. It is the basis for the earlier paradigm's perception of the identity of Jesus. It is also the basis for C. S. Lewis's well-known comment, still encountered in conservative Christian apologetic works:

> A man who was merely a man and said the sort of things Jesus said would not be a great moral teacher. He would either be a lunatic—on a level with the man who says he is a poached egg—or else he would be the Devil of Hell. Either this man was, and is, the Son of God: or else a madman or something worse.[6]

Lewis's comment depends upon the claim that the christological language of the gospels originates with Jesus himself.

But it almost certainly does not. Within the emerging paradigm, this language looks quite different. Four statements are important. First, this language is post-Easter. A strong majority of mainline scholars think it unlikely that Jesus said these things about himself; he probably did not speak of himself as the Messiah, the Son of God, the Light of the World, and so forth. Rather, this is the voice of the community in the years and decades after Easter. It is not the language of self-proclamation, but the community's testimony to Jesus' significance in their lives.

As such, it is very powerful. The community affirms: we have found in this person the light in our darkness, the way that has led us from death to life, the bread of life that nourishes us even now; we have found in this person the word and wisdom of God; we have found in this person the son of God, the promised messiah; he is one with God, and we address him as "My Lord and my God." Indeed, for me this language is more powerful as the testimony of a community than if I try to imagine it as language a man used about himself.

Second, all of this language is metaphorical. We see this most readily by putting a number of these titles in a single sentence: "I believe Jesus is the Lamb of God, the Light of the World, the Bread of Life, the Word of God, and the Son of God." To state the obvious, Jesus is not a lamb or a sheep, not a flame or a candle, not a loaf, not a word (not a sound or writing on a page). These are all metaphors.

To use another example: in John's gospel, Jesus is the "door." In the book of Revelation, Jesus is "standing at the door, knocking."[7] Well, which is he—the door or the one knocking at the door? He cannot literally be both. Even to raise this question is, of course, a mistake, for it is not an "either-or," but a "both-and": Jesus is both the door and the one who stands at the door and knocks. Metaphorically, he is both—really both, even though not literally so.

But we have tended to literalize at least one of the christological titles, namely "Son of God." We have done so in part because of a literal reading of the birth stories and in part because of the prominence of "Son of God" in the creeds and in our language about the Trinity.

But "Son of God" is a metaphor like the rest. It affirms that Jesus' relationship to God is intimate, like that of child to parent. To echo language from John's gospel: the son knows the father, and the father knows the son, and the son is the father's beloved. This relational understanding of "son of God" is found in the Jewish world of Jesus. In the Hebrew Bible, Israel is called son of God, as are the kings of

Israel and Judah. Closer to the time of Jesus, Jewish mystics who were healers were sometimes referred to as God's son. And "son" resonates with agency as well; in his world, a son could represent a father and speak with the authority of the father. To call Jesus "Son of God" means all of this.

Third, christological language is language of confession and commitment. Metaphor means "to see as." To say, "Jesus is the light of the world," is to say, "I see Jesus as the light of the world"; to say, "Jesus is the Messiah and Lord," is to say, "I see Jesus as the Messiah and Lord." Thus it is the language of confession, like the statement attributed to Peter in response to Jesus' question, "Who do you say that I am?": "You are the Christ," that is, "You are the Messiah."[8]

As confessional language, it is also the language of commitment. It would make no sense to say, "Jesus is the light of the world," and then be indifferent to him. To use this language about Jesus is to commit oneself to him. On the other hand, simply to believe that he used this language about himself does not involve commitment. One might believe that he said all of these things about himself and yet think that he was mistaken.

It is important to keep the individual metaphors because of their rich resonances of meaning. Jesus is the light in our darkness, the bread that satisfies our hunger, the vine that is the source of our life, the healer who makes us whole, the door, and the way, and so forth. But it is possible to speak of the cumulative meaning of all of this language combined together.

And this leads to the fourth statement, a crystallization of the meaning of the community's christological language. In a single sentence: Jesus is, for us as Christians, the decisive revelation of what a life full of God looks like. Radically centered in God and filled with the Spirit, he is the decisive disclosure and epiphany of what can be seen of God embodied in a human life. As the Word and Wisdom and Spirit of God become flesh, his life incarnates the character of God, indeed, the passion of God. In him we see God's passion.

And we can say that he is the decisive revelation of God for us as Christians without needing to say that he is the *only* and exclusive revelation of God, as the earlier paradigm affirms. To paraphrase William Sloane Coffin, a contemporary author and activist: for us as Christians, God is defined by Jesus, but not confined to Jesus. To paraphrase Krister Stendahl, a New Testament scholar, former dean of Harvard Divinity School, and bishop of the Church of Sweden: we as Christians can sing our love songs to Jesus with wild abandon without needing to demean other religions.[9] We need not diminish our devotion to Jesus or our affirmation of him as the decisive revelation of God in order to recognize the validity of the other enduring religions.

Glimpsing the Pre-Easter Jesus

The fifth and final reason the historical-metaphorical study of Jesus matters builds upon the cumulative meaning of christological language; namely, because Jesus is for us as Christians the decisive disclosure of what a life full of God looks like, what we can glimpse of the pre-Easter Jesus matters.

To avoid a possible misunderstanding, I do not think that historical Jesus research as practiced over the last two centuries is essential to being Christian. Christians prior to the modern period and to this day have lived lives shaped in the likeness of Christ based on "only" the gospel and New Testament portraits of Jesus—that is, without access to the historical study of Jesus. My claim is more modest: that the historical study of Jesus is relevant for our time in particular. It can help to flesh out the incarnation.[10]

So, what was Jesus like during his historical lifetime? There is no scholarly unanimity about this, but I think we can know the following about him with a reasonable degree of probability. Because I have developed this elsewhere at length, I here provide a compact summary of my five-stroke sketch of the pre-Easter Jesus:[11]

1. He was a *Jewish mystic*. This first stroke is my most compact shorthand phrase for the historical Jesus. I also see it as foundational for the other four strokes. Mystics are people who have vivid and typically frequent experiences of God, "the

One," "the sacred." Found in every culture known to us, they are also central to the Jewish tradition. In the broad sense of the word as I am using it here, the formative figures of the Hebrew Bible were mystics. Stories about Abraham, Jacob, Moses, Elijah, Elisha, and the classical prophets portray them as people for whom God was an experiential reality. Such figures are also known in Judaism in the time of Jesus: Honi the Circle-Drawer, Hanina ben Dosa, Paul, and Peter. Whatever else needs to be said about Jesus, he was one of these. According to the gospels, he had visions, fasted, spent long hours in prayer, spoke of God in intimate terms, and taught the immediacy of access to God—something mystics know in their own experience. As a Jewish mystic, Jesus lived a life radically centered in God; that was its foundation

2. He was a *healer*. Not all mystics become healers, but some do. Even nonreligious scholars agree that Jesus performed paranormal healings and what he and his contemporaries experienced as exorcisms. More healing stories are told about Jesus than about any other figure in the Jewish tradition. He must have been a remarkable healer.

3. He was a *wisdom teacher*. Teachers of wisdom teach a way, a path, of life. The "narrow way" of which Jesus spoke led beyond the "broad way" of convention and tradition. It was the "road less traveled," to use the phrase from Robert Frost that became the title of M. Scott Peck's recent best-selling book. At the heart of the alternative wisdom of Jesus was the path of death and resurrection understood as a metaphor for an internal psychological-spiritual process. It involved dying to an old identity and being born into a new identity, dying to an old way of being and being born into a new way of being. The new identity and new way of being was a life radically centered in God, in the Spirit of God Jesus knew in his own experience. About this, I will say more in Chapter 6.

4. He was *a social prophet*. The historical analogy is the great social prophets of the Hebrew Bible, figures such as Isaiah, Jeremiah, Amos, and Micah. They were God-intoxicated voices of religious social protest against the economic and political injustice of the domination systems of their day. Jesus was a prophet of the Kingdom of God—of what life would be like on earth if God were king and the kings and emperors of this world were not. As such, he was a radical critic of the domination system of his time that channeled wealth to the few and poverty to the many. About this, I will say more in Chapter 7.

5. He was *a movement initiator*. A movement came into existence around him during his lifetime, even though his public activity was very brief (the synoptic gospels suggest one year; John, three or four years). It was a deeply Jewish movement, both in constituency and vision. Remarkably inclusive, it subverted the sharp social boundaries of his day. Its most visible public activity was its inclusive meal practice, often targeted by Jesus' critics. He ate with the marginalized and outcasts. It was eating together as a simultaneously religious and political act done in the name of the Kingdom of God. The meal practice of Jesus affirmed that bread and inclusivity—not the sharply divided and subsistence world of the domination system—is the Kingdom of God.

The Death of Jesus:
The Cross in History and Theology

And Jesus was killed. This is one of those facts that everybody knows, but whose significance is often overlooked. He didn't simply die; he was executed. We as Christians participate in the only major religious tradition whose founder was executed by established authority. And if we ask the historical question, "Why was he killed?" the historical answer is because he was a social prophet and movement initiator, a passionate advocate of God's justice, and radical critic of the domination system who had attracted a following. If Jesus had been only a mystic, healer, and wisdom teacher, he almost certainly would not have been executed. Rather, he was killed because of his politics—because of his passion for God's justice.

In the decades after Good Friday and Easter, the early Christian movement preserved the memory of Jesus' execution, even as it also saw additional meanings in his death. Several interpretations are found in the New Testament itself. Together with subsequent Christian reflection on the significance of the cross, this is the subject matter of "atonement theology." Its most familiar form is the statement, "Jesus died for your sins." But as we shall see, this is not the only interpretation of Jesus' death in the New Testament. Moreover, when this interpretation is understood literally rather than metaphorically, it becomes highly problematic.

In the judgment of the majority of mainline scholars, atonement theology does not go back to Jesus himself. We do not think that Jesus thought that the purpose of his life, his vocation, was his death. His purpose was what he was doing as a healer, wisdom teacher, social prophet, and movement initiator. His death was the consequence of what he was doing, but not his purpose. To use recent analogies, the deaths of Mahatma Gandhi and Martin Luther King Jr. were the consequence of what they were doing, but not their purpose. And like them, Jesus courageously kept doing what he was doing even though he knew it could have fatal consequences.

So we do not think Jesus saw his purpose as dying for the sins of the world. Rather, this interpretation, like the others in the New Testament, is post-Easter and thus retrospective. Looking back on the execution of Jesus, the early movement sought to see a providential purpose in this horrendous event.[12]

At least five interpretations of the cross are found in the New Testament itself.[13] The first stays closest to the political meaning of the cross. It is a simple rejection-and-vindication understanding of Good Friday and Easter. The authorities rejected Jesus and killed him;

but God has vindicated Jesus by raising him to God's right hand. "God has made him both Lord and Messiah, this Jesus whom you crucified."[14] The authorities said "no" to Jesus, but God has said "yes."

The second, sometimes known as "the defeat of the powers" understanding of the cross, also stays close to the political meaning.[15] Now, it is not simply the Roman and aristocratic rulers in Judea who are seen as responsible, but the "powers" they represent and incarnate. The language is found primarily in letters attributed to Paul: the world is in bondage to "the principalities and powers," "the elemental spirits of the universe," "the prince of the power of the air." The contemporary scholar Walter Wink has persuasively argued that the "powers" are systems of domination built into human institutions.[16]

For this view, the domination system, understood as something much larger than the Roman governor and the temple aristocracy, is responsible for the death of Jesus. In words attributed to Paul, God through Jesus "disarmed the principalities and powers and made a public example of them, triumphing over them in the cross."[17] The domination system killed Jesus and thereby disclosed its moral bankruptcy and ultimate defeat.

The third sees the death of Jesus as the revelation of "the way." His death and resurrection are seen as the embodiment or incarnation of the path of internal psychological and spiritual transformation that lies at the center of the Christian life. The path (which I will say more about in the next chapter) is dying to an old way of being and being raised into a new way of being. We find this path of dying and rising throughout the New Testament, perhaps most concisely expressed by Paul: "I have been crucified with Christ; it is no longer I who live, but it is Christ who lives in me."[18] Paul refers to himself as having undergone an internal crucifixion so that the old Paul is dead and a new Paul, now one with Christ, lives. The cross reveals "the way," indeed is "the way."

The fourth also sees the death of Jesus as a revelation: it reveals the depth of God's love for us. For this interpretation to work, one must think of Jesus not simply historically as a Jewish social prophet executed by the authorities, but as the Son of God sent into the world for us and our salvation. How much does God love us? In the familiar words of John 3:16, "For God so loved the world that God gave God's only Son" for us. In Paul's words, "But God proves God's love for us in that while we still were sinners Christ died for us."[19] In the cross, we see God's love for us.

The fifth is the familiar sacrificial understanding of Jesus' death: "Jesus died for our sins." Though its ingredients are in the New Testament, its full development did not occur until about nine hundred years ago. Yet it is the one most emphasized in popular Christianity and is central to the earlier paradigm. In its developed form, it sees the story of Jesus primarily within the framework of sin, guilt, and forgiveness. We have all sinned against God and are guilty. Our sins can be forgiven only if an adequate sacrifice is made. The sacrifice of animals does not accomplish this, nor can the sacrifice of an imperfect human (for such a person would simply be dying for his or her own sins). Thus God provides the perfect sacrifice in the form of the perfect human, Jesus. Now forgiveness is possible, but only for those who believe that Jesus died for our sins.

If taken literally, all of this is very strange. It implies a limitation on God's power to forgive; namely, God can forgive only if adequate sacrifice is made. It implies that Jesus' death on the cross was necessary—not just the consequence of what he was doing, but that it had to happen, that it was part of God's plan of salvation. It also introduces a requirement into the very center of our life with God: knowing about and believing in Jesus and his sacrificial death.

But in its first-century setting, the statement "Jesus is the sacrifice for sin" had a quite different meaning. The "home" of this language, the framework within which it makes sense, is the sacrificial system centered in the temple in Jerusalem. According to temple theology, certain kinds of sins and impurities could be dealt with only through sacrifice in the temple. Temple theology thus claimed an institutional monopoly on the forgiveness of sins; and because the forgiveness of sins was a prerequisite for entry into the presence of God, temple theology also claimed an institutional monopoly on access to God.

In this setting, to affirm "Jesus is the sacrifice for sin" was to deny the temple's claim to have a monopoly on forgiveness and access to God. It was an antitemple statement. Using the metaphor of sacrifice, it subverted the sacrificial system. It meant: God in Jesus has already provided the sacrifice and has thus taken care of whatever you think separates you from God; you have access to God apart from the temple and its system of sacrifice. It is a metaphor of radical grace, of amazing grace.

Thus "Jesus died for our sins" was originally a subversive metaphor, not a literal description of either God's purpose or Jesus' vocation. It was a metaphorical proclamation of radical grace; and properly understood, it still is. It is therefore ironic to realize that the religion that formed around Jesus would within four hundred years begin to claim for itself an institutional monopoly on grace and access to God.

Because the sacrificial metaphor has often been taken quite literally, we in the church have often domesticated the death of Jesus—by speaking of it as the foreordained will of God, as something that had to happen, as a dying for the sins of the world. But it and the other purposive ways of seeing the death of Jesus are post-Easter retrospective providential interpretations. They matter, they're important, and, rightly understood, they continue to be a way of proclaiming the gospel. But they should not be allowed to eclipse the historical reason for his execution.

In her recent book about the working poor in America, Barbara Ehrenreich writes about going to a tent revival meeting in Portland, Maine. The preacher's theme was "Jesus on the cross" and the importance of believing in him in order to go to heaven. As she listened to him and looked around at the mostly impoverished audience, she thought:

> It would be nice if someone would read this sad-eyed crowd the Sermon on the Mount, accompanied by a rousing commentary on income inequality and the need for a hike in the minimum wage. But Jesus makes his appearance here only as a corpse; the living man, the wine-guzzling vagrant and precocious socialist, is never once mentioned, nor anything he ever had to say. Christ

crucified rules, and it may be that the true business of modern Christianity is to crucify him again and again so that he can never get a word out of his mouth.

She concludes:

I get up to leave, timing my exit for when the preacher's metronomic head movements have him looking the other way, and walk out to search for my car, half expecting to find Jesus out there in the dark, gagged and tethered to a tent pole.[20]

Faith in the Cross

About a year ago after I had given a lecture on the meanings of faith, a person asked in the time set aside for questions, "You've been talking about the meanings of faith, but you haven't mentioned faith in the cross. Don't you think faith in the cross is pretty important?"

To clarify her question, I asked, "Do you mean, do I believe that Jesus died for our sins?" She said, "Yes." I then explained, as I have here, that historically, no, I don't think that Jesus literally died for our sins. I don't think he thought of his life and purpose that way; I don't think he thought of that as his divinely given vocation.

And then I continued. But I do have faith in the cross as a trustworthy disclosure of the evil of domination systems, as the exposure of the defeat of the powers, as the revelation of the "way" or "path" of transformation, as the revelation of the depth of God's love for us, and as the proclamation of radical grace. I have faith in the cross as all of those things.

Jesus as Metaphor and Sacrament of God

Thus Jesus is a metaphor of God. Indeed, for us as Christians, he is *the* metaphor of God. Of course, he was also a real person. As metaphor of God, Jesus discloses what God is like. We see God through Jesus.

We are accustomed to speaking of the death of Jesus as the "passion" of Jesus, and the stories of his death as the "passion narratives." When we do so, we typically think of "passion" as meaning "suffering." And it does mean that. But it has an additional meaning as well. The death of Jesus—his execution—was because of his passion for God and God's justice. And because we see Jesus as the revelation of God, we see in his life and death the passion of God. He discloses both the character and passion of God.

It is this figure who is also, for us as Christians, the Word of God, the Son of God, the Wisdom of God, the Light of the World. Now at the right hand of God, one with God, and the second person of the Trinity, he was in his historical life the character and passion of God incarnate. As a metaphor of God, he is the heart of God made flesh.[21]

Jesus is also a sacrament of God, a means through whom the Spirit of God becomes present. He was during his historical life. I am convinced that his followers sometimes experienced the Spirit through him and in him as a palpable presence. And in the centuries since, Jesus continues to be a sacrament of God. The Eucharist of bread and wine is a sacrament of his body and blood whereby we become one with him and thus present to God, and God becomes present to us. The sacred texts about him become a sacrament of God. And the living Christ continues to be known in Christian experience as the presence of God. Like the Bible, the Word of God in words, he is both metaphor and sacrament of God, the Word of God in a person.

I conclude with a story. A year ago my wife and I spent a week in Assisi, a mountain town in Italy and the home of St. Francis and St. Clare. Francis (1182–1226) is commonly seen as the most Christlike of the church's saints. In his early twenties, Francis had a vision of Jesus, renounced his wealth and all of his possessions, and began a life of devotion to God. By the time of his death twenty years later, a religious order numbering in the thousands had sprung up around him, as also around St. Clare, the most important of his women followers.

Francis found God everywhere—in the birds, the animals, the sun, the moon, death—and his life was marked by a contagious joy. He was known for his embrace of "Lady Poverty," as he called her, and his radical identification with the poor. Shortly before his death, according to the stories about him, he received the stigmata, the wounds of Christ in his hands, feet, and side.

Within a few years of his death, a great church was erected in his honor in Assisi. The Basilica of St. Francis is a masterpiece of architecture filled with some of the world's greatest art: not only Giotto's frescoes of St. Francis's life, but also magnificent frescoes by Cimabue, Lorenzetti, and others. To a lesser degree, Clare is also honored by an impressive church. Both would have protested and would have wanted the money to be used for the poor.

And as my wife and I spent hours in this extraordinary and extravagant basilica dedicated to Francis, visiting it again and again, I thought about Francis and his passion for the poor. He would not have wanted such wealth spent on honoring him. He would have said, "It's not about me."

And yet, even though Francis would have opposed its construction, I don't think the basilica is a mistake, something that never should have been. It reminds us of Francis, draws us to Assisi, perhaps even draws us to Francis's vision. And because Francis pointed beyond himself to God and Jesus, we may be drawn into an even larger vision.

To apply the story to the church's adoration of Jesus in our Christology, creeds, worship, art, music, architecture, and so forth: I think Jesus would have said, "It's not about me." During his lifetime, he deflected attention from himself. In an illuminating passage in our earliest gospel, when a man addressed him as "Good Teacher," Jesus responded with, "Why do you call me good? No one is good but God alone."[22]

Yet I do not think the church's extravagant devotion to Jesus is a mistake, for the purpose of the church, of Christology, of the creed is to point us to Jesus. And then Jesus says, "It's not about me." He points beyond himself to God—to God's character and passion. This is the meaning of our christological language and our credal affirmations about Jesus: in this person we see the revelation of God, the heart of God. He is both metaphor and sacrament of God.

---

1. This chapter is a fresh condensation of material I have treated in three books published by HarperSanFrancisco: *Jesus: A New Vision* (1987), *Meeting Jesus Again for the First Time* (1994), and, with N. T. Wright, *The Meaning of Jesus: Two Visions* (1999). Also relevant are my *Jesus at 2000* (Boulder, CO: Westview, 1996) and two books published by Trinity Press International: *Jesus in Contemporary Scholarship* (1994) and *Conflict, Holiness and Politics in the Teaching of Jesus*, rev. ed. (1998).

2. Readers may have encountered this distinction between the pre-Easter and post-Easter Jesus made with different language. Earlier generations of scholars commonly named it the "Jesus of history" (or the "historical Jesus") and the "Christ of faith." However, the use of the word "faith" in the second phrase unfortunately suggests to many people that the latter *can only be believed in* rather than experienced.

3. For a thoughtful study of a sample of twentieth-century experiences of Jesus, see Phillip H. Wiebe, *Visions of Jesus* (New York: Oxford University Press, 1997).

4. Albert Nolan, *Jesus Before Christianity* (Maryknoll, NY: Orbis Books, 1978), p. 117.

5. A few brief comments about the how the emerging paradigm in general sees the gospels. John's gospel is the least historical; it is primarily the testimony of the community to what Jesus had become in their experience. Matthew, Mark, and Luke (called the synoptic gospels) contain more historical memory, though even they are also testimonies of their communities. The earliest layers of the developing tradition are most easily discerned in Mark and Q (a hypothetical collection of the sayings of Jesus reconstructed from material common to Matthew and Luke and perhaps written in the 50s), though some material found only in Matthew or Luke also is likely to be early. For more, see any mainstream scholarly introduction to the New Testament or the gospels. For my own summary, see "The Historical Study of Jesus and Christian Origins" in *Jesus at 2000*, pp. 121–47.

6. C. S. Lewis, *Mere Christianity* (San Francisco: HarperSanFrancisco, 2001; first published in 1952), p. 52.

7. John 10:9; Rev. 3.20. In John, the NRSV uses "gate"; earlier translations use "door."

8. Mark 8:27–29, with slightly different accounts in Matt. 16:13–16 and Luke 9:18–20. Mainline scholars are divided about whether this reflects an exchange during the lifetime of Jesus or whether it is post-Easter. In either case, note that it is not self-proclamation by Jesus, but the confession of a follower.

9. I heard both of these statements in lectures. Coffin's comment was made in a lecture at Trinity Episcopal Cathedral in Portland, Oregon, in May 2002;

Stendahl's in a lecture at Harvard-Epworth Methodist Church in Cambridge, Massachusetts, in March 2001.

10. And thus I reject the "either-or" of some theologians and historical Jesus scholars: that it is *either* the post-Easter Jesus *or* the pre-Easter Jesus who matters. Rather, I affirm a "both-and"; *both* the pre-Easter *and* the post-Easter Jesus matter.

11. See note 1 of this chapter. For my most recent chapter-length summary of the pre-Easter Jesus, see *The Meaning of Jesus: Two Visions*, pp. 53–76.

12. For a striking example of retrospective providential interpretation in the Bible, see the story of the reunion of Joseph with his brothers in Genesis 45. To remind you of the story, Joseph's brothers sold him into slavery in Egypt. Now, decades later, they come to Egypt in search of food. In the meantime, Joseph has risen to a position of power in Egypt, though they do not know this; indeed, they don't even know he's alive. And so when Joseph meets with them, they are frightened; he has the power to do anything to them that he wishes. But instead, he assures them of the providence of God in what has happened. To quote phrases from Gen. 45:5, 7, and 8: "God sent me before you to preserve life"; "God sent me before you to preserve for you a remnant on earth, and to keep alive for you many survivors"; "So it was not you who sent me here, but God." Now, does this mean that it was God's will that Joseph's brothers sell him into slavery? No, it is never God's will to sell a brother into slavery. So also with the cross; was it God's will? No, it is never the will of God that an innocent person be crucified. Yet retrospectively the community can affirm the providence of God in the events of Good Friday and Easter.

13. For my treatment of these in a previous book, see *The Meaning of Jesus: Two Visions*, chap. 8.

14. Acts 2:36.

15. This is also named with the Latin phrase *Christus Victor*, the "Christ victorious" or "Christ triumphant" understanding of the atonement.

16. See his trilogy on the powers, all published by Fortress Press: *Naming the Powers* (1984), *Unmasking the Powers* (1986), and especially the third volume, *Engaging the Powers* (1992). See also his one-volume condensation, *The Powers That Be* (New York: Doubleday, 1998).

17. Col. 2:15, RSV.

18. Gal. 2:19b–20a.

19. Rom. 5:8.

20. Barbara Ehrenreich, *Nickel and Dimed* (New York: Henry Holt, 2001), pp. 68–69.

21. For the phrase, Jesus as the "heart of God become flesh," see Henri Nouwen, *In the Name of Jesus* (New York: Crossroad, 1989), pp. 38–39.

22. Mark 10:18.

Part Two

Seeing the Christian Life Again

SIX

Born Again
A New Heart

In the previous chapter, I concluded my treatment of how the three primary Christian affirmations appear within the emerging paradigm: the centrality of the Bible, God, and Jesus. Now I turn to its way of seeing the Christian life as a relational and transformational vision. In Chapter 2, I described a relational understanding of "faith." In this chapter and the next, I continue this emphasis by speaking of the two transformations at the heart of the Christian life: the individual-spiritual-personal and the communal-social-political.

These two transformations are twins. Though not identical, they are indissolubly linked. In order to stress their linkage, I risk being tediously repetitive:

■ The Bible is both personal and political.

■ The biblical vision of life—of our life with God—is both personal and political.

■ The biblical understanding of salvation is both personal and political. It is about both the individual and society, both spiritual and social. It concerns us as persons; it is about our relationship with God as individuals. And it is also about politics, about our life together as societies, about justice—about political, social, and economic justice.

In this chapter, I emphasize the first of these transformations with the metaphor of being "born again." I use this metaphor for two reasons. One is its centrality in the New Testament. The other is its importance for conservative and fundamentalist Christians. "Born again" is thus a potential bridge metaphor between the two paradigms. If mainline Christians can learn to speak of the importance of being born again, the possibility that these two parts of the church might come together increases.

Unfortunately, mainline Christians have generally allowed their more conservative Christian brothers and sisters to have a near monopoly on "born again" language. There are a number of reasons for this. For some, the language may be too hot and heavy because of its associations with revivals and a "sweaty" kind of Christianity.

Moreover, the notion is sometimes quite narrowly defined. In some Christian circles, to be born again can mean accepting a certain set of beliefs, a particular conservative theology, often expressed in a question using a salvation formula such as, "Do you believe in Jesus Christ as your personal lord and savior?" In charismatic churches, it means receiving the gifts of the Spirit, especially speaking in tongues. In at least the first of the "left behind" novels that have been best-sellers for the last half decade, to be born again is defined even more narrowly by being virtually equated with believing in the "rapture" and the imminent second coming of Jesus.

In addition, most of us have known at least one person who was born again in a remarkably unattractive way. When being born again leads to a rigid kind of righteousness, judgmentalism, and sharp boundaries between an in-group and an out-group, it's either not a genuine born-again experience or it has a lot of static in it.

Born Again: Its Centrality in the New Testament

But rightly understood, being born again is a very rich and comprehensive notion. It is at the very center of the New Testament and the Christian life. We need to reclaim it.

The Classic Text

The need to be "born again" is the theme of the story of Nicodemus and Jesus at the beginning of the third chapter of John's gospel.[1] Because John is more symbolic than historical, this story most probably doesn't go back to Jesus. Though most likely the voice of the community and not the voice of Jesus, the story captures much of what is central to Jesus' message and to the New Testament as a whole.

Like most texts in John's gospel, it is rich in symbolism, missed connections, and double meanings. "Now there was a Pharisee named Nicodemus, a leader of the Jews." Nicodemus appears later in John's gospel as well.[2] He is wealthy, a member of the elite class, and it is interesting that at least a few of this class were attracted to the Jesus movement. There was something about early Christianity that caught their attention.

"He came to Jesus by night." Here is the first of the story's double meanings. It is night: Nicodemus is in the dark. Symbolism of light and darkness abounds in John: Jesus is the light shining in the darkness, the light of the world, the true light that enlightens every person, the one who gives sight to those who are blind. Though Nicodemus comes to the light, he has not yet seen the light. He addresses Jesus in flattering terms: "And he said to Jesus, 'Rabbi, we know that you are a teacher who has come from God, for no one can do these signs that you do apart from the presence of God.'"

In what seems like a misconnection, Jesus responds by changing the subject. It's as if he hasn't heard what Nicodemus is saying—or perhaps has heard beneath his words and heard him very well. In any case, what follows is the key verse of the text: "Jesus answered him,

'Very truly, I tell you, no one can see the kingdom of God without being *born from above.*'"

Like "night," the phrase contains a double meaning: the Greek for "born from above" can also be translated "born again" or "born anew." Translating unfortunately requires choosing between the two, but John intends both meanings: to be born "again/anew" is to be born "from above," that is, to be born of the Spirit.

Nicodemus doesn't get it. He's a literalist, like many other characters in John's gospel. Taking Jesus' words literally, he misses the point: "How can anyone be born after having grown old? Can one enter a second time into the mother's womb and be born?" He's still in the dark.

So Jesus repeats the point: "Very truly, I tell you, no one can enter the kingdom of God without being born of water and Spirit. What is born of the flesh is flesh, and what is born of the Spirit is spirit. Do not be astonished that I said to you, 'You must be born anew.'" The word "water" also has a double meaning. On the one hand, to the readers of John's gospel, it would evoke baptism; on the other hand, parallel to "flesh," it refers to the waters of birth. Though one is born "of water," "of the flesh," one must also be born "of the Spirit"—that is, anew and from above.

As the text continues, Jesus emphasizes the connection to the Spirit: "The wind blows where it chooses, and you hear the sound of it, but you do not know where it comes from or where it goes. So it is with everyone who is born of the Spirit." Yet another double meaning, indeed triple meaning: in Greek, the word for "wind" is also the word for "breath" and "Spirit." The breath of God, the Spirit of God, is the source of rebirth. To be born again is to enter new life through and in the Spirit, a life centered in the Spirit of God.

The point of this classic text is obvious: what Nicodemus needs is a spiritual rebirth, an internal rebirth, a personal transformation. This is what we all need, as I will soon suggest.

Born Again: Dying and Rising

The phrase "born again" occurs only one more time in the New Testament.[3] But the notion, often expressed in the language of dying and rising, death and resurrection, is utterly central in early Christianity and the New Testament as a whole. "Dying and rising" and "to be born again" are the same "root image" for the process of personal transformation at the center of the Christian life: to be born again involves death and resurrection. It means dying to an old way of being and being born into a new way of being, dying to an old identity and being born into a new identity—a way of being and an identity centered in the sacred, in Spirit, in Christ, in God.

In the gospels and in the rest of the New Testament, death and resurrection, dying and rising, are again and again a metaphor for personal transformation, for the psychological-spiritual process at the center of the Christian life. Because of its importance, we shall trace this theme through the New Testament's central witnesses.

Dying and Rising in the Synoptic Gospels

In the synoptic gospels (Matthew, Mark and Luke), the path of death and resurrection is "the way" that Jesus himself taught. According to Mark, the earliest gospel, Jesus said, "If any want to become my followers, let them deny themselves and take up their cross and follow me."[4] So also in a saying found in Matthew and Luke independently of Mark, Jesus said, "Whoever does not carry the cross and follow me cannot be my disciple."[5]

The language is early. It equates following Jesus—being his disciple—with "taking up the cross." In the first century, the cross was a symbol of execution, of death. It had not yet become a loose metaphor for whatever suffering or inconvenience might come one's way, whether arthritis or a difficult in-law. It meant death. To follow Jesus meant to follow him on the path of death. And to make sure that we understand this metaphorically, Luke adds the word "daily" to the phrase to "take up their cross."[6]

The synoptic gospels not only report that Jesus spoke about dying as the path to new life; their literary structure as a whole is also shaped by the theme of death and resurrection as "the way" of Jesus. We see this structure in Mark's gospel, a pattern taken over by Matthew and Luke.

A central theme of Mark's gospel is "the way." He announces it at the beginning of his gospel: it is about "the way of the Lord."[7] Then, in the carefully structured central section of his gospel, the "way of Jesus" is the story of Jesus' journey from Galilee to Jerusalem. Three times in the course of this journey, Jesus speaks of his impending death and resurrection. Each of these three predictions of the passion, as they are called, is paired with teaching about following Jesus. According to the first of these:

> Then Jesus began to teach them that the Son of Man [Jesus himself] must undergo great suffering, and be rejected by the elders, the chief priests, and the scribes, and be killed, and after three days rise again.

To follow Jesus is to follow him on this path:

> Jesus called the crowd with his disciples, and said to them, "If any want to become my followers, let them deny themselves and take up their cross and follow me."

The passage continues with language that makes the same point: "Those who want to save their life will lose it, and those who lose their life for my sake, and for the sake of the gospel, will save it."[8]

The third prediction of the passion is the most detailed. Jesus and those with him are "on the way" to Jerusalem ("road," "way," and "path" are the same word in Greek). According to Mark, Jesus says:

> See, we are going up to Jerusalem, and the Son of Man will be handed over to the chief priests and the scribes, and they will condemn him to death; then they will hand him over to the Gentiles; they will mock him, and spit upon him, and flog him, and kill him; and after three days he will rise again.

Then Jesus asks his disciples: "Are you able to drink the cup that I drink, or to be baptized with the baptism that I am baptized with?"[9] "To drink the cup" and "to be baptized" are both metaphors for death.

Thus for Mark, "the way" of Jesus leads from Galilee to Jerusalem. Jerusalem, the destination of the journey, is the place of death and resurrection, of endings and beginnings, where, to use an old word-play, the tomb becomes a womb. For Mark (and for Matthew and Luke, who repeat and amplify this pattern), the way, the path of personal transformation, is the path of death and resurrection.[10]

Strikingly, Mark frames this central section with stories of blindness and seeing. It begins with the blind man of Bethsaida gradually gaining his sight and ends with blind Bartimaeus, his sight restored, throwing off his cloak and following Jesus.[11] The framing suggests that seeing, having one's sight restored, involves seeing that following Jesus on his journey to Jerusalem is "the way"—the path of transformation leads to and through death and resurrection.

Dying and Rising in Paul's Letters

So also in Paul's letters: dying and rising with Jesus, dying and rising with Christ, is a metaphor for the personal transformation at the heart of the Christian life.[12] He uses the metaphor to speak of his own experience. Paul wrote in his letter to his community in Galatia: "I have been crucified with Christ; and it is no longer I who live, but it is Christ who lives in me."[13] Again, the language is early, written in the 50s, before any of the gospels. Note how the language works: Paul refers to himself as having undergone an internal crucifixion. The old Paul is dead. The result is new life: a new Paul has been born, one in whom Christ lives.

For Paul, this was not only his own experience, but the life to which the community is called. In his letter to Christians in Rome, he correlates dying and rising with Christ with baptism, the ritual of initiation that involved being plunged beneath the waters of death and re-creation:

> All of us who have been baptized into Christ Jesus were baptized into his death. Therefore we have been buried with him by baptism

into death, so that, just as Christ was raised from the dead by the glory of the Father, so we too might walk in newness of life.[14]

Embodied in a ritual, baptism symbolizes the internal transformation of dying to an old way of being and birth into a new way of being.

Death and resurrection—being born again—as a metaphor for personal transformation is the foundation for Paul's shorthand phrase for naming the new life. It is life "in Christ." Paul uses "in Christ" 165 times in his letters and the virtually synonymous phrase "in the Spirit" about 20 times.[15]

The result of being "in Christ," "in the Spirit," is a new way of being and a new identity, a new creation. To the Christian community in Corinth, Paul wrote: "So if anyone is *in Christ*, there is a new creation: everything old has passed away; see, everything has become new!"[16]

"In Christ" also involves a new communal identity that subverts the sharpest boundaries of convention. "*In Christ Jesus* you are all children of God through faith," Paul wrote to the Galatians. They had become so through the ritual that embodies death and resurrection: "As many of you as were baptized *into Christ* have clothed yourselves with Christ." The result: "There is no longer Jew or Gentile, there is no longer slave or free, there is no longer male and female; for all of you are all one *in Christ Jesus*."[17] The deepest divisions of the first-century Roman and Jewish social worlds are overcome "in Christ."

Being "in Christ" is the basis for one of Paul's most famous passages. He asks rhetorically, "What will separate us from the love of Christ?" His answer: *nothing*—nothing can "separate us from the love of God *in Christ Jesus* our Lord"; neither "death, nor life, nor angels, nor rulers, nor things present, nor things to come, nor powers, nor height, nor depth, nor anything else in all creation."[18] Being in Christ, one is reconnected to God, the one who is beyond and beneath death and life, angels and rulers, things present and things to come, beyond and beneath all creation.

And how does one become "in Christ"? For Paul, by dying to our old life, to life "in Adam," and being reborn in Christ. The way to life *in* Christ is by dying and rising *with* Christ. The path is death and resurrection, death and rebirth. When Paul resolved to "preach nothing but Christ and Christ crucified," this is most centrally what he meant: the cross as symbol of the process of personal transformation at the heart of the Christian life.

Dying and Rising in the Gospel of John

John's gospel not only includes the classic born-again text. Like the synoptics and Paul, John also uses the image of death and resurrection as the way to new life. The whole of John is shaped by this theme, even as John also expresses it compactly in a single verse: "Very truly, I tell you, unless a grain of wheat falls into the earth and dies, it remains just a single grain; but if it dies, it bears much fruit."[19]

Indeed, this theme is the key to understanding the well-known verse in John often used as the basis of Christian exclusivism: "I am the way, and the truth, and the life. No one comes to the Father except through me."[20] To set this verse in the context of John's incarnational theology: just as Jesus is the "Word made flesh," so he is "the way" made flesh, the path embodied in a life. The key question then becomes: What is "the way" that Jesus incarnates? What is "the way" that Jesus is? For John, as for the New Testament generally, "the way" embodied in Jesus is the path of death and resurrection. Dying and rising is the only way to God.

Christian exclusivism understands this verse to mean that you must know about Jesus and believe certain things about Jesus in order to be saved. But "the way" that John speaks of is not about believing doctrines about Jesus. Rather, "the way" is what we see incarnate in Jesus: the path of death and resurrection as the way to rebirth in God. According to John, this is the only way—and, as I shall soon suggest, it is "the way" spoken of by all the major religions of the world. Dying and rising is the way. Thus Jesus is "the Way"—the way become flesh. Rather than being the unique revelation of a way known only in him, his life and death are the incarnation of a universal way known in all of the enduring religions.

The Cross and Being Born Again

The cross is the single most universal symbol of Christianity, in the New Testament, in Christian worship and practice, and in Western popular culture. Like all symbols, it has multiple meanings, and Christians have legitimately seen many meanings in it. Literally and historically, the cross—Jesus' crucifixion—was an execution. The authorities killed him. The rulers of this world executed him. But, as described in Chapter 5, the early Christian movement saw a number of meanings in the cross.

In particular, the early Christian movement saw the cross as a symbol of "the way." It embodies "the way": the path of transformation, the way to be born again. The cross, the central symbol of Christianity, points to the process at the heart of the Christian life: dying and rising with Christ, being raised to newness of life, being born again in Christ, in the Spirit. It is no wonder, and yet it is, that Paul vowed to preach "nothing but Christ crucified"; no wonder, and yet it is, that the gospels saw the way of Jesus as the way of the cross; no wonder, and yet it is, that the season of Lent climaxing in Good Friday and Easter is about participating in the death and resurrection of Jesus.

Sometimes this internal process of dying is spoken of as a "dying to self" or the "death of the self." Until perhaps twenty years ago, I did so myself. But I think "dying to self" is too imprecise because it is subject to misunderstanding. "Dying to self" has been used to encourage the repression of the self and its legitimate desires. Oppressed people, in society and in the family, have often been told to put their own selves last out of obedience to God. When thus understood, the message of the cross become an instrument of oppressive authority and self-abdication.

But the cross is the means of our liberation and reconnection. It is not about the subjugation of the self, but about a new self. And so to avoid the potentially negative meaning of "dying to self," I prefer to speak more precisely of an old and new *identity* and *way of being.* The way of the cross involves dying to an old identity and being born into a new identity, dying to an old way of being and being raised to a new way of being, one centered in God.

Not only does this language avoid the negative meanings of "dying to self," but it recognizes that we exist as selves. This is not wrong. I am persuaded that this is one of the meanings of the biblical understanding of creation: we are created to be selves. The problem is not that we are selves. The issue is what kind of selves we are, and what kind we might be.

Born Again: Why We Need This

Why do we need to be born again? Why do we need to die to an old way of being and an old identity and be born into a new way of being and a new identity—into a life centered in God, in the Spirit, in Christ? The reason is because of something that happens in us very early in life and then is intensified by the process of growing up.

What happens early in our lives is the birth of self-consciousness. By this, I mean simply self-awareness, that is, awareness of the distinction between self and world. How early this happens we cannot say with precision, but it clearly seems to happen in the preverbal stage of life. A newborn infant is not yet conscious of being a self. With good parenting, infants initially experience the world as an extension of themselves: they get hungry, they get fed; they get wet, they get changed; they cry, they get picked up. But at some point, infants in the process of becoming toddlers become aware that the world is separate from themselves.

Several years ago I was told a story about a three-year-old girl.[21] She was the firstborn and only child in her family, but now her mother was pregnant again, and the little girl was very excited about having a new brother or sister. Within a few hours of the parents bringing a new baby boy home from the hospital, the girl made a request: she wanted to be alone with her new brother in his room with the door shut. Her insistence about being alone with the baby with the door shut made her parents a bit uneasy, but then they remembered that they had installed an intercom system in anticipation of the baby's arrival, so they realized they could let their daughter do this, and if they heard the slightest indication that anything strange was happening, they could be in the baby's room in an instant.

So they let the little girl go into the baby's room, shut the door, and raced to the intercom listening station. They heard their daughter's footsteps moving across the baby's room, imagined her standing over the baby's crib, and then they heard her saying to her three-day-old brother, "Tell me about God—I've almost forgotten."

The story is both haunting and evocative, for it suggests that we come from God, and that when we are very young, we still remember this, still know this. But the process of growing up, of learning about *this* world, is a process of increasingly forgetting the one from whom we came and in whom we live. The birth and intensification of self-consciousness, of self-awareness, involves a separation from God.[22]

The birth of self-consciousness is the birth of the separated self. When this happens, the natural and inevitable result is self-concern. The two go together: the separated self and the self-centered self.

The birth of self-consciousness, of the separated self, is one of the central meanings of the Garden of Eden story. It is our story. Adam and Eve, living in a paradisiacal state, become conscious of opposites, of good and evil. The result is multifold: they cover themselves, no longer naked and unashamed; they experience life as toil and burden; they are expelled from paradise. The Genesis story ends with them (and us) living their (and our) lives "east of Eden," estranged and in exile.[23]

The birth of the separated self—what we call "the fall"—is something we go through early in our own lives. We have all experienced this. Moreover, it cannot be avoided; it is utterly necessary. Imagining that Adam and Eve could have avoided it misses the point. We cannot develop into mature human beings without self-consciousness. And yet it is a "fall"—into a world of self-consciousness and self-centeredness, estrangement and exile.

The sense of separation and self-concern is intensified by the process of growing up. Commonly called "socialization," this process involves internalizing within the self the central "messages" of one's upbringing. At a foundational level, socialization includes language, whose labels and categories intrinsically divide up the world. It includes a worldview, an understanding of what is real and possible. And, significantly, it includes messages about who we are and what we should be like: parental messages, cultural messages, and for some of us religious messages.

The result: we descend more deeply into the world of self-consciousness and self-concern. Our identity and way of being are more and more shaped by the "world," meaning the "world" as we internalize it in the process of growing up. The world of the child, with its mystery and magic, is left farther and farther behind.

A poem by Billy Collins, poet laureate of the United States, captures the ache of loss at the end of childhood. Its title is significant: "On Turning Ten":

The whole idea of it makes me feel
like I'm coming down with something,
something worse than any stomach ache
or the headaches I get from reading in bad light—
a kind of measles of the spirit,
a mumps of the psyche,
a disfiguring chickenpox of the soul.

You tell me it is too early to be looking back,
but that is because you have forgotten
the perfect simplicity of being one
and the beautiful complexity introduced by two.
But I can lie on my bed and remember every digit.
At four I was an Arabian wizard.
I could make myself invisible
By drinking a glass of milk a certain way.
At seven I was a soldier, at nine a prince.

But now I am mostly at the window
watching the late afternoon light.
Back then it never fell so solemnly
against the side of my tree house,
and my bicycle never leaned against the garage
as it does today,
all the dark blue speed drained out of it.

This is the beginning of sadness, I say to myself,
as I walk through the universe in my sneakers.
It is time to say good-bye to my imaginary friends,
time to turn the first big number.

It seems only yesterday I used to believe
there was nothing under my skin but light.
If you cut me I would shine.
But now when I fall upon the sidewalks of life,
I skin my knees. I bleed.

By the time we are in early adolescence, perhaps earlier, our sense of who we are is increasingly the product of culture. We feel okay or not okay about ourselves to the extent that we measure up to the messages we have internalized. In our culture, these messages center around the three A's of appearance, achievement, and affluence. To recall the issues of adolescence: Are we attractive enough? Do we look good enough? Are we cool? In adulthood the issue of attractiveness continues, now accompanied by issues of achievement and affluence and also issues of intimacy, sensitivity, and caring. Am I enough? Am I good enough?

And throughout this process, we fall farther into the world of separation and alienation, comparison and judgment—of self and of others. We live our lives in relation to what Thomas Keating calls "the false self," the self created and conferred by culture. Or, to use language from Frederick Buechner, we live our lives from the outside in rather than from the inside out.[24]

Our fall into exile is very deep. The biblical picture of the human condition is bleak. Separated and self-concerned, the self becomes blind, self-preoccupied, prideful; worry-filled, grasping, miserable; insensitive, angry, violent; somebody great, or only okay, or "not much." In the dark, we are blind and don't see. We live in bondage in Egypt, in exile in Babylon, and sometimes we become Egypt and Babylon. We can even be both victim and oppressor. Especially as groups, we can be brutal and oppressive. There seems no evil of which we are collectively incapable.

Blaise Pascal (1623–62), a French mathematician, philosopher, and mystic, marveled about our capacity for good and evil: "Our greatness and our wretchedness are so evident that the true religion . . . must account for such amazing contradictions."[25] The biblical vision of our amazing contradiction is that we are created in the image of God, but we live our lives outside of paradise, "east of Eden," in a world of estrangement and self-preoccupation. It is the inevitable result of growing up, of becoming selves. None of us, whether success or failure, escapes it.

Thus we need to be born again. It is the road of return from our exile, the way to recover our true self, the path to beginning to live our lives from the inside out rather than from the outside in, the exodus from our individual and collective selfishness. To be born again involves dying to the false self, to that identity, to that way of being, and to be born into an identity centered in the Spirit, in Christ, in God. It is the process of internal redefinition of the self whereby a real person is born within us.

Born Again: The Process

The born-again experience can be sudden and dramatic. It can involve a dramatic revelation, a life-changing epiphany, as in the case of Saul on the road to Damascus, an experience through which he became Paul. Such dramatic conversions continue to this day; some people can name a day or even an hour when it happened. There is no reason to doubt that such "sudden conversions" occur. William James not only reports many such experiences, but speaks of them as one of the most remarkable psychological phenomena known.[26]

But for the majority of us, being born again is not a single intense experience, but a gradual and incremental process. Dying to an old identity and being born into a new identity, dying to an old way of being and living into a new way of being, is a process that continues through a lifetime. The Christian life as it matures is ever more deeply centered in the Spirit—that is, centered in the Spirit of God as known in Jesus, the Spirit of Christ.

For most of us, this takes time. And even for those who can name an hour when they were born again, the process of living into the new life takes time. Of course, progress is not automatic; one can thwart it, obstruct it, impede it. But in the Christian life, aging, if not interfered with, has a way of deepening our centering in the Spirit. The messages and lures of youth and middle age are muted; we can rest more and more in God, more easily be in silence with God. And by being more centered in God, our lives are transformed. As the Christian life matures, we begin to experience the self-forgetfulness that accompanies a deepening trust in God.

The born-again metaphor not only applies to a single dramatic event or a lifelong process, but also to shorter rhythms in our lives. It is a process that may occur several times in periods of major transition, whatever the cause.

It even applies to the micro-rhythms of daily life. Martin Luther, a major spiritual mentor in my childhood, spoke of "*daily* dying and rising with Christ" and, in language that sounds a bit archaic, of "*daily* putting to death the old Adam," the old self in us. By adding "daily," Luther echoes the gospel of Luke.

The "dailiness" of the process fits my experience, as it does that of many people I know. In the course of a day, I sometimes realize that I have become burdened, and that the cause is that I have forgotten God. In the act of remembering God, of reminding myself of the reality of God, I sometimes feel a lightness of being—a rising out of my self-preoccupation and burdensome confinement. We are called again and again to come forth from our tombs.

This process is at the heart not only of Christianity, but of the other enduring religions of the world. The image of following "the way" is common in Judaism, and "the way" involves a new heart, a new self centered in God. One of the meanings of the word "Islam" is "surrender": to surrender one's life to God by radically centering in God. And Muhammad is reported to have said, "Die before you die." Die spiritually before you die physically, die metaphorically (and really) before you die literally. At the heart of the Buddhist path is "letting go"—the same internal path as dying to an old way of being and being born into a new. According to the *Tao te Ching*, a foundational text for both Taoism and Zen Buddhism, Lao Tzu said: "If you want to become full, let yourself be empty; if you want to be reborn, let yourself die."

This process of personal spiritual transformation—what we as Christians call being born again, dying and rising with Christ, life in the Spirit—is thus central to the world's religions. To relate this to John's affirmation that Jesus is "the way": the way that Jesus incarnated is a universal way, not an exclusive way. Jesus is the embodiment, the incarnation, of the path of transformation known in the religions that have stood the test of time.

Seeing this commonality between the way of Jesus and the ways of the world's religions is sometimes disconcerting to Christians, given our history of "Jesus is the only way." But the commonality is cause for celebration, not consternation. Not only does it mean, to echo an exclamation in the book of Acts, the Spirit has gone out to Muslims, Buddhists, Jews, Hindus, and so forth, but it also adds credibility to Christianity.[27] When the Christian path is seen as utterly unique, it is suspect. But when Jesus is seen as the incarnation of a path universally spoken about elsewhere, the path we see in him has great credibility.

Born Again: Intentionality

Being born again is the work of the Spirit. Whether it happens suddenly or gradually, we can't make it happen, either by strong desire and determination or by learning and believing the right beliefs. But we can be intentional about being born again. Though we can't make it happen, we can midwife the process. This is the purpose of spirituality: to help birth the new self and nourish the new life. Spirituality is midwifery.

Spirituality combines awareness, intention, and practice. I define it as *becoming conscious of and intentional about a deepening relationship with God.* The words are very carefully chosen. *Becoming conscious of our relationship with God:* I am convinced that we are all already in relationship to God and have been from our birth. God is in relationship with us: spirituality is about becoming aware of a relationship that already exists.

Becoming intentional about our relationship with God: spirituality is about paying attention to the relationship. Though God is "Mystery," there is nothing mysterious about paying attention to our relationship with God. We do so in the ways we pay attention in a human relationship: by spending time in it, attending to it, being thoughtful about it. We pay attention to our relationship with God through practice, both corporate and individual: worship, community, prayer, scripture, devotion. About practice, I will say more in Chapter 10.

A *deepening relationship with God:* in what is now a familiar theme, the Christian life is not very much about believing a set of beliefs, but about a deepening relationship with the one in whom we live and move and have our being. Paying attention to this relationship transforms us. This is what our lives are to be about: a transforming relationship to "what is," "the More."

In short, spirituality is about the process of being born again (and again and again). It is at the heart of the Christian life. If we as Christians and as the church took this seriously, we would recover the rich spiritual practices of the Christian tradition. We would learn them and encourage their use. One of the central purposes of our life together as church would be to midwife and nourish the process of being born again.

And this is happening. The recovery of spirituality and spiritual practices in mainline churches in our time is an encouraging sign of the revitalization of Christianity. It is also a sign of the emerging paradigm with its emphasis on a more relational and experiential understanding of faith and the Christian life.

The New Life

Being born again begins a new life. Indeed, newness is its defining characteristic. It is most dramatically experienced and celebrated by those who thought their lives were irredeemably lost, whether prisoners incarcerated for brutal crimes or a slave trader like John Newton, author of "Amazing Grace." The image of being "born again," born of the grace and Spirit of God, is full of hope, of new beginning in the midst of what seems like ending. Always grace and rebirth are possible.

And it is entry into a different kind of life. Dying and rising has consequences. It does not leave us unchanged. It is a transformation that begins a process of continuing transformation sometimes called "sanctification." The New Testament constantly speaks of the new life. As it does so, it is both rhapsodic and realistic. Its realistic treatment can be attested by the fact that the gospels, letters, and book of Revelation all offer explicit or implicit evidence of problems in early Christian communities.

But it is the rhapsodic aspect that I wish to highlight: what the new life is like. It is enormously attractive. It is the life of reconnection with God. It is the life of the returned prodigal, welcomed home from exile; the life of the healed demoniac, restored to his right mind and to community; the life of the bent woman, standing up and restored to health; the life of the woman of the city, redeemed by her love; the life of Lazarus, raised from the dead.

Paul speaks of the new life "in Christ" in the most extraordinary terms. It is marked by freedom, joy, peace, and love, four of his favorite words: freedom from the voices of all the would-be lords of our lives; the joy of the exuberant life; the peace of reconnection to what is, the peace that passes all understanding; and love—the love of God for us and the love of God in us.[28]

Paul and the other authors of the New Testament consistently see these qualities as the "fruits" of the Spirit, as "gifts" of the Spirit. They are the fruit not of human striving, but of a new identity and new way of being—the fruit, the product, of centering one's life in God, in the Spirit.

Paul's most famous description of the new life is found in 1 Corinthians 13, often called Paul's "hymn to love." Its context between chapters 12 and 14 makes the connection to "the gifts of the Spirit" explicit. These gifts include prophecy, wisdom, healing, speaking in tongues, and the interpretation of tongues. Then in chapter 13, unfortunately often read in isolation from its context, Paul says about love in relation to the other gifts of the Spirit:

> If I speak in the tongues of mortals and of angels, but do not have love, I am a noisy gong or a clanging symbol. And if I have prophetic powers, and understand all mysteries and all knowledge, and if I have all faith, so as to remove mountains, but do not have love, I am nothing. If I give away all my possessions, and if I hand over my body so that I may boast, but do not have love, I gain nothing.[29]

The affirmation sounds again at the end of the chapter in Paul's memorable triad of faith, hope, and love: "And now faith, hope, and love abide, these three; *and the greatest of these is love*." For Paul, love is the primary gift of the Spirit, indeed the definitive gift.

The same is true for Jesus. For Jesus, the primary quality of a life centered in God is compassion. When Jesus sums up theology and ethics in a few words, he says: "Be compassionate as God is compassionate."[30] Where Paul uses the word "love," Jesus uses the word "compassion." The associations of the word in Aramaic and Hebrew are strikingly evocative: to be compassionate is to be "womblike": life-giving, nourishing, embracing. So God is; so we are to be.

Thus growth in love, growth in compassion, is the primary quality of life in the Spirit. It is also the primary criterion for distinguishing a genuine born-again experience from one that only appears to be one.

It is the pragmatic test suggested by William James, quoting Jesus: "By their fruits you shall know them." The fruit is love. Indeed, such fruit is the purpose of the Christian life.

---

1. John 3:1–10.

2. John 7:45–52; 19:38–42. In the latter text, he supplies an extravagant amount of burial spices. He is not mentioned in the other gospels.

3. In 1 Pet. 1:22–23. The passage begins with the fruit of having been born again, and the phrase itself appears near the end: "Now that you have purified your souls by your obedience to the truth through the Spirit so that you have genuine mutual love, love one another deeply from the heart. You have been *born anew*, not of perishable but of imperishable seed, through the living and enduring word of God."

4. Mark 8:34.

5. Luke 14:27 = Matt. 10:38. As a saying shared by Matthew and Luke but not derived from Mark, it is thus Q material, which the majority of scholars think was an early collection of the sayings of Jesus, perhaps put into writing in the 50s. Though a minority of scholars deny the existence of Q, all would agree that this is early material.

6. Luke 9:23. The author of Luke is copying Mark 8:34 here, so the addition is deliberate.

7. Mark 1:3.

8. Mark 8:31, 34–35.

9. Mark 10:32–34, 38. The second prediction of the passion is found in Mark 9:31, and is followed in 9:35 by "Whoever wants to be first must be last of all and servant of all."

10. Both Matthew and Luke retain this pattern, and Luke amplifies it by lengthening the story of Jesus' final journey in what is commonly called the travel narrative of Luke. It begins in 9:51 and concludes in 19:27.

11. Mark 8:22–26; 10:46–52.

12. I use both phrases, "dying and rising with Jesus" and "dying and rising with Christ," because for Paul the two terms are virtually interchangeable. "Christ" (that is, "the messiah") becomes for Paul a name of Jesus.

13. Gal. 2:19b–20a.

14. Rom. 6:3–4. See the whole passage, through v. 11.

15. For Paul's use of "in Christ," see my *Reading the Bible Again for the First Time* (San Francisco: HarperSanFrancisco, 2001), pp. 245–51.

16. 2 Cor. 5:17.

17. Gal. 3:26–28.

18. Excerpted from Rom. 8:31–39.

19. John 12:24. It is followed by language of loving one's life and losing it, hating one's life and gaining it.

20. John 14:6.

21. I was initially told this story by a couple in Seattle about ten years ago. Recently, I was told that it appears in a book by Parker Palmer, a contemporary Quaker scholar. I have not had time to track it down, but I am very happy to credit Palmer and to recommend his many fine books.

22. Of possible relevance is a study by K. Tamminen, "Religious Experiences in Childhood and Adolescence," in the *International Journey for the Psychology of Religion* 4.61–85 (1994). The study asked the question of young people of various ages, "Have you at times felt that God is particularly close to you?" The results suggest that growing up involves a diminishment of an experiential sense of God. Of children in the first grade, 84 percent said "yes"; in the fifth grade, 69 percent; in the seventh grade, 57 percent; in the eleventh grade, 47 percent. The study is reported in Benjamin Beit-Hallahmi and Michael Argyle, *Religious Behavior, Belief and Experience* (New York: Routledge, 1997), pp. 149–50. For this reference I thank Ken Vincent, a retired psychology professor at Houston Community College, and author of *Visions of God: The Near Death Experience* (Burdett, NY: Larson, 1994).

23. For this and other meanings of the Eden story, see *Reading the Bible Again*, pp. 77–81.

24. Thomas Keating, *Intimacy with God* (New York: Crossroad, 1997), p. 163. Buechner's remark was made in a lecture at Grace Episcopal Cathedral in San Francisco in 1990; I believe it is also found in his *Telling Secrets* (San Francisco: HarperSanFrancisco, 1991).

25. Richard J. Foster and James Bryan Smith, eds., *Devotional Classics* (San Francisco: HarperSanFrancisco, 1993), p. 172.

26. William James, *The Varieties of Religious Experience*, lecture 10.

27. The passage is Acts 10:45: They "were astounded that the gift of the Holy Spirit had been poured out even on the Gentiles," that is, to those who were not of the chosen people. See also Acts 11:18.

28. For an exceptionally clear exposition of Paul's vision of the Christian life as marked by freedom, joy, peace, and love, see Robin Scroggs, *Paul for a New Day* (Philadelphia: Fortress, 1977), pp. 21–38.

29. 1 Cor. 13:1–3.

30. Luke 6:36. Though most English translations of Luke 6:36 use the word "mercy," the context in Luke points to "compassion" as a better translation. "Mercy" in English suggests a situation of wrongdoing: we can show mercy toward those who have wronged us. But the context in Luke suggests generosity: love your enemies, do good, lend without expectation of return.

SEVEN

The Kingdom of God

The Heart of Justice

We turn now to the other transformation at the center of the biblical vision of our life with God: social and political transformation. To use a central metaphor from the gospels, the Christian life is about the "Kingdom of God." It is about "being born again" and the "Kingdom of God."

The Bible is political as well as personal. It combines sharp political criticism and passionate political advocacy: radical criticism of systems of domination and impassioned advocacy of an alternative social vision. Protesting the nightmare of injustice, its central voices proclaim God's dream of justice, a dream for the earth. Criticism and advocacy are grounded in their understanding of the character and passion of God: a God of love and justice whose passion for our life together is the Kingdom of God.

A Neglected Emphasis: God's Passion for Justice

The claim that the Bible is political and that the God of the Bible is passionate about justice is surprising, even startling, to many Christians. We have often overlooked it; and when it is pointed out, we often resist seeing it. Reflecting about the reasons for our relative blindness is illuminating. Doing so may help us understand why this major stream of the Bible is unfamiliar to many Christians as well as to people outside the church.

One reason is the long period of time during which Christianity was the religion of the dominant culture. It began with the Roman emperor Constantine's embrace of Christianity in the fourth century and lasted until recently. During these centuries, the "powers that be" were Christian. So long as the wedding of Christianity and dominant culture continued, Christians seldom engaged in radical criticism of the social order. Instead, personal salvation in the hereafter was the primary message, an emphasis that continues to this day in many parts of the church. This emphasis incidentally (or not so incidentally) mutes the political voices of the Bible, thereby domesticating its political passion.

Another reason is because of a common misunderstanding of "God's justice." Theologically, we have often seen its opposite as "God's mercy." "God's justice" is understood as God's deserved punishment of us for our sins, "God's mercy" as God's loving forgiveness of us in spite of our guilt. Given this choice, we would all prefer God's mercy and hope to escape God's justice. But seeing the opposite of justice as mercy distorts what the Bible means by justice. Most often in the Bible, the opposite of God's justice is not God's mercy, but human injustice. The issue is the shape of our life together as societies, not whether the mercy of God will supersede the justice of God in the final judgment.

In the United States in particular, there is yet another reason why we often miss the Bible's passion for justice. Our culture is dominated by an ethos of individualism. It is our core cultural value: we are probably the most individualistic culture in human history.[1] Of course, there is much that is good about individualism: the value it gives to individual lives, the importance of individual rights, individual choice and opportunity. It emphasizes freedom, and freedom is one of the gifts of God. But individualism as a core value leads to a way of seeing life that obscures the enormous effect of social systems on the lives of people.

Individualism stresses that the primary factor responsible for our well-being is individual effort. The notion of the "self-made person"— that we are primarily the product of our own initiative and hard work—is widespread in the United States. It is often used to legitimate a social system (both political and economic) that maximizes rewards for individual "success" and minimizes providing a safety net for those who are not "successful." According to this way of thinking, we as individuals get what we deserve. The quality of our lives is the result of how responsibly we make use of our opportunities.

Of course, individual responsibility matters, but none of us is really self-made. We are also the product of many factors beyond our control. These include genetic inheritance, affecting both health and intelligence; the family into which we're born and our upbringing; the quality of education we receive; and a whole host of "accidents" along life's way—good breaks and bad breaks. To think we are primarily the product of our own individual effort is to ignore the web of relationships and circumstances that shape our lives.

Social systems are among the factors beyond the individual that deeply affect people's lives. Seeing this is the key to understanding the Bible's passion for justice. Social systems include political systems, economic systems, and systems of convention, by which I mean cultural attitudes and values enshrined in society. These can be, and often are, oppressive.

We more easily recognize the negative impact of systems on human lives in retrospect. We easily see that the system of slavery was monstrous; but until about two centuries ago, it was practiced in many Christian countries, sanctioned by law and convention, and even legitimated by appeal to the Bible.[2] Given our more recent history, most of us easily see that racism and sexism are systems: both were (and in some ways still are) embedded in political and economic structures and in conventional attitudes. Until recently, people of color and women of any color simply did not have the same opportunities in our society as white men. Their standing in society and what they could become were much more the result of social systems than of individual effort.

The issue is what is commonly called "systemic injustice"—sources of unnecessary human misery created by unjust political, economic, and social systems. Its opposite, of course, is "systemic justice," also known as structural, social, substantive, or distributive justice. The test of the justice of systems is their impact on human lives. To what extent do they lead to human flourishing and to what extent to human suffering?

This is what the political passion of the Bible is about. Its major voices protest the systemic injustice of the kingdoms and empires that dominated their world. They do so in the name of God and on behalf of the victims—slaves in Egypt, exiles in Babylon, exploited peasants in the time of the monarchy and again in the time of Jesus, and the most vulnerable in all times—widows, orphans, the poor, and the marginalized. And in the name of God, the major figures of the Bible advocate a very different vision of our life together.

God's Passion for Justice in the Hebrew Bible

The political passion of the Bible goes back to the origin of Israel. It begins with Moses and the exodus. Ancient Israel's foundation story is a narrative of liberation from bondage in imperial Egypt—an oppression that was political, economic, and religious; and a liberation that was political, economic, and religious.

The political stream continues in the prophets of Israel several hundred years after Moses. Now the target was the injustice created by the monarchies of the kingdoms of Israel and Judah. The classical prophets of ancient Israel—figures such as Amos, Isaiah, Micah, and Jeremiah—were God-intoxicated voices of protest against the human suffering created by the unjust systems imposed by the powerful and wealthy. Egypt had been re-created within Israel. In the eyes of the prophets, this was no less than betrayal of God's covenant with Israel.

What Egypt and the monarchies of Israel and Judah shared in common is that both were forms of the "ancient domination system," the most widespread form of society in the premodern world. Powerful and wealthy aristocracies centered around the monarchy structured the political and economic systems in their own self-interest. Three primary features characterized these premodern domination systems:

- **They were politically oppressive.** Ordinary people had no voice in the structuring of society. Rather, they were ruled by the monarchy and powerful and wealthy elites.

- **They were economically exploitative.** The powerful and wealthy structured the economic system so that approximately one-half to two-thirds of the annual production of wealth ended up in the hands of the wealthiest 1 to 5 percent of the population. The consequences for the lives of peasants (roughly 90 percent of the population, and the primary producers of wealth in these preindustrial societies) were severe: poverty and subsistence living, malnourishment and disease, vulnerability to vicissitude. The quality of life and life expectancy for the peasant class were drastically lower than for the elite classes.

- **They were religiously legitimated.** In most (all?) premodern societies, it was affirmed that the social order reflected the will of God. Kings ruled by divine right, the powers that be were ordained by God, the laws came from God. Of course, it was the elites who saw things this way. From the vantage point of "royal consciousness," their privileged status came from God.[3]

This is the world of Egypt and monarchy. This is the world that the exodus story and the words of the prophets protest.[4]

God's Passion for Justice in the New Testament

Passion for God's justice and criticism of domination systems surface again in the first century in Jesus, Paul, the book of Revelation, and in the New Testament as a whole. But we have been even less likely to see it in early Christianity than in the Hebrew Bible. Yet it is centrally there, a claim I will develop with four points.

The Kingdom of God

The phrase the "Kingdom of God" is perhaps the best shorthand summary of the message and passion of Jesus. As a New Testament scholar has written: "Ask any hundred New Testament scholars around the world, Protestant, Catholic or non-Christian, what the central message of Jesus of Nazareth was, and the vast majority of them—perhaps every single expert—would agree that this message centered in the Kingdom of God."[5]

Its importance for Jesus is underlined by the author of Mark, our earliest gospel. Like the other gospel writers, Mark uses the opening scene of Jesus' public ministry—his "inaugural address"—to state in advance the theme of his gospel. Jesus' first words in Mark are about the Kingdom of God:

> Now after John the Baptizer was arrested, Jesus came to Galilee, proclaiming the good news of God, and saying: "The time is fulfilled, and *the kingdom of God is at hand*; repent, and believe in the good news."[6]

What is the story of Jesus most centrally about? The Kingdom of God. It is also the subject of many of Jesus' parables and short sayings. And it is at the center of the best-known Christian prayer, the Lord's Prayer: "Thy kingdom come."

Like metaphors and symbols generally, the Kingdom of God has more than one meaning in the message of Jesus. Sometimes it points to the power of God active in Jesus' work as a healer and exorcist; sometimes it has a mystical meaning, referring to the presence of God. In other texts, it refers to a community, and it can refer to the kingdom at the end of history or beyond history in which "many from east and west" will eat "with Abraham and Isaac and Jacob in the Kingdom of God."[7]

"Kingdom of God" also has a political meaning, and it is this meaning I wish to highlight. It is, of course, a political metaphor: "kingdom" is a political term. Jesus could have spoken of the "family" of God or the "community" of God, but he chose to speak of the "kingdom" of God. And though we might speak of family politics or church politics, these terms are not intrinsically political. But "kingdom" is.

Moreover, the people to whom Jesus spoke lived in a world in which there were real kingdoms. Kingdoms were a present reality for them, not something "once upon a time." "Kingdom" was not associated with fantasy, as in Disney's "Magic Kingdom." Nor did it refer to a parliamentary democracy presided over by a constitutionally limited monarch, as in today's United Kingdom. Rather, "kingdom" referred to the political system under which they lived: the ancient domination system ruled by powerful and wealthy elites.

Thus when Jesus spoke of the Kingdom of God, his hearers would have heard an immediate contrast. They lived under other kingdoms: the kingdom of Herod and the kingdom of Caesar. They knew what those kingdoms and life in them were like. And here was Jesus speaking of the Kingdom of God.

As Jesus used the phrase, it is also of course a *religious* metaphor: it is the Kingdom *of God*. Thus we might see it as a "religious-political," or "theo-political," metaphor. As scholar John Dominic Crossan puts it: for Jesus, it is never kingdom without God, and it is never God without kingdom.[8]

So what is the political meaning of the Kingdom of God? In a sentence: it is what life would be like on earth if God were king and the rulers of this world were not.[9] The Kingdom of God is about God's justice in contrast to the systemic injustice of the kingdoms and domination systems of this world.

Significantly, the Kingdom of God for Jesus was something *for the earth*. We have often missed this. Among the reasons is a linguistic decision made by the author of Matthew. He preferred to avoid using the word "God," presumably for reverential reasons; many Jews avoided pronouncing or writing the word. Thus, as Matthew wrote his gospel, he most often changed "Kingdom of God" to "Kingdom of heaven." And because Matthew was the synoptic gospel most commonly read in the lectionary of the church through the centuries, generations of Christians have heard Jesus speaking about the Kingdom of *heaven*. The natural assumption was that Jesus was talking about heaven, that is, about an afterlife.

But the Kingdom of God is not about heaven; it is for the earth. This really shouldn't surprise us. We pray for the coming of God's Kingdom on earth every time we pray the Lord's Prayer: "Thy kingdom come, thy will be done, *on earth*, as it already is in heaven." To cite one of John Dominic Crossan's memorable serious quips: "Heaven's in great shape; earth is where the problems are."[10]

The Lord's Prayer as a whole also points to its earthly meaning. To see this most clearly, we need to remember that Jesus' primary audience was the peasant class. The powerful and wealthy elites, along with their support class, lived mostly in cities; the peasant underclass, most of the population, lived in rural areas. Jesus avoided cities, with the exception of Jerusalem. He spoke in small towns, villages, and the countryside. The elites heard of him, and a few of them were attracted to him and even supported him, but he spoke primarily to peasants.

In this context, the Lord's Prayer is pointedly about the exigencies of peasant life. After the petition "Thy kingdom come on earth," the next petition is about bread: "Give us this day our daily bread." Bread, enough food, was always an issue in the peasant class. Moreover, there is reason to think that the peasant quest for adequate sustenance was becoming even more desperate in the time of Jesus. God's Kingdom (in contrast to the other kingdoms they knew) is about enough bread.

The earthly meaning continues in the next petition, about forgive-ness. It is the one during which Christians visiting a different church have to pause to see how it will be worded. Forgive us our debts? Or sins? Or trespasses? Part of the reason for uncertainty is different English translations of the gospel texts. But it is also because there are three versions of the Lord's Prayer in early Christianity. Matthew and Luke each have one, as does the *Didache*, an early Christian document written around the year 100.[11]

In wording that is almost identical, Matthew and the *Didache* both have "debt": "And forgive us our *debts*, as we also have forgiven our *debtors*." Luke's version is different. Luke has "sins" in the first half: "And forgive us our sins, for we ourselves forgive everyone indebted to us." But whether Christians have used Matthew's "debts" or Luke's "sins," we have most commonly understood the "real" meaning to be "sins": just as God forgives our sins, so we should forgive those who sin against us. This is an excellent teaching, and the world is better when it is observed. But it may also be too much of a spiritualization of the notion of "debt." Though it is true that "debt" in some Jewish writings had acquired the metaphorical meaning of "sin" by the first century, it is not at all clear that the metaphorical meaning would have obliterated the literal meaning. Most likely, "debt" still carried the association of financial debt.

Debt, along with bread, was the primary survival issue in peasant life. Indebtedness could lead to the loss of one's land, if one still owned some, and descent into the even more precarious world of the tenant farmer or day laborer. If peasants were landless, indebtedness could cause them and their families to be sold into indentured labor.

Thus the best-known Christian prayer names the two central material concerns of peasant life in the time of Jesus. The coming of God's Kingdom involves bread and debt forgiveness. Like the phrase "Kingdom of God," the Lord's Prayer has a theo-political meaning. Indeed, it is tempting to think that even the first petition, "Hallowed be thy name," is to be heard in this context. How does God's name become holy? The hallowing of God's name involves the coming of the Kingdom, bread, and debt forgiveness. Of course, the prayer also has a more than political meaning. It is not simply a prayer for a better world, a more just world. But it is not less than that.

Almost as well known as the Lord's Prayer are the Beatitudes, part of the Sermon on the Mount in Matthew and the Sermon on the Plain in Luke. They similarly combine the Kingdom of God, the poor, and food. To quote Luke's version:

> Blessed are you who are poor,
> for yours is the kingdom of God.
> Blessed are you who are hungry now,
> for you will be filled.[12]

The coming of God's Kingdom means blessing and happiness for the poor. It means food for the hungry: they will be filled.

The next line also refers to the suffering of the peasant class, the poor: "Blessed are you who weep now, for you will laugh." We naturally associate these words with grief and mourning, dying and death, for these are the primary contexts in which we suffer and weep. But in the lives of impoverished peasants, these were not the primary reason for weeping. Peasant life was marked by daily and desperate sorrow: the suffering of children, worry about food and money, illness with none to help, no way out, hopelessness. They weep now, and not just in the hour of death. But when the Kingdom comes, the poor will be blessed, the hungry will be filled, and those who sorrow will laugh.

Thus the Kingdom of God is what life would be like on earth if God were king. It is God's dream as dreamed by the great figures of the Jewish tradition: Moses, the prophets, and for those of us who are Christians, Jesus. It is a dream for the earth.

Jesus Is Lord

"Jesus is Lord" is the most widespread early Christian affirmation. It is central for Paul and for the rest of the New Testament. Like "Kingdom of God," it has a political meaning as well as a religious meaning.

The key to seeing its political meaning is realizing that "lord" was one of the titles of the Roman emperor: Caesar was called "lord." To say "Jesus is Lord" is to say "Caesar is not lord." To affirm the lordship of Christ is to deny the lordship of Caesar.

Indeed, several of the "titles" of Jesus in the New Testament were also titles of Caesar. On coins and inscriptions, Caesar was referred to not only as "lord," but also as "son of God," "savior," "king of kings," and "lord of lords." Caesar was also spoken of as the one who had brought peace on earth. Early Christians used all of this language to refer to Jesus. Even the Christmas story, so politically domesticated in our observance, contains the challenge to Caesar. In Luke, the angel says to the shepherds, "To you is born this day . . . a *Savior,* who is the Christ, the *Lord,*" who will bring *peace on earth.*[13] The titles of Caesar properly belong to Jesus.

Thus the familiar affirmation "Jesus is Lord," now almost a Christian cliché, originally challenged the lordship of the empire. It still does. To use examples from more recent times, it is like Christians in Nazi Germany saying, "Jesus is *mein Führer*"—and thus Hitler is not.[14] Or in the United States, it would mean saying, "Jesus is my commander in chief"—and thus the president is not. The lordship of Christ versus the lordship of empire is the same contrast, the same opposition, that we see in the Kingdom of God versus the kingdoms of this world

Early Christian Perceptions of Empire

Consistent with the political meanings of "Kingdom of God" and "Jesus is Lord," early Christians had a very negative perception of the Roman Empire. We see this especially clearly in the book of Revelation, an anti-imperial apocalypse written by an early Christian named John. The word "apocalypse" means "revelation" or "disclosure," and Revelation not only discloses what John thought would happen soon, but also discloses the nature of empire.

The Beast from the Abyss: John speaks of the Roman Empire as the "beast from the abyss," the ancient serpent who threatens the creation itself with chaos, as the incarnation and embodiment of Satan.

By doing so, the author turns the empire's perception of itself upside down. In the myth of Apollo slaying Python, Rome saw itself as Apollo: Apollo was the god of light and order, and Python was the ancient serpent. But the author of Revelation reverses this: the empire is not Apollo, but Python. The empire is what threatens to plunge the world into chaos.[15]

The Great Harlot: John continues his indictment of empire by portraying Rome as the "great harlot," the great seducer. She is alluring; dressed in elegant finery, adorned with gold and jewels, she seduces the rulers of this world with her wealth and power. But in John's vision she is allied with the beast of the earlier vision: she rides upon the great serpent, indeed is the great serpent. She is "Babylon the great," a destructive empire of the past, even as she is "the great city that rules over the kings of the earth." She is Rome.[16]

Roma: A third perception of empire is found in an early Christian acrostic. An acrostic is a word made up of the first letters of each word in a phrase or sentence. In this case, the phrase is an early Christian saying in Latin: *radix omnium malorum avaritia. Radix* means "root," *omnium* means "all," *malorum* means "evil," and *avaritia* means "avarice" (or "greed"). Putting it together, it says, "Avarice (or greed) is the root of all evil."[17] And the first letters of each word produce *Roma,* the Latin spelling of Rome. It makes a striking point: Roma—empire—is the embodiment of avarice, the incarnation of greed. That's what empire is about. The embodiment of greed in domination systems is the root of all evil.

Of course, the acrostic exaggerates, as many memorable nuggets do. There are other sources of evil besides the greed built into domination systems, and early Christians knew that. The issues the New Testament addresses are not simply political oppression and economic exploitation. It emphasizes personal issues, personal sins, and the need for personal transformation. What is striking is it also emphasizes political issues, political sins, and political transformation.

As we conclude this section on the political passion of the New Testament and its indictment of empire, it is worth remembering that, as empires go, Rome was not particularly bad. A good case can be made that it was better than most. In terms of its system of law, protection against bandits and pirates, a stable order, public projects such as roads, and so forth, Rome was better than the empires it replaced and better than most of the kingdoms and empires that replaced it. But its policies negatively impacted the lives of millions. Its wars of conquest were brutal. In the world of empire, the rich taxed the poor. Moreover, the imperial economic policy of commercialization led to peasants losing their land to large landowners in the Jewish homeland. In the rest of the empire, it caused the migration of many peasants to cities, where they lived uprooted lives in the midst of urban squalor.[18]

The Political Meaning of the Cross

The anti-imperial ethos of early Christianity can be seen in yet one more way. In some ways, it is the most obvious: Jesus was executed by the empire. The domination system of his day killed him. As I emphasized in Chapter 5, we as Christians participate in the only major religious tradition whose founder was executed by established authority. This is the political meaning of Good Friday: it is the domination system's "no" to Jesus. This is also the political meaning of Easter: Easter is God's "yes" to Jesus and his vision, and God's "no" to the domination system. As the book of Acts puts it in words addressed to the authorities, "God has made him both Lord and Christ, this Jesus whom you crucified."[19] Jesus is Lord; the powers of this world are not.

Thus the cross is both personal and political. It embodies the path of personal transformation, of being born again by dying and rising with Christ; and it indicts the domination systems of this world. Good Friday and Easter have a political meaning, even as they are also more than political. Indeed, it is striking how much of our religious language was, in the first century, theo-political language. It indicts the way domination systems built on power and wealth oppress the world.

Meanings for Our Time

Seeing the political meaning of the Bible leads to seeing a political dimension in the Christian life. If we believe that God is the same today as yesterday and tomorrow, that God's character is consistent, then God's passion for justice is as strong in our time as in the time of Moses, the prophets, Jesus, and the New Testament.

I am defining politics in its broad sense as the social systems in which we live. The English word comes from the Greek *polis*, which means "city," and politics is thus about the shape and shaping of the city. By extension, politics is about the shape and shaping of human community, from smaller communities to nations and the international community.

Politics thus includes systems of government (laws and procedures); economic systems (to a large extent, shaped by the ruling class); and conventional systems of beliefs and attitudes (often embodied in laws). All of these are systems that shape our lives together as communities. And they can be better or worse. All us would be able to agree on a short list of terrible systems, Nazi Germany being an obvious nominee. Systems matter. This is what politics is about.

If we ask why the God of the Bible cares about politics, about systemic justice, the answer is disarmingly simple. God cares about justice because the God of the Bible cares about suffering. And the single biggest cause of unnecessary human suffering throughout history has been and is unjust social systems. What would it mean for us to take this seriously?

Consciousness-Raising in the Church

Taking unjust social systems seriously would mean consciousness-raising in the church about the way they shape and affect the lives of people, including our own. Consciousness-raising about the impact of systems is best introduced with obvious examples, such as the effects of racism and sexism on people's lives, as mentioned earlier in this chapter. The importance of systems can also be illustrated by reflecting about why most gays and lesbians were so deeply closeted until recently—namely, because of a system of negative and deeply ingrained conventional attitudes.

The effects can also be illustrated in relatively minor ways, such as the use of the terms "old maid" and "spinster" until recently to

categorize unmarried women above a certain age. Perhaps such naming did not cause deep suffering, but it did negatively label women
who did not conform to the cultural norm of marriage. Systems affect
how we think, including our perception of ourselves and others.

Systems also affect the material conditions of life. In our time,
consciousness-raising about the way our economic system affects
the lives of people is one of the most important justice issues.
Because of the importance of this point, I treat it at greater length.
Doing so not only illustrates the importance of consciousness-raising
about the impact of systems, but also illustrates the way powerful
and wealthy elites in our time, as in the ancient world, use their
power and wealth to structure the economic system in their own
narrow self-interest.[20]

The title of a very recent book by Kevin Phillips names the problem: *Wealth and Democracy*. Its central argument is twofold. First, the
amount of national wealth owned by the richest 1 percent of our population is increasing dramatically. And second, the growing concentration of wealth in the hands of a few threatens American democracy,
simply because of the political power and influence that go with
wealth. The argument is compelling in part because its author is not a
political liberal; if he were, conservatives might suspect him of skew-
ing the data to support his case.[21]

The book is a rich mine of data supporting his claims. Among the
statistics he reports for the United States:

In the twenty-year period between the late 1970s and the late
1990s, the percentage of total wealth owned by the wealthiest
1 percent of our population nearly doubled, increasing from 21
percent to just over 40 percent.[22]

During the same period, the economic situation of the majority
of Americans worsened. In real dollars, both the annual income
and net wealth of the bottom 60 percent of our population
actually declined.[23]

Why did these changes occur? Clearly not because the wealthiest 1 percent worked harder than everybody else. During this same period, the middle and lower classes worked very hard. According to Phillips, the United States has the highest percentage of two-income families in the industrialized world, as well as the largest number of working hours per year.[24] The primary factor creating a greater concentration of wealth among the very rich is not individual hard work and effort.

Nor is the growing gap the necessary result of an efficient free-enterprise system, as if a natural law, an invisible hand, is responsible for it. Other prosperous democracies with free-enterprise systems have much lower income ratios between the top one-fifth and bottom one-fifth of their populations. In Japan, the ratio is 4.3 to 1; in Belgium, 4.6 to 1; in Canada and France, 7.1 to 1. The United States has the highest income ratio between the top quintile and bottom quintile of any developed nation: 11 to 1.[25]

Rather, the wide and widening gap is a "systems" result, the product of the way our economic system is structured. "Economic system" includes specific economic policies (taxation policy, regulation policy, interest rates, and so forth) as well as the degree of freedom and incentive built into the system. Obviously, the way our economic system has been structured has favored the very wealthy. How else can one account for their accumulation of wealth during a period when the economic situation of the majority of Americans remained stagnant or declined? Though some affirm that "a rising tide raises all boats," the truth seems to be that a rising tide raises all yachts.

Moreover, the structuring of our economic policy in the interests of the very wealthy continues. For example, both the tax cut of 2001 and the proposed tax cut of 2003 benefit primarily the wealthiest 1 percent: approximately one-half of the total dollars involved will go to them. The reason: the very wealthy as a group (there are exceptions) use their political influence to structure tax policy in their own self-interest. But heightened awareness of the justice (or injustice) of economic systems would argue that, if there are going to be tax cuts, the middle and lower economic classes need the extra dollars much more than the very wealthy do.

The issue of wealth is a sensitive point for many people, including many readers of this book. The majority of us are financially comfortable, and some of us may be among the wealthiest 5 percent or even 1 percent. We may feel criticized for being comfortable, as if that were morally wrong. Thus it is important to emphasize that the issue is not the individual goodness or virtue of the wealthy. Wealthy people can be very good as individuals, just as poor people can.

The issue, rather, is a systems issue: the structuring of the economic system and whose interests it serves. For those of us who are well-to-do, the question is: How are we going to use our wealth and influence? Will we use it to bring about change or to support policies in the narrow self-interest of a few?

The New Testament names some from the wealthy and powerful elites who were attracted to Jesus and his vision: Joanna, Susanna, Phoebe, Nicodemus, Joseph of Arimathea. They must have been disenchanted members of the elites. And they can be role models for those of us who are comfortable or wealthy. There's nothing wrong with being a Joanna or a Joseph of Arimathea. Indeed, we need more of them: financially comfortable people disenchanted with systemic injustice and committed to the Kingdom of God.

Advocacy of God's Justice

Second, taking the political passion of the Bible seriously would mean advocacy of God's justice. In a democratic society, this means politics in the narrower sense of the word, namely, participation in the political process in loyalty to the dream of God. I don't have a name for this kind of politics. "Liberal politics" catches a dimension of it, but the word "liberal" has been so vilified in our time as to be virtually unredeemable. Perhaps it could be called "progressive politics," "a politics of compassion," or "the politics of the Kingdom."

It would be a politics suspicious of the ways wealthy and powerful classes use their power and wealth to structure systems largely in their own interest. Elites have always been very good at that. It would be a politics concerned not with privilege, but with compassion for "the least of these."

Its particular details are quite open, but its general form is shaped by a vision of God's passion for the earth: a justice marked by enough bread and freedom from debt, worry, and sorrow. Of course, that is an ideal that we can never achieve. Ultimately, the Kingdom of God always exceeds our grasp, but there are social systems that are closer to and farther from the ideal.

Specific Examples

Third, I provide some examples of what taking the Kingdom of God seriously might mean for us in our time as Christians and residents of the United States. I do so for the sake of being concrete and not simply general. Though of course I would like you to agree with me, I am less concerned with soliciting agreement than I am with provoking thoughtfulness about the way our life together is, and could be, structured.

Health Care: Taking seriously God's passion for the marginalized would mean enacting a system of health care for the uninsured. How best to do this, I do not know, and I do not think that being Christian provides any particular guidance about details. We can learn from the successes and shortcomings of other systems that provide health care for everybody and design the mix that seems best in our setting. But whatever the details, the goal seems incontrovertible. The notion that we cannot afford it is ludicrous. Societies less prosperous than ours, including capitalist countries with productive economies, have found ways to do it. Moreover, we are considering a tax cut that would cost more than extending health care to everybody would. We can afford to establish a Department of Homeland Security that costs more, and as I write this, we have initiated a war that will cost more. It is difficult to avoid the conclusion that fear is a more powerful political motive in our society than compassion.

The Environment: Concern for the environment and the nonhuman world is important both for the long-term self-interest of human beings and because of the biblical understanding of creation. To whom does the earth belong? The Bible's answer is clear: "The earth is the Lord's and the fullness thereof."[26] We are not the owners of the earth, but stewards; and stewards manage that which belongs to some-body else.

But we have most often treated the earth as if it does belong to us. We have seen nature primarily as having instrumental value (its use *for us*) and not as having intrinsic value (its value in itself, that is, its value to God). Our view has been anthropocentric, human-centered, whereas God loves the whole of creation and not simply human beings. And within our anthropocentric view, we think primarily of ourselves and not very much about future generations—our children and our children's children. The earth belongs to God, not simply to us, and not simply to those of us alive today.

Economic Justice: "The earth is the Lord's and the fullness thereof" also requires economic justice. We not only treat the earth as if it belongs to us as a species, but as if it belongs to some of us much more than to others. Economic justice is about the just distribution of God's earth.[27] "Just" does not mean absolutely equal. Differentials can remain, but how great they are matters; they can be more or less just. The just distribution of God's earth is not a utopian and unattainable absolute. But it does mean that everybody is to have the material essentials of life, even if some have more.

The quest for greater economic justice entails insight and action about the growing gap between rich and poor. As I emphasized ear-lier in this chapter, the gap is widening dramatically and threatens American democracy. The gap is also widening globally. Economic justice may be the single most important domestic and international justice issue today.

The Use of Imperial Power: For Christians in the United States, taking the Kingdom of God seriously means critical thinking about what it means to be an imperial power. Like it or not, we are the world's imperial power ever since the fall of the Soviet Union and the end of the Cold War.

Militarily, we are the world's superpower. We are also the world's major economic power. The combination of global military and economic power is the defining characteristic of empire. We are the Rome of our time.

The perennial temptation of empire is the overuse and misuse of imperial power. We need to be as thoughtful, responsible, and creative as possible in the use of our power, for it can be used in two very different ways. We can use it to try to control the world in our own self-interest, to structure the system so that it serves us, to impose our will on the world. Or we can use it to build up. We can use our power with the world's well-being in mind rather than primarily our own.

This includes the use of our military power, an acute issue as I write this chapter. We have begun a war against a weak and impoverished country because we think it is necessary for our security. This is contrary to all accepted Christian teaching on war—not only to early Christian pacifism, but also to the only other legitimate Christian position, namely, the "just war" theory. We are acting like an empire, for it is empires that think they have a right to initiate war in their own perceived interest.

How we use our imperial power includes not only military power, but also the global use of our economic power. Economic globalization is happening and seems to be inevitable, but it can be done in quite different ways. It can be done with the interests of the world's wealthy in mind or with the interests of large numbers in mind. Thus far, the former prevails: the present structures of economic globalization favor the wealthiest 1 percent of the world's population. We could use our economic power differently.

The prophet Ezekiel's indictment of the city of Tyre, famed for its wealth as a center of trade, is chillingly appropriate. About Tyre Ezekiel said, "You corrupted your wisdom for the sake of your splendor."[28] Imperial power and loss of wisdom often go together. It is unusual, and very difficult, for a superpower to be wise, gentle, and compassionate. But that's what we are called to do.

Taking the Kingdom of God seriously means taking the systemic causes of human suffering seriously. Taking the Kingdom of God seriously means taking God's justice seriously. In Chapter 10, I will say more about what this might mean for Christian practice today.

Conclusion

Seeing the political passion of the Bible calls us to a politically engaged spirituality.[29] This phrase combines the two transformations, personal and political, at the center of the Christian vision of life as we see it in the Bible and in Jesus.

If we emphasize only one, we miss half of the biblical message, half of the gospel. The strength of much of conservative Christianity is that it has emphasized the first, personal transformation. Its weakness is that it has often neglected the Kingdom of God. The strength of much of liberal Christianity has been that it has often emphasized the second. Its weakness is that it has often neglected being born again. A politically engaged spirituality affirms both spiritual transformation and political transformation. The message of Jesus, and the Bible as a whole, is about both. What we see in Jesus and the Bible answers our deepest personal longing, to be born again, and the world's greatest need, the Kingdom of God.

1. Robert Bellah et al., *Habits of the Heart* (Berkeley: University of California Press, 1985).

2. For an account of the church's wrestling with the question of slavery and the Bible, see Peter Gomes, *The Good Book* (New York: William Morrow, 1996), pp. 84–101.

3. I owe the phrase "royal consciousness" to Walter Brueggemann, the foremost Hebrew Bible scholar in the United States today. See his *The Prophetic Imagination* (Philadelphia: Fortress, 1978).

4. This is a common emphasis of mainstream scholarship on the Hebrew Bible. For my more extended treatments of justice in the Hebrew Bible, see *Reading the Bible Again for the First Time* (San Francisco: HarperSanFrancisco, 2001), chaps. 5–6; and *The God We Never Knew* (San Francisco: HarperSanFrancisco, 1997), pp. 132–41.

5. John Reumann, *Jesus in the Church's Gospels* (Philadelphia: Fortress, 1968), p. 142.

6. Mark 1:14-15. A brief comment on the word "repent" in this verse: the word means something quite different from the common meaning of "being sorry for one's sins." It is related to the Hebrew Bible's understanding of "return": returning to God, returning from exile; and its Greek roots suggest "to go beyond the mind that you have."

7. Quoted words from Matt. 8:11; see also Luke 13:28-29. For my slightly fuller sketches of the meanings of the "Kingdom of God," see *The Meaning of Jesus: Two Visions*, with N. T. Wright (San Francisco: HarperSanFrancisco, 1999), pp. 74-75; and *Jesus in Contemporary Scholarship* (Valley Forge, PA: Trinity Press International, 1994), pp. 86-88.

8. In an Internet debate with Luke Timothy Johnson and me in March 1996.

9. Crossan, in a lecture at Trinity Episcopal Cathedral in Portland, Oregon, June 2002. See his comment in *Excavating Jesus*, co-authored with Jonathan Reed (San Francisco: HarperSanFrancisco, 2001), p. 172: "Be it called the Kingdom of God or of Heaven, it means the divine will for this earth, for here below, for here and now. How, in other words, would God run the world if God sat on Caesar's throne?"

10. Remark made by Crossan in a lecture. See also *Excavating Jesus*, pp. 274-75: "The Kingdom of God is about God's will for this earth. Heaven is in great shape, it's the earth that's problematic."

11. Matt. 6:9-15; Luke 11:2-4; *Didache* 8:1-2. For a display of the three versions on the same page, see Burton H. Throckmorton, ed., *Gospel Parallels*, 5th ed. (Nashville: Thomas Nelson, 1992), p. 31.

12. Luke 6:20-21. For Matthew's somewhat different version, see Matt. 5:3-12. In addition to having more beatitudes, Matthew also spiritualizes the beatitudes about the poor and the hungry: "Blessed are the poor *in spirit*" (5:3); and "Blessed are those who hunger and thirst *for righteousness*" (5:6). That Luke is speaking about real poverty and real hunger is clear from the "woes" that immediately follow his beatitudes: "Woe to you who are rich. . . . Woe to you who are full now. . . . Woe to you who are laughing now" (Luke 6:24-25).

13. Luke 2:11, 14. For the political meaning of the birth stories as a whole, see especially Richard Horsley, *The Liberation of Christmas* (New York: Crossroad, 1989).

14. Once again, Crossan is the source of this way of putting it (in a lecture at Trinity Episcopal Cathedral in Portland, Oregon, in 2000). He hears the political meaning of early Christian language with remarkable sensitivity.

15. Rev. 12-13. For my own more extended comments on these chapters, see *Reading the Bible Again*, pp. 281-84.

16. Rev. 17, with her destruction portrayed in Rev. 18. In both chapters, note how her wealth, power, and material glory are emphasized. For further comments, see *Reading the Bible Again*, pp. 286–89.

17. And thus it is very close to the familiar saying "The love of money is the root of all kinds of evil" (1 Tim. 6:10). I first became aware of this acrostic in a Beliefnet column by Phyllis Tickle in the summer of 2002.

18. For a striking picture of life in the large cities of the Roman Empire, see Rodney Stark, *The Rise of Christianity* (San Francisco: HarperSanFrancisco, 1996), chap. 7.

19. Acts 2:36.

20. In order to avoid a possible misunderstanding: the issue is not capitalism versus socialism, but the particular ways in which our system of capitalism is structured.

21. Kevin Phillips, *Wealth and Democracy: A Political History of the American Rich* (New York: Random House, 2002). Phillips identifies himself as a Republican. For another book that very helpfully raises consciousness about the effects of our economic system on the working poor, see Barbara Ehrenreich, *Nickel and Dimed* (New York: Henry Holt, 2001).

22. Phillips, *Wealth and Democracy*, p. 123.

23. Phillips, *Wealth and Democracy*, pp. xviii, 111.

24. Phillips, *Wealth and Democracy*, p. 113.

25. Phillips, *Wealth and Democracy*, p. 124.

26. Ps. 24:1 (RSV).

27. Phrasing owed to Dominic Crossan in a lecture at Trinity Episcopal Cathedral in Portland, Oregon, June 2002.

28. Ezek. 28:17.

29. A phrase I owe to William Sloane Coffin. See his most recent book, full of memorable insights, and with a great title: *The Heart Is a Little to the Left* (Hanover, NH: University Press of New England, 1999).

EIGHT

Thin Places
Opening the Heart

"Open hearts" and "thin places" suggest much of what is central to being Christian. Together, these two metaphors express the emerging paradigm's relational and transformational vision of the Christian life. They name both the goal and means of transformation, the purpose and practice of the Christian life for us as individuals and in our life together as church.

The Heart: A Metaphor for the Self

The word "heart" appears well over a thousand times in the Bible. Most often, it is a comprehensive metaphor for the self. It covers much more than does the metaphorical meaning of "heart" in contemporary English. In our usage, the heart is most commonly associated with love, as in Valentine hearts; courage, as in brave hearts; and grief, as in broken hearts. But in the Bible, the "heart" includes these and more: it is a metaphor for the inner self as a whole.

A selection of short quotations from the Hebrew Bible and Christian Testament illustrates this comprehensive meaning of the "heart":

"The thoughts of their hearts were only evil continually"
(Gen. 6:5).

"The inclination of the human heart is evil from youth"
(Gen. 8:21).

"Keep these words that I am commanding you today in your
heart" (Deut. 6:6).

"Serve the Lord your God with all your heart" (Deut. 10:12).

"Incline your hearts to the Lord, the God of Israel" (Josh. 24:23).

"Return to the Lord with all your heart" (1 Sam. 7:3).

"The Lord looks on the heart" (1 Sam. 16:7).

"I will give thanks to the Lord with my whole heart" (Ps. 9:1).

"Let the words of my mouth and the meditation of my heart be
acceptable to you" (Ps. 19:14).

"In God my heart trusts" (Ps. 28:7).

"Your law is within my heart" (Ps. 40:8).

"Create in me a clean heart, O God" (Ps. 51:10).

"So teach us to count our days that we may gain a wise heart"
(Ps. 90:12).

"Search me, O God, and know my heart" (Ps. 139:23).

"Incline your heart to understanding" (Prov. 2:2).

"Trust in the Lord with all your heart" (Prov. 3:5).

"My child, give me your heart" (Prov. 23:26).

"The heart is devious above all else" (Jer. 17:9).

"I will put my law within them, and I will write it on their hearts"
(Jer. 31:33).

"Where your treasure is, there your heart will be also"
(Matt. 6:21).

"Out of the heart come evil intentions" (Matt. 15:19).

"Mary treasured all these words and pondered them in her heart"
(Luke 2:19).

"God searches the heart" (Rom. 8:27).

"The God who said, 'Let light shine out of darkness,' has shone
in our hearts" (2 Cor. 4:6).

"God has sent the Spirit of God's Son into our hearts, crying,
'Abba! Father!'" (Gal. 4:6).

"May you be strengthened in your inner being with power
through God's Spirit, that Christ may dwell in your hearts"
(Eph. 3:16–17).

The heart is an image for the self at a deep level, deeper than our perception, intellect, emotion, and volition. As the spiritual center of the
total self, it affects all of these: our sight, thought, feelings, and will.

The Closed Heart

The Bible has many pairs of metaphors for the human condition and
our need. These pairs of images portray our predicament and the solution. In bondage, we need liberation. In exile and estranged, we need
to return and reconnect. Blind, we need to have our sight restored. In
the dark, we need enlightenment. Sick and wounded, we need healing. Hungry and thirsty, we need food and drink. Sinful and unclean,
we need forgiveness and cleansing. Dead and entombed, we need to
be raised into new life.

Yet another of the Bible's correlative metaphors for our condition
and the solution is "closed hearts" and "open hearts." The condition of
the heart matters. The heart, the self at its deepest level, can be turned
toward God or away from God, open to God or closed to God. But its
typical condition is that it is turned away from God and "closed." The
Bible speaks of this condition with a rich collection of synonymous
metaphors. Our hearts can be "shut." They can be "fat," as if encrusted
within a thick layer. They can be "proud," puffed up and enlarged. They
can be "made of stone" rather than made of flesh. They are often "hard."
The Greek word for this condition is *sklerokardia*: we have sclerosis of
the heart.

What goes with a closed heart? What is this condition like? In the
Bible, it is a particularly rich image with many associations. Many connect to the other correlative images of our condition and our need. As
I suggest the qualities of a closed heart, I invite you to consider the
extent to which they fit your experience, for this language seeks to
describe a condition, a way of being.

■ Blindness and limited vision go with a closed heart. We do not see clearly when our hearts are closed. A shut heart and shut eyes go together; we have eyes but do not see. So also we have ears and do not hear. Enclosed in our own world, we neither see nor hear very well.

■ A closed heart affects the mind, the reasoning process itself. Rather than the mind being in charge of this deeper layer of the self, the heart controls the mind. The heart can even deceive the mind in the process we call "rationalization," that is, self-interested self-justification. We often believe our own deceptions. The phenomenon of self-deception (always easier to recognize in others than in ourselves) is fascinating: there is something "in me" that can deceive me. Thus the closed heart is associated with lack of understanding and a darkened mind.

■ A closed heart and bondage go together. As in the exodus story, we can be in bondage because of the hardness of Pharaoh's heart. And Pharaoh can also live within us: we are often in bondage to the desiring of our own hearts.

■ A closed heart lacks gratitude. If successful in life, a person with a closed heart often feels self-made and entitled; or if life has gone badly, bitter and cheated. But gratitude is far from it.

■ A closed heart is insensitive to wonder and awe. The world looks ordinary when our hearts are closed.

■ A closed heart forgets God. It does not remember the one in whom we live and move and have our being; it loses track of the Mystery always around us.

■ A closed heart and exile go together. Self-preoccupied, turned inward upon itself, the shut heart is cut off from a larger reality. Separated and disconnected, it is estranged and in exile.

■ A closed heart lacks compassion. In the Bible, compassion is the ability to feel the feelings of another at a level lower than one's head, "in the womb," "in the bowels," and then to act accordingly. A closed heart does not feel this. Though it can be charitable, it does not feel the suffering of others.

■ For the same reason, a closed heart is insensitive to injustice. Closed hearts and injustice go together. The prophets and Jesus, champions of God's justice, often indict the condition of the hard heart.

The "closed heart" is a striking image for our condition. It is as if our selves are normally encased in a hard rind, in a tough shell. Why is this so? Why do we commonly have closed hearts? For some, it is the result of a chaotic childhood marked by abuse or radical instability. The self builds up layers of protection to defend itself against an unreliable and hurtful world.

But the condition does not develop only in people with difficult childhoods. The closed heart is the natural result of the process of growing up. The birth and development of self-awareness involves an increasing sense of being a separated self. We live within this separated self, as if the self is enclosed in a dome, a transparent shell: the world is "out there," and I am "in here." Like an invisible shield, the dome is a boundary separating the self from the world. It can become hard and rigid. It closes us off from the world, and we live centered in ourselves. The same process of growing up that creates the need to be born again creates the need for our hearts to be opened. To mix metaphors, the reason we need to be born again is because we have closed hearts.

The condition of a closed heart covers a spectrum of hardness. Not all hearts are equally hard. In severe form, hard hearts are associated with violence, brutality, arrogance, and a rapacious world-devouring greed. These all have milder forms. The mild form of violence is judgmentalism; of brutality, insensitivity; of arrogance, self-centeredness; of rapacious greed, ordinary self-interest.

It is also interesting to reflect about what opens and closes our hearts on a daily basis. I am aware that some days my heart is more open than other days. Even in the course of a single day, there are moments when my heart is more open or more closed. Sometimes it is closed because of tiredness, worry, or busyness. I know that my heart is closed whenever I feel grumpy or self-preoccupied, when the world looks ordinary, or when the critical voice is strong in my head, whether directed at myself or others. When I stand in a supermarket checkout line and all the people I see look kind of ugly, I know that my heart is closed.

When our hearts are closed, we live within a shell. To extend the egg metaphor: the shell needs to be broken open if the life within it is to enter into full life. What we need is the "hatching of the heart."[1] And if the heart is not hatched, we die. The hatching of the heart—the opening of the self to God, the sacred—is a comprehensive image for the individual dimension of the Christian life.

The yearning, promise, and imperative of an open heart, a new heart, a pure heart, runs though the Bible:

"Create in me a clean heart, O God, and put a new and right spirit within me" (Ps. 51:10).

"Get yourselves a new heart and a new spirit! Why will you die?" (Ezek. 18:31).

"A new heart I will give you, and a new spirit I will put within you; and I will remove from your body the heart of stone and give you a heart of flesh" (Ezek. 36:26; see also 11:19).

How does this happen? How do hearts become open? The biblical answer: the Spirit of God does it. And the Spirit of God operates through thin places.

Thin Places

I owe the metaphor of "thin places" to Celtic Christianity, a form of Christianity that flourished in Ireland and parts of Scotland, Wales, and northern England beginning in the fifth century. An underground current in that part of the world ever since, Celtic spirituality is being rediscovered in our time.[2]

"Thin places" has its home in a particular way of thinking about God. Deeply rooted in the Bible and the Christian tradition, this way of thinking sees God, "the More," as the encompassing Spirit in which everything is. God is not somewhere else, but "right here." In words attributed to Paul in the book of Acts, God is "the one in whom we live and move and have our being." Note how the words work: we are in God, we live in God, we move and have our being in God. God is a nonmaterial layer of reality all around us, "right here" as well as "more than right here."[3] This way of thinking thus affirms that there are minimally two layers or dimensions of reality, the visible world of our ordinary experience and God, the sacred, Spirit.

One of my favorite quotations expressing this understanding of God is from Thomas Merton, a twentieth-century Trappist monk:

> Life is this simple. We are living in a world that is absolutely transparent, and God is shining through it all the time. This is not just a fable or a nice story. It is true. If we abandon ourselves to God and forget ourselves, we see it sometimes, and we see it maybe frequently. God shows Himself everywhere, in everything—in people and in things and in nature and in events. It becomes very obvious that God is everywhere and in everything and we cannot be without Him. It's impossible. The only thing is that we don't see it.[4]

But occasionally we do "see it," do experience God shining through everything. "Thin places" are places where these two levels of reality meet or intersect. They are places where the boundary between the two levels becomes very soft, porous, permeable. Thin places are places where the veil momentarily lifts, and we behold God, experience the one in whom we live, all around us and within us.

Thin places can literally be geographical places. For Celtic Christianity, the island of Iona off the west coast of Scotland is a classic thin place. So also are traditional destinations of pilgrimage: for Christians, Jerusalem, Rome, Canterbury, and others; for Muslims, especially Mecca, but also Medina and Jerusalem. Mountains and high places are thin places in many religious traditions, including the Bible and Native American traditions.

But the notion refers to much more than geographical locations. A thin place is anywhere our hearts are opened. To use sacramental language, a thin place is a sacrament of the sacred, a mediator of the sacred, a means whereby the sacred becomes present to us. A thin place is a means of grace.

There are many kinds of thin places. Some are "secular" in that they are not explicitly religious. For example, nature, especially wilderness areas, can sometimes become a thin place. The combination of an untamed world with solitude and quiet can yield moments when we experience "the earth filled with the glory of God." For some, the arts can become a thin places. Music, poetry, literature, the visual arts, and dance can all become thin places in which the boundary between one's self and the world momentarily disappears.

For Thomas Merton, a street corner in downtown Louisville became a thin place. The most prolonged thin place I have experienced was on an airliner flying across the Atlantic. They can happen anywhere. Even times of serious illness, suffering, and grief can become thin places. They do not always, of course; but sometimes our hearts are broken open by such experiences.

People can become thin places. Many of us have known at least one or two people through whom we experienced the presence of the Spirit at particular junctures in our lives. Jesus in particular must have been a remarkable thin place; his followers' devotion flowed out of their experience of him as such. And the saints, known and unknown, Christian and non-Christian, were (and are) thin places.

Thin Places and Christian Practices

What I wish to emphasize is how this notion helps us to understand traditional Christian practices, both corporate and individual. My claim is that their central purpose is to become a thin place where our hearts are opened. In Chapter 10, I will say more about some of these practices, but for now my primary purpose is to illustrate how they function as thin places.

Worship can become a thin place. Indeed, this is one of its primary purposes. Of course, worship is about praising God. But worship is not about God needing praise. I recall hearing a radio preacher talking about how "God just loves to be praised." He made God sound like a narcissist. Rather, worship has the power to draw us out of ourselves. Worship is directed *to God*, but is in an important sense *for us*.

Worship is about creating a sense of the sacred, a thin place. The diverse forms of Christian worship do this in different ways. At one end of the spectrum, the enthusiasm of Pentecostal worship can become a thin place by mediating an almost palpable sense of the presence of the Spirit. At the other end of the spectrum, Quaker silence serves the same purpose. In liturgical and sacramental forms of worship, the use of sacred words and rituals creates a sense of another world.

The primary role of music within worship, whether performance or participatory, is to become a thin place. We can be deeply moved by a performance of Handel's *Messiah*, Durufle's *Requiem*, Bach's *Mass in B Minor*, acapella chanting, gospel music, and so on.

The primary purpose of participatory music—congregational singing—is to provide a thin place. More Protestants report being moved by hymn singing than by any other element in the service. We sing to God, and our hearts are opened. The hymns that do this best combine two features: words that move us and music that can be easily sung.

If we took this seriously, it would affect our selection of hymns. Hymns that are difficult to sing are very unlikely to work as a thin place. Hymns intended for congregational participation need to be accessible to musically untrained and musically challenged voices. I am among them, often uncertain that I am on pitch. But if the music is accessible so that the congregation can sing their hearts out, then I can join in with all my heart, unafraid that my voice will stand out in an unseemly way.

The issue is not contemporary versus traditional hymns. Many traditional hymns are wonderfully accessible and can therefore become a thin place. To cite some examples from earlier centuries: "Of the Father's Love Begotten," "Be Thou My Vision," "O Come, O Come Emmanuel," "A Mighty Fortress Is Our God," O Sacred Head Now Wounded," "Come Down, O Love Divine," and "O Come, All Ye Faithful."

Participation in the sacraments of baptism and the Eucharist can become a thin place. Indeed, this is their officially defined function: they are means of grace. We do not always experience them this way. But whether or not we experience them as such in the moment, they are nevertheless means of grace, thin places.

Sermons can become thin places. Of course, they do not always do so, but sometimes, whether because of their intensity, evocative quality, or the work of the Spirit, hearing them, we find ourselves addressed. The preaching of the Word is meant to become a thin place, a place where our hearts are opened.

The Bible can become a thin place. This is its sacramental function and is most obvious in its private devotional use, but the Bible can also become a thin place in the worship life of the church. When read well, the lectionary readings can become sacramental, as can biblical preaching.

Liturgical words—by which I mean words that are a regular part of worship services—can become thin places. For virtually all Christians, this includes the Lord's Prayer; and for most Christians, it also includes the creed, a confession of sin, and a few responses (such as "And also with you" or "Thanks be to God"). When we say words that we know "by heart," it is not an intellectual exercise in which we think about the meaning of the words. Liturgical words are not about intellectual content. They serve a different function.

When we pray the Lord's Prayer together, the point is not to "think hard" about the meanings of the words and to mean them. As a child, I remember being told that it was important not simply to *say* the Lord's Prayer, but to *pray* the Lord's Prayer—that is, to really *mean* it. So my attention became focused on *thinking hard* about the words. I no longer say or pray the Lord's Prayer in such an effortful manner. Rather, the point is to let the drone of these words that we know by heart become a thin place. For Simone Weil, one of the twentieth century's remarkable Western spiritual figures, saying the Lord's Prayer consistently brought her into a thin place, and not because she was paying attention to the meaning of the words.

So also saying the creed together can become a thin place. I know that many mainline Christians have difficulties with the creed, and I understand why. If one thinks that saying the creed commits one's intellect to the propositional (literal?) truth of all of its statements, it is impossible for a thoughtful modern person to do so. To use two obvious examples, Jesus did not "descend" into hell (hell is not "down") or "ascend" in to heaven (heaven is not "up"). And, of course, many mainline Christians also have trouble with "born of the Virgin Mary," "he will come again some day," and "raised bodily from the dead."

But affirming all of these to be literally true propositions is not the purpose of saying the creed in the context of worship. Of course, the creed does have propositional content: minimally, it affirms the co-centrality of God, Jesus, and the Spirit. But its primary purpose in worship is not propositional but sacramental: through these clunky words that stumble in the presence of Mystery, God is mediated. These words that we know by heart can become a thin place as we join ourselves in the sound of the community saying these words together. As we do so, we also join ourselves with a community that transcends time, all of those centuries of Christians who have heard and said these words. We become part of the communion of saints, together in a thin place.

Just as liturgical words can become thin places, so also can liturgical time, sacred time. For Christians, the great festivals of the church year, Easter and Christmas, are often experienced as thin places. We attend Christmas and Easter services in great numbers not simply for conventional reasons, but because they move us. Though filled with nostalgia for many of us, they are not simply about sentiment, but often open us up at a deep level of ourselves. They touch our hearts. The symbolism is remarkable and remarkably powerful. Both begin in darkness and proclaim new life. In the midst of our winter darkness, the midnight service on Christmas Eve celebrates Jesus, the light in our darkness and the light of the world who, in Paul's words, shines in our heart. The Easter Vigil service begins in the darkness of the tomb and climaxes in a flood of light as the congregation sings, "Christ the Lord Is Risen Today," with its soaring "alleluias" rising like Jesus from the dead.

These times have great power, as do the liturgical seasons leading up to Christmas and Easter. During Advent, we yearn for and prepare for the coming of the light. We sing "O come, O come, Emmanuel, and ransom captive Israel, that mourns in lonely exile here," "Let every heart prepare him room," and "Be born in us today." During Lent, we journey with Jesus from Galilee to Jerusalem and participate in Holy Week with its inevitable climax of death and resurrection. The purpose of Lent and Advent is to become thin places.

If we took seriously that a major purpose of worship is to become a thin place, it would affect how we would conduct our worship services. Like several denominations, the Episcopal church, to which I belong, has a relatively fixed order of worship. But even within this, there are choices to be made: the selection of hymns, the amount of silence in the service, whether the liturgy is sung or said, the care with which the lectionary texts are read. In general, the spoken word is the least effective way of opening the heart. The spoken word, unless it is poetry or story, tends to address the head, and we have to pay attention with our minds. Of course, sermons and readings are important, but as much of the rest of the service as possible should be designed to become a thin place.

In addition to the collective practices of the church, individual practices can also become thin places. This is one of the central functions of prayer: to become a thin place in which our hearts are opened. Though this can happen in the context of verbal prayer in which we talk to God, this is especially the purpose of the prayer of internal silence. The silence becomes a thin place in which we sit in the presence of God: "Be still and know that I am God."

So also a primary function of many other Christian practices is to become a thin place: journaling, retreats, pilgrimage, fasting. Their purpose is to bring intention and attention together for the opening of the heart.

In a comprehensive sense, the opening of the heart is the purpose of spirituality, of both our collective and individual practices. The Christian life is about the "hatching of the heart," the opening of the self to the Spirit of God by spending time in "thin places"—those places and practices through which we become open to and nourished by the Mystery in whom we live and move and have our being.

The Open Heart

What goes with open hearts? What are we like, what are our lives like, when our hearts are open? It's the opposite of the characteristics of the closed heart described at the beginning of this chapter. But rather than treating the whole list, I provide some examples.

An open heart and seeing go together. We see more clearly when our hearts are open—see the person right in front of our face, see the landscape stretched out before us. We move from darkness to light, from night to day, when we "see with the eyes of our heart enlightened."[5] An open heart and enlightenment go together.

An open heart is alive to wonder, to the sheer marvel of "isness." It is remarkable that the world is, that we are here, that we can experience it. The world is not ordinary. Indeed, what is remarkable is that it could ever look ordinary to us. An open heart knows "radical amazement."[6]

An open heart and gratitude go together. We can feel this in our bodies. In the moments in my life when I have been most grateful, I have felt a swelling, almost a bursting, in my chest.

An open heart, compassion, and a passion for justice go together. An open heart feels the suffering and pain of the world and responds to it. Compassion and a passion for justice are the ethical impulse and imperative that go with an open heart. Indeed, they are the primary fruit of the Spirit. "Be compassionate as God is compassionate," Jesus said. Paul said the same in different words: "Now faith, hope, and love abide, these three; and the greatest of these is love."[7] The purpose of the Christian life, of life in Christ, is to become more and more compassionate beings.

Christian devotion through the centuries has yearned for an open heart, a new heart, a transformed heart. In the words of a song remembered from childhood:

Into my heart, into my heart;
Come into my heart, Lord Jesus;
Come in today, come in to stay;
Come into my heart, Lord Jesus.

In prayers known as collects, used at the beginning of the service in many denominations, we pray for the coming of the Spirit into our hearts:

Send your Holy Spirit and pour into our hearts your greatest gift, which is love, the true bond of peace and all virtue, without which whoever lives is accounted dead before you.

Create and make in us new and contrite hearts.

Pour into our hearts such love toward you, that we, loving you in all things and above all things, may obtain your promises, which exceed all that we can desire.[8]

And the heart is the subject of a moving prayer from Dag Hammarskjöld, a Swedish diplomat and Secretary General of the United Nations in the middle of the last century. Hammarskjöld was also a Christian mystic, though few knew this during his lifetime. He kept a journal that was discovered after his death in a peacekeeping mission in the Congo. In it, he wrote:

Give us pure hearts, that we may see you;
Humble hearts, that we may hear you;
Hearts of love, that we may serve you;
Hearts of faith, that we may abide in you.[9]

The Christian life is about a new heart, an open heart, a heart of flesh, a heart of compassion. The Christian life is about the Spirit of God opening our hearts in thin places.

---

1. I owe the phrase "hatching of the heart" to Alan Jones, *Exploring Spiritual Direction* (New York: Seabury, 1982), pp. 127–30, who got it from Frederick Buechner's novel *Godric* (New York: Atheneum, 1980).

2. There are many recent books on Celtic spirituality. See, for example, Edward C. Sellner, *Wisdom of the Celtic Saints* (Notre Dame, IN: Ave Maria Press, 1993); Philip Newell, *Listening for the Heartbeat of God* (London: SPCK, 1997); Esther de Waal, *Celtic Light* (London: HarperCollins, 1997).

3. See also Chapter 4, pp. 65–69.

4. From an audiotape of Merton made in 1965. I thank Rev. David McConnell, a United Methodist pastor in Montana, for providing me with the quotation.

5. Eph. 1:18.

6. Abraham Heschel, *Man Is Not Alone* (New York: Farrar, Straus and Giroux, 1951), esp. pp. 11–17.

7. Luke 6:36; 1 Cor. 13:13. For the use of "compassionate" in this passage from Luke, see Chapter 6, n. 30.

8. From *The Book of Common Prayer*, the collects for the seventh Sunday after the Epiphany, Ash Wednesday, and the sixth Sunday of Easter.

9. Dag Hammarskjöld, *Markings*, trans. W. H. Auden and Leif Sjoberg (London: Faber and Faber, 1964), p. 93.

NINE

Sin and Salvation
Transforming the Heart

"Sin" and "salvation" are very familiar words to Christians. Loaded and multilayered in meaning, they have been central to Christian vocabulary from the beginning. Yet both are often poorly understood. Some understandings obscure their meanings, even trivialize them.[1]

Thinking About Sin

We begin with sin. The language of sin (and forgiveness) dominates the Christian imagination. Its centrality in Christian thought and practice is evident. Virtually every Christian worship service includes a confession of sin. If we grew up Lutheran, as I did, we said every Sunday morning, "Almighty God, our Maker and Redeemer, we poor sinners confess unto thee, that we are by nature sinful and unclean, and that we have sinned against thee in thought, word, and deed. Wherefore we flee for refuge to thine infinite mercy, seeking and imploring thy grace. . ."

Catholics until recently were expected to make formal confession to a priest before receiving the Eucharist. And though denominations with more liturgical freedom (like Presbyterians, Baptists, Methodists, and other Protestants) do not have such formalized rituals of confession, sin still looms large. From the vantage point of other religions, the Christian emphasis upon sin looks strange. As a friendly Buddhist quip puts it, "You Christians must be very bad people—you're always confessing your sins."[2]

And it's not only liturgical confessions that give a central place to sin. In the most familiar wording of the Lord's Prayer, we pray for the forgiveness of our sins (or trespasses). Sin is the problem from which we need deliverance. It is commonly understood as the reason for Jesus' death: he died for our sins. Indeed, in many forms of Christianity, we could not be forgiven if it were not for Jesus' sacrifice on the cross. Sin is thus the reason for the incarnation. If we had not sinned, Jesus' life and death would not have been necessary. God would not have needed to "send the only begotten Son." Thus for centuries, Christians have seen the central issue separating us from God as "sin."

In recent decades in some churches, sin has not been emphasized quite as much. Some welcome this development. Others wonder about it and lament the loss, asking, "Whatever happened to sin?"[3] To the extent that the lament names a diminishing sense that there's anything "wrong" with us, it is merited. There is much that is wrong with us. As one of my wife's favorite childhood stories put it, "'Something is not right,' said Miss Clavell in the middle of the night."

Miss Clavell's perception is shared by the Bible. It is unequivocal about the fact that something has gone wrong. To use Frederick Buechner's words to describe the Bible's central plot:

> I think it is possible to say that in spite of all its extraordinary variety, the Bible is held together by having a single plot. It is one that can be simply stated: God creates the world; *the world gets lost*; God seeks to restore the world to the glory for which God created it.[4]

The world gets lost. We are lost.

The question I raise in the first part of this chapter is whether "sin" is the best way to name what is wrong and why we are lost. Is the dominant place of the language of sin and forgiveness in the Christian imagination helpful and important? Does its centrality illumine what the Christian life is about or cloud it?

What Is Sin?

The word "sin" has several nuances of meaning. When I have asked Christian groups what they think of when they hear the word "sin," their most common association is "disobedience." For most of them, the first thing that comes to mind is that sin is "disobeying God's laws," "breaking the rules," "being bad," even though it may also mean more than that. This isn't surprising, of course. We learn about keeping rules early in life. And rules matter. We couldn't live together without them.

Among these rules, if we grew up Christian, are "God's laws," including, for example, the Ten Commandments. Sin is our failure to keep God's laws. The problem in the Garden of Eden was disobedience; Eve and Adam disobeyed the commandment God gave them. God's laws are often extended to thoughts, so that anger and sexual desire are just as much sins as killing and adultery. This is "sins" in the plural, understood as specific acts (internal or external) of wrongdoing.

In the history of Christian thought, sin has also been thought of in more "root ways"—not so much in the plural as specific behaviors, but as a "state" or "condition" that produces the more specific behaviors that we commonly call sins. This is "sin" in the singular. Two theologians from the mid-twentieth century, Reinhold Niebuhr and Paul Tillich, illustrate insightful ways of seeing the "root sin." Both go far back into the Christian tradition.

For Reinhold Niebuhr, heir to a school of thought reaching back at least to Augustine, the "root sin" is "pride," *hubris*, to use the Greek term. *Hubris* is self-centeredness. It names the primal self-concern that flows inevitably out of our nature as finite creatures who are also aware of our finitude and vulnerability. The result is we become anxious, very early in life, and in this state of primal anxiety become self-centered.[5]

The more specific behaviors that we typically label as sins flow out of this primal self-centeredness.

For Paul Tillich, the root meaning of "sin" is separation, to be put asunder. Tillich's term for this state is "estrangement," very deliberately chosen to suggest being *separated from that to which we belong.* Our lives are estranged from God. We live in exile, east of Eden. And our sense of separation leads to centering in the self or the world (or both) rather than in God and the more specific behaviors we commonly call sins.[6] Tillich emphasizes the importance of this "root sin" by suggesting that "sin" be used in the singular only, never in the plural.

Sometimes the root sin is named as "unfaithfulness" to God. This is sin as *not* "loving the Lord your God with all your heart, life force, strength, and mind," but devoting this love to somebody or something else. Thus the primal sin is "idolatry" and "adultery" in the sense used in Chapter 2: centering in something other than God. Sometimes the root sin is seen as lack of trust in God, as "un-faith."[7]

All of these formulations are right and wise, it seems to me. Each "catches" a comprehensive dynamic at work in who we are. The problem is disobedience. The problem is estrangement. The problem is pride. The problem is infidelity. The problem is lack of trust. And they complement each other very nicely. The history of Christian thought about sin is filled with wisdom.

Is "Sin" the Best Term for Our Problem?

But now to return to the question: Is "sin" the best comprehensive term for naming our problem? Or would we understand our problem (and its solution) better if we used multiple images to speak about it?

To avoid a possible misunderstanding, I emphasize that the issue isn't whether there is something seriously wrong with us. If to say, "We're all sinners, we're all sinful," is our way of saying, "Something is not right, something is radically wrong, we are lost," I agree. The question, to risk being repetitive, is whether sin is the most helpful way of naming what is wrong.

I raise the question because the Bible has many rich images for naming our problem, one of which is sin. It is a major image. In the

Hebrew Bible, the three most common words translated "sin" appear almost a thousand times.[8] But there are other images for the human condition.

To list some but not all of them: we are blind, in exile, in bondage; we have closed hearts; we hunger and thirst; we are lost. Each of these images for our problem has a correlative image; that is, each implies a remedy, a solution. If we are blind, we need to see; if we are in exile, we need to return; if we are in bondage, we need liberation; if we have closed hearts, we need to have our hearts opened; if we hunger and thirst, we need food and drink; if we are lost, we need a way, we need to be found.

So also "sin" has a correlative image in the Bible and in the Christian imagination—"forgiveness." Thus, when sin is named as the issue, the logic of the image suggests that the solution is forgiveness. When sin becomes the one-size-fits-all designator of the human condition, then forgiveness becomes the one-size-fits-all remedy. And this is the problem. If the issue is blindness, what we need is not forgiveness, but sight. If the issue is bondage, what we need is not forgiveness, but liberation, and so forth.

To illustrate with a story: in a church service a couple of years ago, I was struck again by the way the language of sin and forgiveness dominates Christian thinking. I had just preached a sermon on the "closed heart" and our need for an "open heart." In the pastoral prayer following the sermon, one of the clergy prayed, "We ask you, O Lord, to forgive us our closed hearts." I thought, "Well, okay, but it misses the point. If we have closed hearts, we don't need forgiveness as much as we need to have our hearts opened."

Of course, one can make a case that sin is often involved in the other images for the human condition in the Bible. Our blindness can be the result of our own doing; it can become willful, a refusal to see. Our estrangement can become hardened by how we live; we often indulge our self-centeredness. But many of these are not simply (or not at all) the result of our deeds. Estrangement, the birth of the separated self, is the natural result of growing up; it cannot be avoided. For the same reason, we develop closed hearts, a shell around the self. There is a sense in which we are blinded by the imprinting of culture on our psyches and our perception. In a sense, we fall into bondage through no fault of our own. It's the inevitable result of growing up.

The story of Israel's bondage in Egypt is particularly instructive here. There is no suggestion in the story that the Hebrews' enslavement was their own fault. What they needed in Egypt was not forgiveness, but liberation. I have sometimes remarked that if Moses had gone into Egypt and said to the Hebrew slaves, "My children, your sins are forgiven," they would have said, "Well, that's nice, but you see, our problem is bondage." Of course, we can deepen our bondage by our actions or inactions. But in an important sense, we could not avoid bondage itself, or exile, or blindness, or developing closed hearts.

The message of sin and forgiveness doesn't address these issues very well. To the extent that we are responsible for these conditions, the message of forgiveness does mean that we are accepted by God even though our hearts are closed, even though we're in bondage, even though we're self-centered, and so forth. This message is true and important.

But forgiveness doesn't address the problems themselves. We may pray, "Forgive us our blindness," but if we're blind, we need to see—forgiveness doesn't help us to see. So also, if our problem is a closed heart, bondage, or exile, we need more than forgiveness.

Thus the question once again: Should we use "sin" as the blanket designator, the common denominator, the root diagnosis of what ails us? Or should we use it as one designator among the many biblical images for what ails us? For very practical reasons, I favor letting go of sin as the umbrella description for the human problem. It would remain as one way of speaking about what is wrong.

I am persuaded that our understanding of the heart of the Christian vision of life is enriched by using multiple biblical images for the human problem and its remedy. The problem is not simply that we have been bad and have rebelled against God (though that may be true), but that we are blind, estranged, lost, in exile, self-centered, wounded, sick, paralyzed, in bondage, grasping, and so forth. Forgiveness doesn't speak to these issues. But the central images of the Christian life as a "way" do: it is a way of return from exile, of reconnection; it is way of liberation from bondage; a way in which our sight is restored; a way of having our hearts opened by spending time in thin places; a way that leads from being lost to finding and being found.

Concretely, taking these multiple biblical images seriously would affect the words we use in worship. Sin and forgiveness would become only one way that we talk about our problem. The nearly universal liturgical element of "confession of sins and absolution" might be replaced or complemented by a "declaration of what ails us and God's promise to us."[9] One Sunday the declaration might emphasize sin, another Sunday bondage, another Sunday estrangement, another Sunday blindness, and so forth. Or many of the images could be combined into a single declaration. So also eucharistic liturgies could be modified so that the sacrificial language of sin and forgiveness is not the primary or exclusive emphasis.

There are at least two more reasons for using sin as one image among several rather than as the comprehensive image for our problem. The first is that "sin" sometimes (and perhaps often) does not fit our experience very well. I have already mentioned that "sin" would not have been a good description of the Hebrew slaves' predicament in Egypt. So also for us.

For many, the central existential issue is not a sense of sin. Yet, though the language of sin may not speak very powerfully to them, the language of blindness, exile, alienation, a closed heart, or captivity to culture may speak with great power. Also for some, the issue is not their own sin, but their victimization by others. For example, what does the message of sin and forgiveness mean to victims of domestic abuse? Though at some point they may need to forgive their abusers in order to get on with their own lives, an emphasis upon sin may lead them to focus on what they have done to cause their abuse. For them, the message they need to hear is not that they have sinned and need forgiveness, but that it is not God's will that they live under an abusive and oppressive Pharaoh. God wills their liberation and safety.

The other reason is that sin in popular Christianity is often understood individualistically, obscuring the reality of "social sin."[10] An emphasis upon sin most often leads to introspection about what I have done wrong. Of course, such introspection can be helpful, but it clouds the fact that much of human suffering and misery is not because of our individual sins, but because of collective sin. For example, when it is emphasized that Jesus "died for our sins" (and thus for your sins and my sins), our sins are seen as responsible for Jesus' death.

But it wasn't individual sins that caused Jesus' death. He wasn't killed because of the impure thoughts of adolescents or our everyday deceptions or our selfishness. The point is not that these don't matter. The point, rather, is that these were not what caused Jesus' death. Rather, Jesus was killed because of what might be called "social sin," namely, the domination system of his day. The common individualistic understanding of sin typically domesticates the political passion of the Bible and Jesus.

The purpose of these suggestions is not a weakening of the notion of sin, but an enriching of our understanding of the condition from which we need deliverance. There is great value in using the Bible's rich multiplicity of images. Fixating primarily on sin impoverishes our understanding.

Salvation

Like the word "sin," "salvation" is loaded and multilayered. And like the word "sin," its most common association hides rather than illuminates the rich meanings of the term in the Bible and the Christian tradition. Salvation is most often associated with "heaven" or "going to heaven." The question "Are you saved?" most often means "Are you confident that you'll go to heaven when you die?" Salvation is about the next world.

Salvation as Heaven?

About a year ago on a lecture trip, I found myself saying in response to a question, "If I were to make a list of Christianity's ten worst contributions to religion, on that list would be popular Christianity's emphasis on the afterlife." Since then, I have received a number of e-mails and letters asking me, "What are the other nine?" Well, I don't have a list, but I can provide three reasons why I made the remark.

The first reason I already mentioned in Chapter 1. Whenever the afterlife is emphasized, the almost invariable result is that it turns Christianity into a religion of requirements. If there is a heaven, it doesn't seem right that everybody gets to go there regardless, so there must be something that separates those who do get to go from those who don't, namely, something that we believe or do. The second reason is that such an emphasis creates a distinction between an in-group and an out-group: there are those who are saved and those who aren't. The third reason is that emphasizing the afterlife focuses our attention on the next world rather than on transformation in this world.

My critique of what happens when the afterlife is emphasized involves no denial of an afterlife. My point, rather, is to highlight what happens when heaven is made central and when salvation is virtually identified with going to heaven.

Salvation in This Life

The biblical understandings of salvation are focused on this world, not the next. Though salvation is central to the Bible, heaven as life after death is not. For a long time now, mainstream biblical and theological scholarship has recognized that belief in an afterlife did not emerge until nearly the end of the writing of the Hebrew Bible. The first unambiguous reference occurs in the last chapter of Daniel, seen by most scholars as the latest document of the Hebrew Bible, written around 165 BCE. Though the authors of the Psalms and other books often pray for deliverance from death, there is no clear affirmation of an afterlife until Daniel.[11]

This means that for all the previous centuries of the biblical period, people in ancient Israel didn't believe in life after death. To state the obvious, "going to heaven" could not have been their motive for taking God seriously. To add another obvious remark: though they often talked and wrote about salvation, salvation couldn't have meant "going to heaven."

By the time of Jesus' public activity, two centuries after Daniel, a majority of the Jewish people did believe in an afterlife. A major reason for growth in the belief was the continuing experience of oppression and persecution. Indeed, belief in an afterlife within Judaism originated in the context of martyrdom, beginning in the time of Daniel. Jewish martyrs (and there were many) were being killed by foreign powers precisely because of their deep loyalty to God and the Torah. If it is precisely those who refuse to compromise their loyalty to God who are being killed, how can one reconcile that with God's justice? And so the notion of an afterlife arises as compensation for those killed for their loyalty to God. The possibility was soon extended beyond martyrs to others.

Jesus himself seems to have believed in an afterlife, but he doesn't talk about it very much. Most often in the gospels, the topic is brought up by somebody else. And when Jesus does talk about it, it's not clear whether we should understand him as providing "information" about the afterlife, or whether we should hear him primarily as subverting overly confident notions of what it will be like.[12] In any case, it's clear that his message was not really about how to get to heaven. It was about a way of transformation in this world and the Kingdom of God on earth. If he also believed in heaven, it would not be remarkable. But Jesus wasn't very much concerned with life beyond death, either his own or that of others.

The writers of the New Testament (and thus the early Christian movement for whom they wrote) believed in an afterlife. Paul spoke of being with Christ forever.

> Listen, I will tell you a mystery! We will not all die, but we will all be changed, in the twinkling of an eye, at the last trumpet. For the trumpet will sound, and the dead will be raised imperishable, and we will be changed. . . . Then the saying that is written will be fulfilled: "Death has been swallowed up in victory."[13]

For to me, living is Christ and dying is gain. If I am to live in the flesh, that means fruitful labor for me; and I do not know which I prefer. I am hard pressed between the two; my desire is to depart and be with Christ, for that is far better.[14]

And so we will be with the Lord forever.[15]

In the gospel of John, "eternal life" is a major theme. And the Christian Bible concludes with a magnificent vision of the "new Jerusalem" in the last chapters of Revelation. In that city of light, every tear will be wiped away and death shall be no more.

But even though the affirmation of an afterlife is found in the New Testament, it does not seem to have been the primary message of early Christianity. Paul affirms an afterlife, yet his letters suggest that his primary emphasis was new life "in Christ" in this life, a metaphor that has both personal and social dimensions. It involves dying and rising with Christ and becoming part of the "body of Christ," a new communal reality. The joys he celebrates are known in this life: freedom, peace, love, joy itself. When we read Paul attentively in his first-century context, he doesn't sound like a preacher proclaiming, "Here's what you must do to get to heaven." He speaks primarily of the new life in the now.

So also in John's gospel. Though it affirms life after death, his phrase "eternal life" (or "everlasting life") does not mean primarily that.[16] The English phrase translates a Greek phrase that in turn expresses a Jewish notion: "the life of the age to come." "Eternal life" means "the life of the age to come." Thus, for example, John 3:16 could be translated:

> For God so loved the world that God gave God's only begotten Son; whoever believes in him shall not perish, but shall have *the life of the age to come*.

An important further connection: in John, "eternal life" is often spoken of in the present tense. "The life of the age to come" *has come*. It is here. Eternal life does not refer to unending time beyond death, but to something that can be known now. "This *is* eternal life," John affirms, and then adds, "to know God."[17] To know God in the present is to experience the life of the age to come. It is a present reality for John, even as it also involves a future destiny. We can know it now, experience it now. The point is that even John's language about "eternal life" has a strong present dimension.

Thus salvation in the Bible is primarily a this-worldly phenomenon. It happens here. But what is it? The root of the English word is helpful. It comes from a Latin word that means "wholeness" or "healing" (the same root from which we get the word "salve," a healing agent). In its broadest sense, salvation thus means becoming whole and being healed. The language of "wholeness" suggests movement beyond fragmentation, and the language of "healing" suggests being healed of the wounds of existence.

The meanings of salvation are also suggested by the correlative images of the human condition and the remedy. Salvation is:

Light in our darkness
Sight to the blind
Enlightenment
Liberation for captives
Return from exile
The healing of our infirmities
Food and drink
Resurrection from the land of the dead
Being born again
Knowing God
Becoming "in Christ"
Being made right with God ("justified")

In the Bible, salvation is all of the above.

Stories of Salvation

The biblical meanings of salvation are also suggested by what I have elsewhere called the "macro-stories" of scripture.[18] These stories shape the Hebrew Bible as a whole and, because of the centrality of the Hebrew Bible for early Christianity, the New Testament as well.

The first of these is the story of the exodus from Egypt. It images the human problem as bondage and slavery. Though there was a historical Pharaoh, Pharaoh is also a metaphor for what holds us in bondage, internally and externally. Our problem is that we live in Egypt, the land of bondage. Life in Egypt is marked by hard labor. It is a life of bitter herbs and meager rations; you get enough to live on, but that's all. It's a life of powerlessness and victimization.

The solution is, of course, liberation, exodus, a "way out," as the Greek roots of the word suggest. But liberation is not the end of the story. Liberation brings us into the wilderness. The wilderness is not only a place of freedom beyond the domestication of culture, but also a place of insecurity where we are tempted to erect one golden calf after another. The exodus story involves a long journey through the wilderness (forty years), climaxing in entry into the promised land, the place of God's presence. The story of salvation begins in bondage and ends in the land of God's promise, a land flowing with milk and honey.

The second is the story of exile in Babylon, which images the human problem as exile. Anticipated in the Garden of Eden story, which ends with us living our lives "east of Eden," it is based on the Jewish experience of exile in Babylon in the sixth century BCE. Life in exile, in Babylon, is living under an alien empire. A story of separation from one's homeland and longing for home, it is marked by yearning, grief, loneliness, anger, and despair. Psychologically and spiritually, exile is a condition of alienation, a sense of being cut off from a center of meaning and energy. The solution is a journey of return, a journey that God both invites and energizes. The journey, "the way," once again leads through the wilderness, and in the wilderness we are nourished by God. The story of salvation is a story of reconnection with the one in whom we live and move and have our being, the one who has always been here even though we have been estranged.

The third is what I call the temple story.[19] It images the human problem as sin and impurity. Unlike the first two stories, which are based on the historical memory of slavery in Egypt and exile in Babylon, this story is centered in an institution, namely, the temple in Jerusalem as the place of sacrifice for sins and impurities. Though sin and impurity were not the same thing, both prevented entrance into the presence of the holy God, and both were dealt with through temple sacrifice. Psychologically and spiritually, this story addresses our sense of being stained and soiled, of being sinful and unworthy. The story of salvation is thus a story of being cleansed, forgiven, accepted.

It is this third story that has dominated popular Christianity through the centuries and the earlier paradigm in our day. And though it continues to speak powerfully to some people, others are more powerfully addressed by the stories of bondage and exodus, exile and return.

Strikingly but not surprisingly, the New Testament understandings of Jesus correlate with the macro-stories of the Hebrew Bible. The story of Jesus thus becomes a story of salvation:

- Jesus as liberator has its metaphorical home in the exodus story: he is the one who has come to set the captives free. The gospel is about liberation. Salvation is liberation.

- Jesus as "the Way" has its metaphorical home in the exile story: in his life, death, and resurrection, he embodies the way of return. The gospel is about homecoming. Salvation is homecoming.

- Jesus as the sacrifice has its metaphorical home in the temple story: his death as "the once for all" sacrifice for sin replaces the temple and temple sacrifice. The gospel is about forgiveness and acceptance. Salvation is about forgiveness and acceptance.

The meanings of salvation are also suggested by more specific images of Jesus. Each speaks of our problem and the remedy. Salvation as:

Light in our darkness: Jesus is the light of the world.
The satisfaction of our hunger: Jesus is the bread of life.
The quenching of our thirst: Jesus is living water.

Finding the way: Jesus is the way, the door.

Connection to the source of life: Jesus is the vine.

Being born again: Jesus is the path of dying and rising.

New life out of death: Jesus is the resurrection and the life.

Healing: Jesus is the one who makes us whole.

Entry into God's presence: Jesus is the new temple, even as he is also the sacrifice.

All of these, the stories and the images, are metaphors of salvation. Put most simply, salvation means to be saved from our predicament. But these images put it more richly, suggesting the multiple nuances of this multilayered affirmation of the transformation of our lives in this world.

Salvation as Both Social and Personal

Salvation is personal, but this hardly needs emphasis. We are accustomed to hearing it in personal terms. For example, as you read the previous section, my hunch is that most of you thought of ways that these images connect to your personal experience of bondage, blindness, alienation, unworthiness, and so forth. That's good, and I make these connections myself. They do apply to our personal lives in a powerful way.

What does need emphasis is that salvation in the Bible is also social. Ancient Israel's story is a story of the creation of a new people, a nation, a community. Salvation is about life together. Salvation is about peace and justice within community and beyond community. It is about *shalom*, a word connoting not simply peace as the absence of war, but peace as the wholeness of a community living together in peace and justice. Salvation is never only an individual affair in the Hebrew Bible.

The emphasis upon social salvation continues in the New Testament. In the teaching of Jesus, social salvation is expressed in the theopolitical metaphor at the heart of his activity, the Kingdom of God.[20] For Paul also, salvation is social (as well as personal). He was creating new communities "in Christ" whose life together embodied an alternative vision to that of empire. And these—the movement around Jesus, the communities of Paul, and all of the early Christian communities of which we know—were communities of bread as well as Spirit. Food and Spirit, bread and breath: the sharing of the necessities of life in a new community that transcended the conventional boundaries of this world, all in allegiance to an alternative Lord. The Bible is not about the saving of individuals for heaven, but about a new social and personal reality in the midst of this life.

Salvation and Response

Salvation comes from God, even as it involves our response. It is God who liberated the slaves from Egypt, God who created a way of return, God who provided a way of overcoming our sins and impurities, God who is the source of light, healing, and so forth.

Yet salvation always involves our response. If the slaves in Egypt had not responded to the message that God was liberating them, they would be there still. If the exiles in Babylon had not set foot on their journey of return, they would be there still. If blind Bartimaeus had not called out, "Son of David, have compassion on me," he would still be blind. Without our response, little or nothing will change in our lives or in the life of the world. Salvation is the work of God, and yet we must respond.

A few years ago in a lecture, Archbishop Desmond Tutu quoted St. Augustine: "God without us will not, as we without God cannot."[21] The statement applies to both the personal and the social dimensions of salvation. Without us, without our response, God will not do it; and we, without God, cannot do it. Without us, without our response, God will not transform us or rescue us, either as individuals or societies. We without God cannot bring about transformation. But God without our response will not bring about transformation.

Sin, Salvation, and Repentance

The trivialization of sin sees it individualistically as "breaking God's rules" and thus as deserving God's punishment. It is a much richer and more perceptive notion. The trivialization of salvation sees it as being about individuals "going to heaven" because they have believed or done what is necessary. It is a much richer, more life-affirming, and hopeful notion. In the richer sense of these words, the Christian life leads from sin to salvation—from living within our predicament to living in a transforming relationship with God.

In the Christian imagination, the word "repentance" belongs to the same vocabulary as "sin" and "salvation." We need to repent of our sins in order to be saved. Rightly understood, this is correct. But repentance too has been trivialized. In the minds of many Christians, its first association is introspective guilt. It means feeling really sorry for what you have done or left undone, feeling really bad about the horrible person that you are.

But the biblical meaning of "repent" is not primarily contrition, but resolve. In the Hebrew Bible, to repent means primarily to return to God. Its metaphorical home is the exile. To repent means to return from exile, to reconnect with God, to walk the way in the wilderness that leads from Babylon to God.

In the New Testament, repentance continues to have the meaning it has in the Hebrew Bible. The gospel of and about Jesus sees repentance as following the way of Jesus. Our earliest gospel, Mark, begins with language from the exile: "In the wilderness, prepare the way of the Lord." The story of Jesus then follows. The way is the way of Jesus, the path of dying and rising, and it is the way of return.

And repentance in the New Testament has an additional nuance of meaning. The Greek roots of the word combine to mean "go beyond the mind that you have." Go beyond the mind that you have been given and have acquired. Go beyond the mind shaped by culture to the mind that you have "in Christ."

Repentance is the path of salvation. It is the path of reconnection, the path of transformation, the path of being born again, the path of dying and rising, the path of response to the message of the Kingdom of God: "Jesus came to Galilee proclaiming . . . , 'The time is fulfilled; the Kingdom of God is at hand; repent.'"[22] The Kingdom is at hand: go beyond the mind that you have. Repentance, like sin and salvation, is both personal and social.

Salvation and the Afterlife

So what about an afterlife? It is one of the ten most frequent questions I am asked by the largely Christian groups to whom I speak. The question seems to arise not out of a strong concern that it's central and that Christianity makes no sense without it, but from seeking to figure out where it fits into the Christian vision of life. To speak very personally, I don't have a clue about what happens after death. Having said that, I nevertheless say more.

I am intrigued by the research that has been done on near-death experiences. Of people who have been near death, about 40 percent report a common pattern: a sense of journeying through a tunnel, a burst of light, a sense of being in the presence of a loving reality, quite often accompanied by a sense of being out of one's body. The last item sometimes includes a sense of being able to view one's body from a vantage point beyond the body. A significant number of reports include details about what was going on that the person could not have witnessed from within his or her body. For me, this is the most impressive part of the experience. All of the other features could be accounted for as regression to our initial birth experience. But if our consciousness and perception can even momentarily be separate from our bodies, then the modern intrinsic linkage between brain and consciousness is called into question, and we have no idea what is possible beyond death.

Nevertheless, I have no idea what this might mean for life beyond death. I know quite a lot about the diverse ways that Christians have thought about or believed in this, as well as those of people of other religions. Some Christians have believed that we're all simply dead until the second coming of Jesus, the resurrection of all the dead, and judgment. This was the dominant belief for the first thousand years of Christianity. But around the year 1000, belief began to shift to judgment at the moment of death. Which is it? Moreover, the majority of Christians throughout history have believed in at least three possible postdeath states: heaven, hell, and purgatory. Only Protestants, a small percentage of the Christians who have ever lived, have rejected purgatory. Are they right? And though we associate reincarnation primarily with Asian religions, some Christians throughout history and to the present day believe in reincarnation. So, if there is life after death, is it reincarnation, or instant heaven or hell, or purgatory?

Beyond this, does heaven involve the survival of personal self-awareness? If so, is that desirable or undesirable? The best times in my life have been times during which I have been so wholly caught up in the experience that self-awareness—awareness of being a particular separated self—has momentarily disappeared. Would a heaven in which I know I'm "me" be a superior or inferior state of affairs?

Does heaven involve reunions with family? Funeral sermons sometimes suggest so. If so, is this good news or bad news? For those who have had a family filled with love and affection, it may be good news. But for those for whom family has been a great source of misery, it is difficult to hear this as good news. Eternity with these folks? And if it should be suggested, "Well, they'll all be perfected," will they then be the same people?

I see no way of deciding among these different ways of imagining what lies beyond death. Nor can one resolve this by believing one way or the other. Of course, one may believe what one wishes, but believing that such and such is the case has nothing to do with whether it really is that way.

Thus I see no persuasive reason for thinking that one way of seeing the afterlife is the way it's really going to be. Who could know? How can we know anything about it? The different visions cancel each other out, even as they also join in a symphony affirming a "moreness."

And the sense of a "More" is the ground of our hope, and even more of our trust. We live in God. We move in God. We have our being in God. And when we die, we do not die into nothingness; we die into God.

Salvation is "the dream of God."[23] It is a dream for the earth. And it is a dream for us. It is about being born again and about the Kingdom of God. Salvation is about the transformation of life, individually and together, here and now. And the Bible speaks of these two transformations as an experience now, and as a hope for history, and as a hope that leads beyond history.

It does so in the language of metaphor and poetry, which is the only language we have for speaking of what lies at the end of history and beyond history.

Jesus said, "I tell you, many will come from east and west and will eat with Abraham and Isaac and Jacob in the Kingdom of God."[24] This is a kingdom beyond history that transcends the generations and time itself.

In Revelation, the magnificent concluding chapters speak of the New Jerusalem, the holy city, descending from the sky in a world that has become new. In this city that stands in contrast to Rome and the empires of this world, every tear will be wiped away, death will be no more, and mourning and crying and pain will be no more. It will be a city of light.[25]

So also Paul speaks of this hope in poetic language that cannot be unified into a system, even as it names God's dream and our dream. He affirms the salvation of the whole of creation: "We know that the whole creation has been groaning in labor pains until now; and not only the creation, but we ourselves, who have the firstfruits of the Spirit, groan inwardly while we wait for adoption, the redemption of our bodies. For in hope we are saved."[26]

For Paul, our hope, and God's promise, is that "God may be all in all."

> Then comes the end, when Christ hands over the kingdom to God the Father, after Christ has destroyed every ruler and every authority and power. For Christ must reign until he has put all his enemies under his feet. The last enemy to be destroyed is death. . . . So that God may be all in all.[27]

What does this mean? We do not know; at best, we have but a glimpse. To cite Paul's rhapsodic language one more time: "For *now* we see in a mirror dimly, but *then* we will see face to face. *Now* I know only in part; *then,* I will know fully, even as I have been fully known."[28]

We are known by God already. In that lies our hope, for God's knowing is forever.

Salvation is about life with God, life in the presence of God, now and forever.

---

1. I have treated some of the themes of this chapter elsewhere, especially in the last chapters of *Meeting Jesus Again for the First Time* (San Francisco: HarperSanFrancisco, 1994) and *The God We Never Knew* (San Francisco: HarperSanFrancisco, 1997). For my treatment of the Genesis stories of "the fall" in particular, see *Reading the Bible Again for the First Time* (San Francisco: HarperSanFrancisco, 2001), chap. 4.

2. I cannot recall where I read or heard this. I do recall that it did not seem mean-spirited.

3. *Whatever Became of Sin?* (New York: Hawthorne, 1973) is the title of a book by psychiatrist Karl Menninger. The question has been picked up by a number of Christian writers.

4. Frederick Buechner, "The Good Book as a Good Book," in *The Clown in the Belfry: Writings on Faith and Fiction* (San Francisco: HarperSanFrancisco, 1992), p. 44.

5. This understanding of human nature is central to Niebuhr's work and is most fully described in his two-volume *The Nature and Destiny of Man* (New York: Scribner, 1941, 1943). I can still vividly remember the excitement with which I read these two volumes as a twenty-three-year-old graduate student. I found them to be the most intellectually compelling analysis of human nature and history that I had yet encountered, and I recall thinking that anybody who read them would become convinced of the truth of the Christian perception of humankind.

6. Paul Tillich, *Systematic Theology*, vol. 2 (Chicago: University of Chicago Press, 1957), pp. 44–59. He then speaks of estrangement as "unbelief" (meaning "unfaithfulness"), "*hubris*" (pride), and "concupiscence," which he defines as "the unlimited desire to draw the whole of reality into one's self" (p. 52).

7. For a wonderfully readable and insightful "case study" of the spiritual and social dimensions of sin, including an integration of Tillich and Niebuhr, see Langdon Gilkey's account of his experience as a civilian prisoner in an internment camp in China during World War II, *Shantung Compound* (New York: Harper & Row, 1966). For a recent book on sin, see Ted Peters, *Sin: Radical Evil in Soul and Society* (Grand Rapids: Eerdmans, 1994).

8. For details, see "Sin, Sinners (OT)," by Robin C. Cover, in *The Anchor Bible Dictionary*, ed. David Noel Freedman (New York: Doubleday, 1992), 6:31–40. It is often pointed out that a common biblical word for sin means "missing the mark" (as an archer might miss a target). Though this is true, I have thus far been unable to see much profundity in this. What is the "mark" that we miss? In some Christian teaching, the "mark" seems to be perfection. Because none of us is perfect, we are in this sense all sinners. But are we really supposed to be perfect? Is that an attainable goal? Are we really supposed to apologize to God continually for not being perfect? Or is the Christian gospel that God accepts us in the midst of our imperfection and provides means for overcoming our blindness, exile, bondage, closed hearts, and so forth?

9. I am not suggesting these exact words as "liturgical headings." I would hope more elegant phrases could be found, but I am suggesting the notion that lies behind these words.

10. At a more theologically sophisticated level, sin is not simply understood individualistically. For example, Tillich and Niebuhr both have a strong sense of the social consequences of sin, or of "social sin."

11. The notion of resurrection appears in earlier documents, perhaps most memorably in Ezek. 37: the vision of "the valley of dry bones" being reassembled and clothed with flesh. But this is a metaphor for the nation of Israel (or Judea) being reconstituted beyond the experience of defeat, captivity, and exile in the Babylonian period (sixth century BCE). It is thus a corporate hope, not affirmation of a future existence for individuals who have died.

12. Three examples: Mark 12:18–27; Matt. 25:31–46; Matt. 8:11–12 = Luke 13:28–30.

13. 1 Cor. 15:51–52, 54.

14. Phil. 1:21–23.

15. 1 Thess. 4:17.

16. "Eternal life" is used by the Revised Standard Version, "everlasting life" by the King James Version.

17. John 17:3.

18. *Meeting Jesus Again*, chap. 6.

19. In *Meeting Jesus Again*, I called this the "priestly story." I mean the same thing.

20. See Chapter 7.

21. Desmond Tutu in *God at 2000*, ed. Marcus Borg and Ross Mackenzie (Harrisburg, PA: Morehouse, 2000), p. 131.

22. Mark 1:14–15.

23. I owe the phrase to the title of a fine book by Verna Dozier, *The Dream of God: A Call to Return* (Boston: Cowley, 1991).

24. Matt. 8:11, with Matthew's "heaven" (his synonym for "God") changed to "God."

25. The concluding vision is in Rev. 21:1–22:5. Echoed words are found in 21:1–2, 4, and 22:5.

26. Rom. 8:22–24.

27. 1 Cor. 15:24–26, 28.

28. 1 Cor. 13:12.

TEN

The Heart of the Matter
Practice

What does it mean to love God? In her important recent book *The Silent Cry,* with the provocative subtitle *Mysticism and Resistance,* Dorothee Soelle comments that we Christians have generally been pretty good at proclaiming God's love for us, but that we have been less good at emphasizing the importance of our love for God.[1]

What does it mean to love God? We all know that both the Hebrew Bible and Jesus commend and command us "to love the Lord your God with all your heart, and with all your life force, and with all your mind, and with all your strength."[2] Indeed, it is the "greatest commandment." But what does it mean to do this? In a word, it means "practice." Loving God means paying attention to God and to what God loves. The way we do this is through "practice."

As I have suggested throughout this book, Christianity is a "way," a path, a way of life. Practice is about the living of the Christian way. And "practice" really should be thought of as plural: practice is about practices, the means by which we live the Christian life.

Modern Western Christianity, especially Protestantism, has not made practice central. This is very different from other religions. Judaism, especially orthodox Judaism, is primarily about practice, about following the "way of Torah." At the center of being Buddhist is the "eightfold path," all of it practice. So also for Muslims: of the five "pillars" of Islam, four are about practice, one of which is praying five times a day. I have been told that the five prayers together take about forty minutes, and I have often wondered how we as Christians would be different if we spent forty minutes a day in prayer.

A major reason that Protestantism has paid little attention to traditional Christian practices goes back to the Reformation, which sharply contrasted "faith" and "works." We are saved by "faith," not "works." To many Protestants, practices sound like "works." But the point of practice is not to earn one's salvation by accumulating merit by "works." Rather, practice is about paying attention to God.

A second reason is that within much of modern Western Christianity, faith came to be understood as "belief" and was thus not about "doing." But if we take seriously that faith is not primarily about belief, but about "beloving God," then faith and practice are not opposites. Rather, practice is how we "belove" God.[3]

There is yet another reason for the lack of attention to spiritual practices in particular. The notion that God is a reality who can be known (and not simply believed in) has become quite foreign in the modern world and in much of modern theology. Often there is even uncertainty about the reality of God. In skeptical form, it leads to a vision of Christianity as primarily "ethics." In most generic form, the Christian way of life becomes "being good," "being nice," "loving people." In strong form, it can become a passion for justice. But whether in generic or strong form, living the Christian life is seen basically as being about our behavior in the world. But Christian practice historically is about our relationship to both God and neighbor, about both Spirit and behavior, about both God and the world.

An encouraging sign of renewal in the church in North America is the recovery of practice as central to the Christian life. Such recovery goes hand in hand with the relational and transformational vision of the Christian life at the heart of the emerging paradigm. If the Christian life is about relationship and transformation, practice will be central.

By practice, I mean all the things that Christians do together and individually as a way of paying attention to God. They include being part of a Christian community, a church, and taking part in its life together as community. They include worship, Christian formation, collective deeds of hospitality and compassion, and being nourished by Christian community. They include devotional disciplines, especially prayer and spending time with the Bible. And they include loving what God loves through the practice of compassion and justice in the world.

The Purposes of Practice

To list the purposes of practice in the Christian life before I detail them, practice is about:

- Paying attention to God

- The formation of Christian identity and character

- Nourishment

- Compassion and justice

- Living "the way"

Practice is paying attention to God. Most concisely and broadly, this is its central purpose. As mentioned in an earlier chapter, the relational vision of life with God is analogous in an important way to a human relationship: it grows and deepens to the extent that we pay attention to it. It involves attending to the relationship, spending time in it, being intentional and thoughtful about it, valuing it, and, ideally, enjoying it.

Paying attention to our relationship with God matters because we as selves are ultimately relational. It is not that we first become selves and then have relationships. Rather, we are constituted by our relationships; they shape and form us. So also paying attention to our relationship with God will shape us.

Practice is about the formation of Christian identity. For newcomers to the church, the process is the initial formation of Christian identity. For long-term Christians it involves the deepening (and sometimes reformation) of Christian identity. Identity is simply (and not so simply) our sense of who we are. To use the title of a searching poem written by Dietrich Bonhoeffer in a Nazi prison, "Who Am I?" Who are we?

All of us already have an identity, though it may be difficult to name it concisely. We acquire a sense of who we are from our socialization and our ongoing life, from the relationships and forces that shaped and continue to shape us. These include relationships with family and friends, the effects of school and work and perhaps church, and also the impact of the wider culture in which we live. Culture has a powerful effect on us. Our culture bombards us with messages that shape our sense of who we are and what is worth valuing. In the United States, the central values of our culture are the "three A's": attractiveness, achievement, and affluence. For many of us, our sense of who we are depends upon how well we measure up to these identity-conferring values that operate in our psyches, as well as to the other messages we have received about who we are and what we should be.

Thus, no matter how good our parenting was, we grow up wounded. Our socialization and life in culture confer conflicting and conflicted identities. Not only are we not whole, but many of us have a low, sometimes desperately low, sense of self-worth. As a result, all of us need the formation of a new identity.

The formation of Christian identity will thus also always involve a transformation of identity—from an identity given by the "world" to an identity in God, in Christ. The Christian life is about "conversion." Conversion is not primarily about converting to Christianity from another religion (or no religion at all). Rather, it is a continuing process that goes on throughout the course of the Christian life.[4]

Christian identity formation involves the deepest level of the self, the heart. It addresses what is perhaps our deepest psychological wound: our sense of not being "enough." The sense of not having measured up is sometimes the result of a requirements-and-rewards version of the Christian message, one that emphasizes that "we are all sinners" much more than it emphasizes the love of God. But it's not just people who have grown up with a finger-shaking God who feel less than what they should be. Even secular people often have a strong sense of not being "enough." It is the result of the internalization of standards of identity and worth flowing from the world in which we live.

Addressing this deep sense of identity, this lack of self-worth, is basic to Christian identity formation. Indeed, it is the most basic message of the gospel. To express it in simple familiar words:

You are created by God.
You are a child of God.
You are beloved by God.
You are accepted by God.

The Christian message is that these statements are unconditionally the case. Of course, if we don't see this, if we don't internalize this, nothing of significance will change in our lives. But when deeply internalized, this basic message not only frees us from preoccupation with the whole project of measuring up, but is also profoundly egalitarian. What is true about us is also true about everybody else.

Christian identity formation also involves something more specific. Its purpose is not only to confer an identity shaped by God's acceptance of us, but to internalize an identity increasingly shaped by the Christian tradition. To use language I will also use in the next chapter, being Christian means living within Christianity as a "cultural-linguistic tradition." It is a little bit like being part of a national group with its language and culture and ethos. To be French means to live within a French cultural-linguistic world, a French ethos.

So also to be Christian means to live within a Christian cultural-linguistic world, a Christian ethos, and to be increasingly shaped by it.

In this, the Bible plays a special role. Its stories and vision and dream are to shape our sense of who God is, who we are, and what life is about. More fully, Christian identity formation means living within the Christian tradition as a whole as a metaphor and sacrament of the sacred.

Practice is about the formation of Christian character. Character—the kind of person we have been shaped to be—is the foundation of ethics. How we behave is a function of the kind of person we have become and are becoming. Character and identity are closely connected: the internalization of a deeper Christian identity shapes character.

The shaping of character also happens through deeds of compassion. Such deeds are not only good in their own right, but also contribute to character formation. We become what we do. The formation of character through practice will also involve internalizing the classic Christian virtues: prudence, justice, temperance, fortitude, faith, hope, and love. Character and virtue go together.[5]

The process of Christian identity and character formation leads from a limited identity to a larger identity, from a limited self to a larger self. The self with which we begin is the result of what has been given and done to us, the wounded self, the false self, the small self of culture. Our character is shaped by entering into a larger identity and larger self through life "in Christ." Practice is the way this happens. The Spirit of God works through practice.

The result will be a growing "counteridentity" to the one formed by culture. Or, if "counteridentity" seems like too aggressive a term, an "alternative identity." The character and values given to us by our culture are very different from Christian character and values. Christian formation leads to an identity in God as disclosed in the Bible and Jesus, and not in culture. Even more compactly, one's identity will increasingly be "in Christ" and not in the self or the world. Christian formation thus intrinsically involves transformation of character.

Practice is about nourishment. Practice is not simply something we do. Rather, it nourishes us. This happens in collective Christian practices such as worship as well as individual devotional practices. To speak for myself even as I reflect the experience of many, Christian worship nourishes me. Daily prayer nourishes me. Daily devotional time with the Bible nourishes me. Retreats and pilgrimages nourish me. Paying attention to my dreams and journaling nourish me. We are fed by practice. And we hunger and thirst, to use one of the Bible's central images of the human condition. Even as practice is about paying attention to God, it also nourishes and nurtures us.

Practice can become a "thin place"—sometimes so thin that we never forget the experience. At other times, we may not be aware of anything "thin," but practice nevertheless has its effect. The Spirit works in us even when we are not aware of it. Practice is a sacrament of the sacred.

Practice is about compassion and justice. Compassion and justice are the primary ethical fruits of the Christian life. They are central to paying attention to God, which is not only about loving God, but about loving that which God loves and becoming passionate about that which God is passionate about. Practice is about becoming more compassionate and about doing justice. About this, I will say more later in this chapter.

In short, *practice is about living "the way."* The aim and purpose of practice is the twofold transformation at the center of the Christian life: being born again, opening the heart, dying to an old identity and being born into a new identity; and becoming passionate about God's passion, the life of compassion and justice in the world. Practice is about paying attention to God and living the Christian path.

Practices: Formation and Nourishment

We move from the singular, "practice," to the plural, "practices," as the more specific means that serve these purposes.

Being part of a church: In my judgment, the single most important practice is to be part of a congregation that nourishes you even as it stretches you. Some of you already are involved in such a church. But if you are not involved in any church or are part of one that leaves you hungry and unsatisfied, find one that nurtures and deepens your Christian journey. Find one that makes your heart glad, so that you can wake on Sunday morning filled with the anticipation of the psalmist: "I was glad when they said to me, 'Let us go to the house of the Lord.'"[6] Choosing a church is not primarily about feeling good, of course, but church is meant to nourish us, not to make us angry or leave us bored. If your church gives you a headache, it may be time to change.

The kind of Christian community that will nurture us depends upon our background and psychological temperament. Some Christians are nourished by sacramental and liturgical worship, some by more informal or contemporary worship, some by charismatic worship, some by worship with a lot of silence. So also our intellectual and devotional needs vary. Some Christians very much need a church that addresses the head as well as the heart, and vice versa.

There are many reasons why being part of a church matters. Participation in worship is vital for Christian formation. In worship, we internalize the tradition through liturgy, hymns, scripture readings, and preaching. We join in praise of God. Praise is *doxology*, and it not only draws us out of ourselves, but is also profoundly subversive: doxology affirms that God alone is the source of all blessing, that God is Lord and the lords of this world are not. In worship, we enter a potential thin place. In worship, we are nourished.

Being part of a Christian community provides a setting for Christian education. This matters for both children and adults. Regarding children, I am often asked, "How do we educate our children in the church?" I have no expertise or experience in this area, but I offer a few general remarks. First, it is important that children not be taught in such a way that they will later need to unlearn many things. We should not put unnecessary obstacles in their path. Second, there are an increasing number of excellent Sunday school curricula that reflect the emerging paradigm. Third, equally as important as a good curriculum is training for the teachers who will teach it. If Sunday school teachers are still operating out of the earlier paradigm, then no matter how good the curriculum, children will still be taught, in harder or softer forms, a literal-factual under-standing of Christianity.

Finally, we should not assume that children are basically literal-ists. Younger children have great appreciation for books with talking animals, talking toys, and so forth; and older children enjoy fantasy. They don't simply dismiss such stories as "silly." When children ask about a biblical story, "Is that a true story?" they may be asking, "Did it happen?" But they are likely to be satisfied with an answer like, "Well, I don't know if it happened or not, but I know it's a true and important story."

Education also matters for adults, particularly in our time of change and transition. For many in the church, education will involve reeducation from a way of seeing Christianity learned as children to a way of seeing Christianity that makes persuasive sense to us as adults at the beginning of the twenty-first century. This is a pressing need in our time. As I mentioned in an earlier chapter, it is difficult to give one's heart to something that one's head rejects.

Adult education commonly includes classes at church, whether on Sunday mornings or weekday evenings. Though it is fine that churches offer courses on topics like parenting and relationships, the heart of Christian education should be strongly relevant to the formation of Christian identity and character: the Bible, theology, Christian lives, Christian spirituality, Christian caring for the world, Christianity and religious pluralism, and so forth.

Adult education can also take place in small groups meeting in homes or at the church, often focused on reading and discussing books together. Reading groups do not need "expert" or church-staff leader-ship. If the books are accessible to an ordinary adult reader with no theo-logical training, all that is needed is a commitment on the part of the group and good facilitation of group discussion. Small groups can also be more than educational. Bible study groups and faith-sharing groups combine formation with nourishment and intimacy. Indeed, the small-group movement is increasingly part of church life in America.

Being part of a church also creates opportunities for the collective practice of compassion and justice. These include caring for people within the church, outreach programs for people beyond the doors of the church, and advocacy of justice.

My purpose here is not to provide a complete account of the purpose of church. Rather, it is to illustrate why being part of a church is important for Christian formation and life. It is the foundational practice. We need to be part of a community of memory that affirms a vision of life very different from modern culture. A church that is faithful to God is a community of resocialization.

Prayer: Moving to more individual Christian practices, prayer is central. Like other practices, prayer is primarily about paying attention to God. There are three major types of Christian prayer. The first is *verbal prayer,* in which we address God with words, whether out loud or silently. Traditionally, there are five categories of verbal prayer: adoration or praise, thanksgiving, confession, intercession, and petition.

Two of these kinds of verbal prayer, petition and intercession, create problems for many modern Christians. These are prayers in which we ask for something for ourselves or others or the world. Ironically, these are also probably the most common forms of prayer. They are a "wish list" addressed to God, and to some Christians it seems silly. After all, they say, God already knows our needs and wishes, so why do we need to tell God about them? Even larger in their minds is the problematic notion of God that such prayer often presupposes; namely, it suggests an almost magical notion of God—that God is an interventionist who sometimes answers prayers.

Not only is the interventionist notion difficult in itself, but the reality of unanswered prayers is a huge problem. Think of all the people who prayed for deliverance from the Holocaust, all the people who prayed for peace and safety in the midst of war, all the people who prayed for healing—and whose prayers were not answered. And thus many modern mainline Christians have problems with this kind of prayer.

I sympathize with the problem, and, as I said in Chapter 4, I do not and cannot believe that God is an interventionist. And yet I do petitionary and intercessory prayer all the time, by which I mean "daily." I do it for myself, for family and friends, for people I've been asked to pray for, for peace and justice, and so forth. Why, if God is not an interventionist?

I do so for several reasons, if "reason" is the right word here.[7] Petitionary and intercessory prayer feel natural; they seem like a natural form of caring. Not to do them would seem like an absence of love. As author Anne Lamott remarks, the two most common prayers are "Help me, help me, help me" and "Thank you, thank you, thank you."[8]

Moreover, I think prayers for healing sometimes have an effect, and perhaps other kinds of prayer do as well. The statistical data about the effect of prayers for healing are very interesting, even though not conclusive.[9] We have good reasons to affirm that "paranormal" healings have happened throughout history and continue to happen today, many of them involving prayer as a factor. So I think these kinds of things happen.

But I refuse to use interventionism as the explanation. I also refuse to use psychosomatic explanations. Of course, some are psychosomatic; body and mind are related in ways that we do not fully understand. Yet some healings are not so readily explained. But the point is that interventionism and psychosomatic explanation both claim to know too much. Both claim to know the "mechanism" at work in the relation between prayer and healing. I myself have no clue what the explanatory mechanism is, and I am content not to.[10]

And this leads to my final reason for continuing to do prayers of petition and intercession. To refuse to do them because I can't imagine how prayer works would be an act of intellectual pride: if I can't imagine how something works, then it can't work. To think thus involves more than a bit of *hubris*.

But regardless of their efficacy, petition and intercession serve the central purpose of prayer: intimacy with God. Indeed, ideally, the whole of verbal prayer is about intimacy. And verbal prayer can be intimate in the more specific sense of just talking to God about our day. It doesn't have to be confession in the sense of, "Here's where I have fallen short," but can simply be reporting out, as one would to an intimate confidant, one's thoughts about the day, concerns and desires for oneself or others. Of course, one might say, "But God knows about my day already," but this misses the point—namely, to state the obvious, being intimate is part of having an intimate relationship. Our relationship with God deepens through such intimacy, through disclosure, through conversation. By doing these things we spend time in the relationship, remind ourselves of it, remember it.

The second and third categories of Christian prayer are *meditation* and *contemplation*. Though central in the history of the Christian tradition, they have been quite neglected in modern Western Christianity. Until recently, the practice of meditation and contemplation occurred primarily in religious orders. Now they are being recovered by both laity and clergy in Protestant and Catholic churches. What they share in common is that they are not about talking to God, but listening for God. They do this in different ways.

Meditation: Meditation involves reflecting on an image or phrase, sitting with it, holding it, remaining with it. A classic example is "Ignatian meditation," named after St. Ignatius, the founder of the Jesuit order in the sixteenth century. Very concisely, it provides a structure for meditation on the images in a biblical text. We enter into the text, and the images of the text become a means for the Spirit to speak to us.

Another classic example of meditation is *lectio divina*. It can be done in either group settings or individually. It involves meditating on a biblical text until a word or a phrase emerges, and then staying with it for as long as one does the exercise and perhaps beyond it. In an informal sense, this is what much of private Christian devotional time with the Bible is about. People who have never heard the phrase *lectio divina* nevertheless do it.

Contemplation: Contemplation is the prayer and practice of internal silence. The purpose of contemplation is to sit silently in the presence of God, of "what is." Contemplation typically involves the silent repetition of a mantra, whether a single word, a short phrase, or a series of short phrases. But the words of the mantra are not to be meditated upon; rather, they are used to give the mind a focus so that the rest of the self can sink into silence. Their purpose is to lead one to the place beyond and beneath all words and images. Ultimately, the purpose of contemplative prayer is to descend to the deepest level of the self, of the heart, where we open out into the sea of being that is God.

The Christian resource of contemplative prayer is being redis-covered in our time. One of the most common forms is called "center-ing prayer," associated especially with the contemporary Benedictine monk Thomas Keating.[11] There are other forms as well. Many churches offer training in contemplative prayer, and in most areas of the country one can find workshops on it.

A *Daily Discipline*: There is great value in establishing a regular daily practice, a specific time set aside each day for paying attention to God. For some Christians, this is a period of contemplative prayer. For others, it combines prayer and spending time with Christian read-ing (primarily the Bible). In my case, I do "morning reading," which always includes prayer and the lectionary texts from the Bible for the day and typically includes a devotional reading from the history of the Christian tradition.[12] During this time, I am not reading for informa-tion or analysis, but unhurriedly, quietly, receptively. It nourishes me. My day begins with a reminder of God. A daily practice is important for both Christian formation and nourishment.

Practice in the Dailiness of Life: There are also many ways of remembering God in the course of the day and week, including brief prayers or rituals of one kind or another. A recent book describes a variety of such practices:

Honoring the body, including, for example, washing one's face "in the name of the Father, and of the Son, and of the Holy Spirit."

Learning how to say no for the sake of saying yes to God.

The practice of hospitality, individually and as a church.

Singing our lives, together and alone; even the songs we sing in silence can shape our lives.

Household economics, including minimizing the amount of "cumber" in our lives.

Testimony—telling one's story and listening to others tell theirs.

Keeping the sabbath, either as a day of the week or in "sabbath moments" spread throughout our days.[13]

All of these and more can shape us, form us, nourish us.

Christian Friendship: By Christian friendship I do not mean simply having friends who are Christian, but the more specific practice of "Christian companionship"—having one or more friends with whom one can share intimately about one's Christian journey. In Celtic Christianity, such friendship is called *anamchara.* In one of his books, Frederick Buechner recalls overhearing a conversation during his visit to an evangelical college in which one student asked another what God had been doing in his life lately.[14] Christian friendship provides a context in which such questions can be asked, talked about, reflected on, and prayed about.

Practicing Compassion and Justice

Paying attention to God means the practice of compassion and justice. They are God's passion. Loving God means participating in God's passion. God's passion is not the redemption and salvation (to use two words that mean the same thing) of individuals *from the world,* but the redemption and salvation *of the world.* God loves the world, not just you and me and us.

The practice of compassion and justice is important both within the internal life of the church and in the world beyond the community of the church. Within the church, compassion is to be the primary virtue shaping our relationships with each other. Among other things, compassion means inclusiveness and inclusive caring. Justice is the social or systemic form of compassion. Thus, within the church, justice means a concern for the structures or systems of the church— church governance and organization. To use an example from recent history, the ordination of women was (and is) a justice issue. In our time, the status of gays and lesbians in the church is a justice issue, as is the role of the laity in the governance of the Catholic church.

Beyond the church, the practice of compassion means both charity and justice. The distinction between the two is important. About a hundred years ago, a Christian activist and author named Vida Scudder listed three ways that Christians can respond to a growing awareness of human suffering: direct philanthropy, social reform, and social transformation. Direct philanthropy means giving directly to those who are suffering, social reform means creating and supporting organizations for their care, and social transformation is about justice—changing society so that the structures do not privilege some and cause suffering for others.[15]

The first two are about charity, the third is about justice. All three are important. Charity is always good and will always be necessary, but historically Christians have been long on the first two and short on the third. One reason is that charity never offends; a passion for justice often does. To paraphrase Roman Catholic bishop Dom Helder Camara from Brazil: "When I gave food to the poor, they called me a saint; when I asked why there were so many poor, they called me a communist."

Charity means helping the victims. Justice asks, "Why are there so many victims?" and then seeks to change the causes of victimization, that is, the way the system is structured. Justice is not about Caesar increasing his charitable giving or Pilate increasing his tithe. Justice is about social transformation. Taking the political vision of the Bible seriously means the practice of social transformation.

Christians in our time are thus called to be political. This does not mean that we are all called to be political activists. To use language from Paul, there is one body and many members, one Spirit and many gifts. But we are all called to be political in the broad sense of being aware of the impact of systems on people's lives and of God's passion for those who are disadvantaged and victimized by systems. As argued in Chapter 7, the practice of justice involves consciousness-raising within the church about the effects of social systems (economic, political, and conventional) on people's lives, and then acting on that awareness in ways appropriate to who we are.

In particular, we need to develop an imaginative sympathy for the poor. Most of us do not have that. It's not that we are "bad people," but we have difficulty imagining what life is like for those with little money. For the most part, we don't personally know the poor, whether the unemployed poor or the working poor. Our neighborhoods are increasingly divided by income. So also are our churches, not by design, but by circumstance. And when we travel, we may see poor people, even become curious about them and moved by them, but we don't know their lives.

This is not something to feel guilty about, as if we've been bad again and need forgiveness. Rather, it's something to do something about. Raising consciousness about the plight of poor people can be done to some extent through education and reading. For example, reading a book like Barbara Ehrenreich's *Nickel and Dimed* in a group setting can be a consciousness-raising exercise.[16]

Another example: median family income in the United States is about $40,000 a year, which means that half of families earn more, half less. An adult-education class or study group in a relatively afflu-ent congregation can be asked to imagine what it would be like to live in a metropolitan area on a before-tax family income of $40,000 or less. Mortgage or rent payment? Car payment? Day care, if both par-ents work, as most do? Public or private school? Food? Clothing? Then they should try to imagine living on $20,000 a year. That amount is what a couple, both working full-time at minimum wage, earn. And it is illuminating to be asked to imagine living on what work-ing full-time at minimum wage generates in a year: a bit over $10,000. Imagining this can soften our hearts and lead to a new way of seeing our political and economic structures.

The most effective consciousness-raising activity is direct contact with the poor and disadvantaged. This can happen through volun-teering to work in church programs or other agencies directly serving the poor, through work projects with poor people locally or overseas, or through serious, respectful intimate partnering with a congregation of lower-income membership. Through such experiences we learn that the difference between "us" and "them" is not about how hard people work, but something both more random and more systemic. Consciousness-raising is learning about people and the way systems affect their (and our) lives.

To move from consciousness-raising to some specific examples. Minimally, in a democratic society, the practice of justice would affect the way we vote. There are issues of justice in local, state, and national elections. Adequate funding of public schools is a justice issue, simply because public schools are the only option for children whose parents cannot afford private schools. So also is adequate funding for health care and prescription medicines for those without health insurance, adequate support for people who are mentally or physically disadvantaged, food for the impoverished, and so forth. The need for a living wage is a justice issue. Tax policy is a justice issue. International policy, both economic and military, is a justice issue. Christians are to be thoughtful about the positions of political candidates and the effect of ballot measures on issues such as these.

The practice of justice should also affect our financial contributions. To use an arbitrary number, we as Christians could resolve to contribute 50 percent of our total giving to organizations whose purpose is to change the world in the direction of greater justice. Most of us do not do that. Most of our giving goes to "our kind" of charities: the church, the arts, museums, public broadcasting, alma maters, soup kitchens, rescue missions, and so forth. These are worthy causes and deserve support, but they are not about justice.

To return to Vida Scudder's language, some organizations seek to care for people who are suffering, and others seek to transform the conditions that produce suffering. Both matter, and it is important to support the latter as well as the former. Groups or committees within Christian congregations could do a study, for the purpose of making recommendations to their congregations, of humanitarian organizations whose purpose is transformation and not simply aid, important as aid is. Ideally, rather than dividing our present giving, we would increase our total giving so that, to use the arbitrary number again, 50 percent of it would support changing the world.

The world's need for systemic transformation is great, but it is important not to become passive or discouraged ("without heart") because the need is so great. None of us is called to be knowledgeable about all of it or capable of doing something about all of it. To use a metaphor I owe to the contemporary theologian Sallie McFague, we might think of the task as like that of women gathering to make a patchwork quilt. Nobody is responsible for doing the whole quilt; rather, it is the product of a host of people working together. The important thing is for each of us to do our patch.

So the practice of compassion and justice is central. It is both something to be done as well as the primary fruit of the Spirit. We participate in the passion of God, loving that which God loves. It is the Spirit becoming incarnate in the lives of Christians.

Concluding Comments

A list of practices can seem like a list of chores to be done. Most of us are already too busy, and we may find it hard to imagine making time to do even more things. But people who practice one or more of these disciplines consistently report that they are nourished by them and have more energy and presence than when they don't practice. Moreover, it is not necessary to undertake all of them at once. The practices I have mentioned are not a list of requirements. Rather, they are for the deepening of our life with God and our love for God.

A famous passage from the prophet Micah is one of the most compact expressions of biblical faith. In a few words it combines the practice of paying attention to God with kindness and justice. Micah asks, "What does the Lord require of you?" His answer:

> To do justice,
> To love kindness,
> To walk humbly with your God.[17]

Christian practice is about walking with God, becoming kind, and doing justice. It is not about believing in God and being a good person; it is about how one becomes a good person through the practice of loving God.

---

1. Dorothee Soelle, *The Silent Cry: Mysticism and Resistance*, trans. Barbara and Martin Rumscheidt (Minneapolis: Fortress, 2001), pp. 1–2.

2. Deut. 6:5; Mark 12:30; Matt. 22:37; Luke 10:27.

3. See the closing section of Chapter 2.

4. The title of Jim Wallis's book makes this point: *Call to Conversion* (San Francisco: HarperSanFrancisco, 1992). It is addressed to Christians. So also William James in *The Varieties of Religious Experience* speaks of "conversion" not as "changing religions," but as something that happens within a tradition: the process of moving from a divided self to an integrated, whole self, the process whereby "the More" becomes ever more central in one's life.

5. For a wise and insightful treatment of the classic Christian virtues, see Peter Gomes, *The Good Life* (San Francisco: HarperSanFrancisco, 2002), especially pp. 211–343.

6. Ps. 122:1.

7. I also treat this subject in *The God We Never Knew* (San Francisco: HarperSanFrancisco, 1997), chap. 5.

8. Anne Lamott, *Traveling Mercies* (New York: Random House, 1999), p. 82.

9. Larry Dossey, *Healing Words* (San Francisco: HarperSanFrancisco, 1993).

10. For a helpful and very readable book on how prayer "works" within a noninterventionist framework, see Marjorie Hewitt Suchocki, *In God's Presence: Theological Reflections on Prayer* (St. Louis: Chalice, 1996).

11. See his *Intimacy with God* (New York: Crossroad, 1997) and *Open Mind, Open Heart* (New York: Continuum, 1997). Contemplative Outreach is an organization furthering the teaching and practice of centering prayer.

12. There are several sources of daily scripture readings. In my own denomination, lists of biblical texts for each day of the year are provided in *The Book of Common Prayer* (New York: Oxford University Press, 1979), pp. 934–95. The two-volume *Daily Office Book* (New York: Church Publishing, 1986, 2002) includes the

biblical texts themselves. There are many collections of readings from the postbiblical traditions. Two that I have found very helpful are *Glorious Companions: Five Centuries of Anglican Spirituality,* ed. Richard Schmidt (Grand Rapids: Eerdmans, 2002), and *Devotional Classics,* ed. Richard J. Foster and James Bryan Smith (San Francisco: HarperSanFrancisco, 1993). I also have been nourished by Dag Hammarskjöld's *Markings,* trans. W. H. Auden and Leif Sjoberg (London: Faber and Faber, 1964), and several of Frederick Buechner's books. His *Listening to Your Life* (San Francisco: HarperSanFrancisco, 1992) contains brief readings for each day of the year. Finally, collections of sermons make excellent daily readings. Many of us have favorites. Mine include collections by Barbara Brown Taylor, Martin Luther King Jr., and Paul Tillich.

13. Dorothy C. Bass, ed., *Practicing Our Faith* (San Francisco: Jossey-Bass, 1997). For more on the recovery of sabbath observance in our work-dominated lives, see especially Wayne Muller, *Sabbath: Finding Rest, Renewal and Delight in Our Busy Lives* (New York: Bantam, 1999). For helpful treatments of specific Christian practices, see Marjorie Thompson, *Soul Feast* (Louisville, KY: Westminster John Knox, 1995) and Tilden Edwards, *Living in the Presence* (San Francisco: Harper and Row, 1987).

14. Frederick Buechner, *Telling Secrets* (San Francisco: HarperSanFrancisco, 1991), pp. 81–82.

15. Vida Scudder, in *Glorious Companions,* p. 222.

16. Barbara Ehrenreich, *Nickel and Dimed* (New York: Henry Holt, 2001).

17. Mic. 6:8.

ELEVEN

Heart and Home

Being Christian in an Age of Pluralism

Throughout this book I have been suggesting a way of being Christian today. To use the five adjectives with which I have described the emerging paradigm, it involves a historical, metaphorical, and sacramental way of seeing the Christian tradition, and a relational and transformational way of seeing the Christian life.

In this chapter, I move from "what" to "why": from *what it means to be Christian* to *why be Christian*. The Christianity of my childhood had a clear and compelling reason: it was the only way to salvation. To put it bluntly, one risked going to hell if one wasn't Christian. The stakes were high. It is difficult to imagine a more powerful sanction and persuasive motive.

But I no longer believe that; nor do a majority of Christians in North America. Though there is more than one reason, a primary one is our growing awareness of religious pluralism. We know about other religions in various ways, from college courses and television series and increasingly through personal acquaintance with people from other religions. Of course, this is happening in Europe and other parts of the world as well, but I will focus on the North American context. In our setting, why be Christian?

A central claim in this concluding chapter is that we understand Christianity most clearly when we see it in the context of religious pluralism. Religious pluralism is both a demographic fact in our time even as it also provides a way of seeing religions (and Christianity) anew. When we see Christianity within the framework of religions as a whole, we see Christianity—its nature and purpose—more clearly, and we better understand, "Why be Christian?" My answer has several building blocks: the demographic reality of religious pluralism; a way of seeing religions since the Enlightenment; an understanding of their similarities and differences; and the role of religion in our life with God.

Religious Pluralism

The religious landscape in the United States is rapidly changing. We have historically been Christian, Jewish, and secular, with the first far outnumbering the second and third. But in the last thirty-five years, we have become the most religiously diverse nation in the world. This is one of the central claims of an important recent book by Diana Eck, a professor at Harvard and director of the Pluralism Project. In *A New Religious America*, Eck describes the growing presence of religions other than Christianity and Judaism in the United States.[1]

The key event that sparked this growth was the Immigration Act of 1965, which opened up immigration to people from nations outside of Europe. The result was a dramatic increase in the number of immigrants from Asia, the Middle East, and to a lesser extent Africa. Most of these brought religions with them other than Christianity and Judaism. Together with their children born in the United States since 1965, they have made religious pluralism a fact of life for us today. Eck's statistics include the following:

There are approximately six million Muslim Americans. There are as many Muslim Americans as Presbyterians and Episcopalians combined, two of the historically most influential Protestant denominations. There are (or soon will be) about as many Muslim Americans as Jewish Americans.

There are four million Buddhist Americans. Though the majority are recent immigrants and their American-born children, many are American converts to Buddhism. There are more Buddhists in the United States than either Presbyterians or Episcopalians.

In lesser numbers, there are about a million Hindus in the United States (about as many as the United Church of Christ or the Christian Church–Disciples of Christ). There are about 300,000 Sikhs.

Moreover, the phenomenon of religious diversity is not confined to major metropolitan areas. People of religions other than Christianity and Judaism are found in regional cities and rural areas as well. Eck writes about a huge mosque in Toledo, Ohio; a great Hindu temple in Nashville, Tennessee; a Cambodian Buddhist temple and monastery in the farmlands of Minnesota; a Sikh *gurdwara* in Fremont, California; Muslim, Hindu, and Buddhist centers in Salt Lake City and Dallas; Cambodian Buddhist communities in Iowa and Oklahoma; and Tibetan Buddhist retreat centers in Vermont and Colorado. Eck comments, "This is an astonishing new reality. We have never been here before."[2]

This is very different from the world of my childhood. Almost fifty years ago, a book on religious diversity in the United States carried the title *Protestant, Catholic, Jew.*[3] Muslims, Buddhists, and Hindus were not part of the picture. And in the small town in which I grew up, religious diversity consisted of Catholics and Protestants, the latter of whom were mostly Lutherans. But now we are experiencing religious pluralism more than any generation of Christians since the early centuries of Christianity.

A second set of statistics underlines both the fact and impact of religious pluralism. According to a poll taken in the United States in 2002:[4]

Those who personally knew somebody who was Christian: 94 percent.

Those who personally knew somebody who was Jewish: 51 percent.

Those who personally knew somebody who was Muslim: 28 percent.

Those who personally knew somebody who was Hindu or Buddhist: 17 percent.

The poll also included questions designed to measure the acceptance of religious pluralism:

"Should Christians seek to convert people of other faiths or leave them alone?" 22 percent said "convert," and 71 percent said "leave them alone."

To the statement "All religions have elements of truth," 78 percent said yes.

To the statement "My religion is the only true religion," only 17 percent said yes.

Of course, public opinion polls do not establish truth; they only report what people think. And this poll not only indicates that many know people of other traditions, but also that most have let go of the notion that only one religion is the true religion.

The fact of religious pluralism in our society creates an imperative to understand other religions and the people who practice them. Understanding other religions is no longer primarily an intellectual interest in religions we've heard of but might never encounter, but an immensely practical need. The imperative has been underlined and made more urgent by the events of September 11, 2001.

Moreover, the need exists for more than cultural and political reasons. For those of us who are Christians, understanding other religions can enrich our understanding of Christianity and what it means to be Christian. Religious pluralism can help us to see our own tradition better.

Three Ways of Seeing Religions

I widen my focus to how religion has been seen in Western culture in the modern period. In broad strokes, three ways of seeing religion (and religions) have emerged since the Enlightenment of the seventeenth century. Describing these options will also provide a concise introduction to the nature and function—the essence and purpose—of religion.

The Absolutist Understanding of Religion

The absolutist understanding of religion affirms that one's own religion is the absolute and only truth. Most familiar to readers of this book in its Christian form, it also exists in Jewish and Muslim forms, though historically the last two have less often seen their religion as "the only true religion" than have Christians.[5] For absolutists, the truth of one's own religion is grounded in God's infallible revelation: God has disclosed God's will in the scriptures of that tradition as nowhere else. This is essentially what I have called the earlier Christian paradigm, especially in its harder form. Against all other claims, whether religious or secular, this religion—our religion—is the true religion. Within this framework, only one religion can be right.

The Reductionist Understanding of Religion

The reductionist view reduces religion to a human invention. It sees all religions as human constructions, as human projections. They were created by us in part out of ignorance about the way things really are, but also to serve strong psychological and social needs. This is the dominant secular understanding of religion, within both secular culture and the secular academy. The psychological and social factors that generate religions include the desire or need for:

Explanations (religion as "primitive science")
Protection from vulnerability and death
Reinforcement of the social order by giving it divine sanction
Meaning

And perhaps other desires could be included as well, such as the desire to sing and dance in praise of creation. But whatever the complete list of factors might include, the final truth about religion is "we made it all up." Religion is reduced to a human psychological and social construction. Thus, for the reductionist view, the religions are all built on a mistake, for there is no God, no sacred, no "More."

Though the reductionist view rejects the foundational claim of the religions, reductionists can be appreciative of religion. Some admire its contributions to thought, wisdom, ethics, art, music, architecture, and so forth. Other reductionists are dismissive of religion, whether politely or contemptuously. To be colloquial, for some it's "just a bunch of crap." But for appreciative and dismissive reductionists alike, none of the religions is right, none of them is true. They are all mistaken, no matter how beautiful and elegant and compassionate they might be.

Much of the conflict about religion in the Christian West in the modern period has been between absolutist and reductionist views of religion. Beginning in the seventeenth century, Christians felt threatened by the emergence of secularism and responded by insisting on the absolute truth of Christianity. In the nineteenth century, many Protestants began to affirm the Bible's infallibility, and the Roman Catholic church explicitly affirmed the infallibility of papal authority. Both absolutism and reductionism are the products of modernity. And to many modern people, they seem like the only two options.

The Sacramental Understanding of Religion

There is an alternative to the first two ways of seeing religion. Within modernity, a third view of religion and the religions is emerging. It sees religions as sacraments of the sacred. As sacraments, the religions are not "absolute." Rather, like the bread and wine of the Eucharist, they are finite products, finite means, of mediating the sacred. This is the sacramental understanding of Christianity that I have been describing in this book.

Though not always named in this way, this way of seeing religion is shared by many scholars of religious pluralism, others within the religious academy, and increasingly within mainline churches. Seven statements describe this understanding of religion and the religions.

First, it sees religions as *human creations*. In this, it is like the second option, the reductionist view. The scriptures, teachings, doctrines, rituals, practices, and so forth, of all the religions are human products. To express this widely accepted view with a phrase from Harvard theologian Gordon Kaufman, religions are "imaginative human constructions."[6] Here "imaginative" does not mean "fanciful" or "fantasy," but "creative," filled with images that come from and address the human imagination—that faculty within us within which our images of reality reside.

Second, unlike the second option, it affirms that religions are human constructions *in response to experiences of the sacred*. Although they are human constructions, they are not simply mistaken human projections generated by psychological and social needs. Of course, they have been shaped and sometimes distorted, often in very destructive ways, in order to serve human desires, but they are not ultimately built on a mistake. Religions are human products created in response to the sacred in the particular cultures within which each came into being. Thus the sacramental understanding of religion robustly affirms the reality of God, the sacred, "the More." Without "the More," there would be nothing to mediate.

Third, religions are *"cultural-linguistic traditions,"* a phrase used by Yale theologian George Lindbeck to express another widely accepted notion.[7] As I understand the phrase, it refers to both the origin and function of religions. Each religion originates within a particular culture and uses the language of that culture to express itself, even if it might also be challenging dominant convictions of that culture. Even more important, the statement refers to the function of religion; namely, a religion that survives over time becomes a cultural-linguistic tradition in its own right, and to be part of that religion is to live within the cultural-linguistic world created by that religion. It means to live within its scriptures, its language, its stories, its vision, its rituals, its practice—in a comprehensive sense, to live within its *ethos*.

To use an only partially apt analogy, as I suggested in the previous chapter, being Christian (or Muslim or Jewish, and so forth) is a bit like being French (or Korean or Ethiopian, and so forth). Being French involves knowing French as a language, but also much more: there is a cultural ethos, a cultural-linguistic world, involved in being French. So also being Christian means living within the ethos of a Christian cultural-linguistic world.

Fourth, the enduring religions of the world are *"wisdom traditions,"* a phrase from Huston Smith, perhaps today's best-known historian of religions. Wisdom and knowledge are not identical. Wisdom is more foundational. It is about the two most important questions in life: "the real" and "the way." What is real? And what is the way—how shall we live? Deeply rooted in the past, the religions that have stood the test of time are repositories of such wisdom. Though they contain the ideas of a much earlier time, some of which from our point of view are mistaken or no longer applicable, they also enshrine the wisdom of the past about "the real" and "the way." They articulate a vision that can deliver us from the partial and provincial view of "flatland" modernity.[8]

Fifth, religions are *aesthetic traditions*. All of the enduring religions have valued and created beauty: in their music, poetry, stories, art, architecture, worship, and rituals. They see beauty as a mediator of "the real."

Sixth, religions are *communities of practice*. All of them provide practical means for living the religious life: the "thin places" and practices of worship, prayer, deeds of compassion, and more specific spiritual practices.

Seventh, and directly connected to the sixth, religions are *communities of transformation*. Religions are "means of ultimate transformation."[9] They have the very practical purpose of transforming the self and the world—the transformation of the self from an old way of being to a new way of being, and the transformation of the world through compassion. These two transformations are central to all of the enduring religions.

All seven of these aspects are included in seeing religions as sacramental. Religion's purpose is to mediate the sacred and, by so doing, to inform, engender, and nourish a transforming relationship to "the More." The enduring religions share these characteristics in common. Each is a massive and magnificent sacrament of the sacred, a finite means of mediating the sacred, a "treasure in earthen vessels."[10]

This realization helps us to understand religious pluralism, even as it also helps us to understand Christianity. Each of the enduring religions is a mediator of "the absolute," but not "absolute" itself. Applying this understanding to being Christian, the point is not to believe in Christianity as the only absolute and adequate revelation of God. Rather, the point is to live within the Christian tradition as a sacrament of the sacred, a mediator of the absolute, whom we name "God" and who for us is known decisively in Jesus. Christianity is not absolute, but points to and mediates the absolute.

Are All Religions Thus the Same?

There is an easy, almost nonchalant acceptance of religious pluralism in some quarters in our time. Some say, "The religions are all the same—just different roads to the same place. It doesn't matter what you are." Rightly understood, the statement contains some truth. But as commonly understood, it's too simple. It is sometimes made by people to whom religion doesn't matter very much; for them, there's no point in spending much energy on whether one religion is better than another or in being part of any religion. And the "place" to which the various religions lead is often thought of as "heaven," and so they are all thought of as ways to "the next world," not really as being about "this life" and transformation in this world.

The statement is too simple for another reason as well. Religions are not all "the same." Though the enduring religions of the world share many common elements, they are very different in important respects. To be very elementary and basic, they are both alike and different. It is important to recognize both.

Their similarity in terms of sacramental function has just been described. Here I provide a compact fivefold summary of their most central similarities:

1. They all affirm "the More," "the real," "the sacred"; and they all affirm that the sacred can be known—not known completely or exhaustively, but known in the sense of being experienced. The religions are grounded in glimpses and visions of the sacred, experiences of seeing and reconnection.

2. They all affirm a way, a path; and the paths are all recognizable variants of the same path, the same way. As suggested in Chapter 6, the way of the cross, the way of Lao Tzu, the way of the Buddha, the way of Islam, and the way of Judaism all speak of the same path: the path of dying to an old identity and way of being and being born into a new identity and way of being. All refer to the same transformation of the self.

3. They all provide practical means (the practices of worship, rituals, prayer, and so forth) for undertaking the way, living the path, undergoing a sacred journey.

4. They all extol compassion as the primary ethical virtue of life. We see this not only in their teachings, but also in the saints of the various traditions who are consistently embodiments of compassion.

5. They all contain a collection of beliefs and teachings. These typically include scripture, what Christians commonly call "doctrines," as well as ethical teachings. To put this point most simply, the religions are all "put into words."

Yet they are not all the same. They're very different, as different as the cultures and histories that shaped them. Each is a distinctive cultural-linguistic world with its own stories, rituals, practices, and ethos. Worshiping in a Hindu temple or a Jewish synagogue is a very different experience from worshiping in a Muslim mosque or a Christian church.

As a way of thinking about the similarities and differences among the religions, I suggest three complementary approaches. All are expressions of the same point of view.

In *The Varieties of Religious Experience,* William James includes some comments about the world's religions. Based on his study of religious experience, he concludes that the religions of the world are most similar in the experiences they report, the path they teach, the practices they commend, and the behavior they produce, the "fruit" of compassion. These are the first four of the similarities I suggested.

They are most different, he concludes, in their beliefs and doctrines (our fifth point). When one thinks about it, this is only what one would expect, for beliefs and doctrines are what are most affected by the particularities of culture and language. What is most affected is what is put into words. For James, their words differ, but their views of reality and the lives they mediate are similar.

Along with others, Huston Smith uses the phrase the "primordial tradition" as a key concept for thinking about similarities and differences among the religions. The "primordial tradition" is a set of core understandings underlying all the enduring religions. These core understandings are twofold. The first is a multilayered understanding of reality: what is real includes more than the space-time world of matter and energy. The second is a multilayered understanding of the self: we are more than our bodies and brains, and open out in our depths into the sea of being that we name God, Spirit, Allah, and so forth. The enduring religions are all different expressions of this primordial wisdom; it is the core underlying their different forms.

A third and closely related way of expressing the same point is the language of "internal core" and "external form." The internal core, the heart of religion, is the experience of the sacred, "the real," "the More." The external form is the particular expression of the religion: it includes the particularities of what is done in worship, the particular words (scripture, stories, teachings) in which the tradition is articulated, the particular practices enjoined, and so forth. Religions are similar in their internal core, different in their external forms.[11]

To return to the statement "The religions are all the same—just different roads to the same place," we are now in position to see its truth as well as its limitations. To use the metaphor of paths going up a mountainside, the enduring religions are all paths up the same mountain. Envision a mountain, broad at the bottom, narrow at the top, the peak finally disappearing into air, space, emptiness. At the bottom, the paths are farthest apart (the external forms). But as the paths lead higher, they become closer together until they converge on the mountaintop. And then, of course, they disappear.[12] And the place to which they lead, the mountaintop, is not "heaven," but "the sacred." The religions are not primarily about the next life, not about paths to an afterlife, but to life centered in the sacred in the here and now.

Significantly, the external forms matter. Serious religious pluralism (as distinct from nonchalant pluralism) involves recognizing that the external forms of religions are quite different. Respecting the integrity of the "other" involves such recognition. Though we might affirm that "human beings are all the same" in some important sense, to refuse to recognize that being French or being Iraqi is different from being English or American is to fail to recognize the distinctiveness of the "other." So also among religions: to be Muslim or Jewish or Buddhist or Christian involves being different from one another. Not only are the religions different; we might even learn to appreciate and relish their distinctiveness. The world is richer because of its distinctive cultural-linguistic traditions.

Additionally, the external forms matter for both a negative and positive reason. Negatively, when the external forms are emphasized, then the differences between religions are more apparent than their similarities. When the external forms (especially scripture and doctrines) are absolutized, as they are in religious fundamentalism, then religious exclusivism is the inevitable result. Authentic dialogue becomes impossible, conversion is the goal, and conflict is often the result. Our time is such a time, "a clash of fundamentalisms," as the title of a recent book puts it.[13]

Positively, the external forms matter because they are sacraments of the sacred. They mediate the sacred, and they mediate the path. In a primary sense, they are the path: practical means for living life with and in God.

This point is important because of a common contemporary contrast between spirituality and religion. Most of us have heard people say, "I'm spiritual, but not religious." We know what they mean: they have a spiritual interest or sensitivity, but they're not part of any particular religion. And the contrast often contains a value judgment as well: spirituality is "good"; religion is "bad," or at least unnecessary. The first is seen as personal, the second as institutional, and we live in a time when many don't think much of institutions.

In an important sense, religions are "institutions." Their external forms—their scriptures, rituals, teaching, practices, organization—are to a large extent "institutionalized." They are "traditions," and traditions are intrinsically "institutions." Religion is "organized religion."

But the contrast between spirituality and religion is both unnecessary and unwise. To use an analogy I owe to Huston Smith, religion is to spirituality as institutions of learning are to education. One can learn about the world, become educated, without schools, universities, and books, but it is like reinventing the wheel in every generation. Institutions of learning are the way education gets traction in history; so also religion (its external forms) is the way spirituality gains traction in history.[14] Religion—its external forms—not just spirituality, matters. Its forms are vessels of spirituality, mediators of the sacred and the way.

Why Be Christian?

I return to the question with which I began this chapter: "Why be Christian?" For centuries, the conventional Christian answer has been that Christianity is the only way to salvation. In the Catholic church, it has been expressed in the Latin phrase *extra ecclesiam nulla salus est*, "Outside of the church there is no salvation." The Second Vatican Council (1962–65) moved away from this position, though recent developments in Rome have moved back toward it.

From their birth in the Reformation, Protestants have rejected the Catholic church's claim to have a monopoly on salvation. But they have nevertheless most commonly claimed a Christian monopoly: "Salvation is only through Jesus, and we've got Jesus." Most premodern and many modern Christians affirm some version of "Christian exclusivism": only through Jesus can one be saved.

But taking religious pluralism seriously calls Christian exclusivism radically into question and, in my judgment, negates it. It is impossible for many of us to believe that only Christians can be in saving relationship to God. Knowing about other religions and especially knowing people of those religions have made it impossible. Moreover, there is a "commonsense" reason for rejecting Christian exclusivism. When we think about the claim that Christianity is the only way of salvation, it's a pretty strange notion. Does it make sense that "the More" whom we speak of as creator of the whole universe has chosen to be known in only one religious tradition, which just fortunately happens to be our own?[15]

And there is a specifically Christian reason for rejecting Christian exclusivism: the classic Christian emphasis on grace. If one *must* be a Christian in order to be in right relationship with God, then there is a requirement, and we are no longer talking about grace, even though we might use the language of grace. If our relationship with God is based on grace, then it is not based on requirements, not even the requirement of being Christian. Of course, deepening the relationship depends upon paying attention to it, but the relationship is not about requirements.

And so my reasons for being Christian have nothing to do with it being the only way. I am convinced, as one who sees Christianity within the emerging paradigm, that God, the sacred, "the More," is known in all of the major religious traditions, not simply in our own. Indeed, if I thought I had to believe that Christianity was the only way, I could not be Christian. Moreover, it seems to me that seeing the similarities between Christianity and other religions adds to the credibility of Christianity rather than threatening it.

When Christianity is seen as one of the great religions of the world, as one of the classic forms of the primordial tradition, as a remarkable sacrament of the sacred, it has great credibility. But when Christianity claims to be the only true religion, it loses much of its credibility. The similarities, it seems to me, are cause for celebration, and not for alarm.

Within this framework, what happens to the passages in the New Testament that proclaim Jesus to be "the only way"? We should remember that they are relatively few. Moreover, passages in both the Hebrew Bible and the New Testament suggest a larger view of God's presence and accessibility. But the "only way" passages are there, most famously John 14:6: "I am the way, and the truth, and the life; no one comes to God except through me." Also well known is Acts 4:12, which says about Jesus, "There is salvation in no one else, for there is no other name under heaven given among mortals by which we must be saved." We can understand these as expressions of both truth and devotion.

Truth: the path seen in Jesus is *the way*—the path of death and resurrection, that path of dying to an old identity and way of being and being born into a new identity and way of being that lies at the heart of Christianity *and* the other religions. This is "the way" expressed in Christian form. For us as Christians, Jesus is *the way*, even though not the only expression of the way.

Devotion: to say "Jesus is the only way" is also the language of devotion. It is the language of gratitude and love. It is like language used by lovers, as when we say to our beloved, "You're the most beautiful person in the world." Literally? *Most* beautiful? Really? Such language is "the poetry of devotion and the hyperbole of the heart."[16] Poetry can express the truth of the heart, but it is not doctrine. And such language, when not hardened into doctrine, can continue to express Christian devotion. To echo Krister Stendahl again, we can sing our love songs to Jesus with wild abandon without needing to demean other religions.

So why be Christian? Here I offer my own reasons, my own "testimony." I suspect it is shared by many.

The first is the importance of being part of a religious community and tradition of practice. This is really a set of reasons that would also be motives for being deeply involved in any of the enduring religions. Though one can be in relationship with God apart from participation in community and tradition, community and tradition matter. They mediate and nourish the relationship.

We need a path. We are lost without one. Community and tradition articulate, embody, and nurture a path. They provide practical means of undertaking the path, not as a requirement for entering the next world, but as a path of reconnection and transformation in this life.

Religious community and tradition put us in touch with the wisdom and beauty of the past. They are communities of memory. There is value in being in touch with the past. Not only does it contain wisdom, but it can deliver us from the provinciality of the present, our limited way of seeing that we seldom recognize as a form of blindness. There is much to be said for being part of a tradition centuries old rather than one made up yesterday.

And, though all the traditions have their monsters and have at times been distorted in brutal directions, they also have incubated lives remarkably filled with compassion, courage, and joy. The saints of the traditions are the most remarkable people who have ever lived. The vision of life articulated by the traditions is both appealing and important, not only for us as individuals but for us as sharing the earth.

All of these are among my reasons for being Christian, even though they are not reasons for being specifically Christian. Rather, they are reasons for being religious—for being part of a community of memory and practice. It is important to be part of a tradition and to live more deeply into the life that it mediates.

When a Christian seeker asked the Dalai Lama whether she should become a Buddhist, his response, which I paraphrase, was: "No, become more deeply Christian; live more deeply into your own tradition." Huston Smith makes the same point with the metaphor of digging a well: if what you're looking for is water, better to dig one well sixty feet deep than to dig six wells ten feet deep. By living more deeply into our own tradition as a sacrament of the sacred, we become more centered in the one to whom the tradition points and in whom we live and move and have our being.

A Christian is one who does this within the framework of the Christian tradition, just as a Jew is one who does this within the framework of the Jewish tradition, a Muslim, within the framework of the Muslim tradition, and so forth. And I cannot believe that God cares which of these we are. All are paths of relationship and transformation.

So why be Christian? In my case, for all of the above reasons and more.

The Christian tradition is familiar; it is "home" for me. I was born into it and grew up in it. Its stories, language, music, and ethos are familiar. It nurtured me, even as I have had to unlearn some of what I was taught.

In adulthood, I have grown to appreciate its extraordinary richness: its antiquity and wisdom; the beauty of its language and music and forms of worship; its passion for compassion and justice; the sheer goodness of its most remarkable lives. Its worship nourishes me; its hymns move me; its scripture and theology engage my imagination and thought; its practices shape me. For me, it mediates the good, the true, and the beautiful; and through all of these, it mediates the sacred. It is for me a sacrament of the sacred.

And it is home. It is familiar to me in a way that no other religion could ever become. I know that other religions could have been home for me; had I been born a Buddhist or a Muslim or a Jew, for example,

I am quite sure that I would still be one. And I am aware that some who grew up Christian were so abused by the experience that Christianity could never seem like home, except as a home that one needs to escape. For them, another way of being religious may be necessary. But for me, Christianity is "home" like no other tradition could be. For me, the ethos of Christianity—its vision and way of life, its scripture, worship, language, music, thought, vision, and so forth—is home.

And we do not need to feel that our home is superior to every other home in order to love it. A twentieth-century hymn, "This Is My Song," expresses this love of home very powerfully. To the wonderful melody of Sibelius's "Finlandia," it sings of the love we have for our homeland:

> This is my song, O God of all the nations,
> A song of peace for lands afar and mine.
> This is my home, the country where my heart is;
> Here are my hopes, my dreams, my holy shrine;
> But other hearts in other lands are beating
> With hopes and dreams as true and high as mine.
>
> My country's skies are bluer than the ocean
> And sunlight beams on cloverleaf and pine;
> But other lands have sunlight, too, and clover,
> And skies are everywhere as blue as mine.
> O hear my song, O God of all the nations,
> A song of peace for their land and for mine.[17]

We need only substitute the word "religions" for "nations," "lands," and "country." Of course, in terms of syllables, the substitution doesn't work, but in terms of affirmation, it does. Religions are homes, and Christianity is home for me.

And home is about more than familiarity and comfort. We sometimes sentimentalize home. "I'll be home for Christmas," "There's no place like home for the holidays," "Home, sweet home." Home is that.

But home is also about growing up, about maturation, about learning and living a way of life that one takes into the larger world. Christianity is a way of life; that is its heart. To be Christian means living "the path" within this tradition. At the heart of Christianity is the way of the heart—a path that transforms us at the deepest level of our being. At the heart of Christianity is the heart of God—a passion for our transformation and the transformation of the world. At the heart of Christianity is participating in the passion of God.

1. Diana Eck, A New Religious America (San Francisco: HarperSanFrancisco, 2001).

2. Eck, A New Religious America, p. 5.

3. Will Herberg, Protestant, Catholic, Jew (Chicago: University of Chicago Press, 1983; first published in 1955).

4. The poll was commissioned jointly by PBS's Religion and Ethics Newsweekly and U.S. News and World Report, and reported in The Christian Century (May 8–15, 2002): 16. It included 2002 adults.

5. For a study of fundamentalism in the three religions, see especially Karen Armstrong's important and impressive book The Battle for God (New York: Knopf, 2000).

6. Gordon Kaufman, Essay on Theological Method (Missoula, MT: Scholars Press, 1975, 1979); The Theological Imagination (Philadelphia: Westminster, 1981); God-Mystery-Diversity (Minneapolis: Fortress, 1996).

7. George Lindbeck, The Nature of Doctrine (Philadelphia: Westminster, 1984). I am very appreciative of this important and illuminating book, even though Lindbeck and I almost certainly disagree about a major element in his argument.

8. "Flatland" refers to a view of reality that denies the transcendent, "the More." It is the title of a book written in the late nineteenth century that invites us to envision "Flatland": a two-dimensional universe inhabited by two-dimensional figures (squares, triangles, circles, rectangles, and so forth). One day a sphere passes through this two-dimensional universe. The author invites us to imagine what the Flatlanders would experience and then how they would explain it within a two-dimensional framework. "Reductionistic" explanations would, of course, be offered. The analogy to reductionistic explanations of religion in the modern

West is apparent: we often seek to explain the human sense of "the More" within the framework of the space-time universe of matter and energy, psychology and sociology. The book is *Flatland*, authored appropriately by "A. Square," actually by Edwin A. Abbott (New York: New American Library, 1984; originally published in 1884).

9. Frederick J. Streng, *Understanding Religious Life,* second ed. (Encino, CA: Dickenson, 1976), p. 7.

10. A phrase from Paul in 2 Cor. 4:7, RSV.

11. A number of scholars use this language, and I am uncertain whether it is traceable to a particular scholar. René Guénon and Frithjof Schuon use the language of "esoteric (internal) core" and "exoteric (external) forms." Seyyed Hossein Nasr makes extensive use of the notion in his brilliant *Knowledge and the Sacred* (Albany: State University of New York Press, 1989).

12. I owe the metaphor of the ways and the mountain to Seyyed Hossein Nasr, who in turn credits Marco Pallis, *The Way and the Mountain* (London: Peter Owen, Ltd., 1991; first published in 1960), a book now out of print, so that I was unable to locate it in time to read it for this book.

13. Tariq Ali, *The Clash of Fundamentalisms: Crusades, Jihad and Modernity* (London and New York: Verso, 2003). The title echoes and challenges the title of a well-known book about the conflict between Islam and the West called *The Clash of Civilizations,* by Samuel Huntington (New York: Simon and Schuster, 1998).

14. For the whole point, see Huston Smith, *Why Religion Matters* (San Francisco: HarperSanFrancisco, 2001).

15. For a superb treatment of Christian theology and religious pluralism, see Paul F. Knitter, *No Other Name?* (Maryknoll, NY: Orbis, 1985).

16. I owe the quotation to John Hick, but I cannot locate the book or essay in which I found it over a decade ago. Hick is a Christian philosopher of religion and a wonderfully lucid author of many books. He articulates a point of view very compatible with this chapter. See, for example, *God Has Many Names* (Philadelphia: Westminster, 1982), *The Fifth Dimension* (Oxford: Oneworld, 1999), and *An Interpretation of Religion* (New Haven: Yale University Press, 1989).

17. Lyrics by Lloyd Stone, 1934.

Index

A

Abbott, Edwin A., 224*n*.8
absolutist understanding of
  religion, 211
Adam and Eve, 50, 51, 114, 166
Advent, 160
afterlife, 10, 171–75;
  salvation and, 181–84
agnosticism, 63
Ali, Tariq, 226*n*.13
anamnesis, 60*n*.7
Apostles' Creed, 39
Argyle, Michael, 124*n*.22
Armstrong, Karen, 8, 21*n*.5, 65,
  225*n*.5
assensus, faith as, 28–31, 37–39
atheism, 63, 69
atonement theology, 92–96
Auden, W. H., 206*n*.12
Augustine, St., 166, 179

B

Babylon, exile in, 49, 176, 185*n*.11
Barth, Karl, 2, 20*n*.1

Bass, Dorothy C., 206*n*.13
"beast from the abyss," 136–37
being part of a church, 193–96
Beit-Hallahmi, Benjamin, 124*n*.22
Bellah, Robert, 146*n*.1
belief, 29; faith as, 25–27, 39–41
Bethlehem, 52
Bible, 3, 4, 7, 15, 17, 38, 43–60, 81;
  Christian life and, 59–60; earlier
  paradigm, 7–12, 15, 18, 43–44;
  emerging paradigm, 13–14, 15,
  43–60; heart of the tradition,
  43–60; historical, 13, 43, 45–46,
  48–49; justice and, 126–48;
  literalism, 4, 8–9, 12, 15, 16,
  43–44, 49–57, 81–82;
  metaphorical, 13, 43, 49–57, 59,
  60; sacramental, 13, 43, 57–59,
  60; as sacred scripture, 47–48;
  sin and salvation, 164–86
Bonhoeffer, Dietrich, 190
Book of Common Prayer, 58
born again, 103–25; dying and
  rising, 107–13; intentionality,
  119–21; new life, 121–23;

born again (*cont.*)
in New Testament, 105–6;
process, 117–19; why we
need this, 113–17
Brueggemann, Walter, 146*n*.3
Buber, Martin, 72, 79*n*.13
Buddhism, 25, 80, 119, 188, 209,
210, 216, 223
Buechner, Frederick, 73, 79*n*.14,
116, 125*n*.24, 163*n*.1, 165,
184*n*.4, 206*n*.12, 206–14
Burke, Kenneth, 19, 21*n*.8

C

Caesar, 132, 136, 201
Calvin, John, 42*n*.12
Camara, Dom Helder, 201
Castelli, Jim, 20*n*.3
Catholics, 6, 7, 21*n*.6, 28, 51, 60*n*.7,
165, 198, 201, 209, 212
Celtic Christianity, 155, 156
change, time of, 1–21
character formation, Christian, 192
charity, 201, 203
childhood, end of, 114–16
Christmas, 160
christological language, meaning of,
86–89
closed heart, 151–54
Coffin, William Sloane, 148*n*.29
Collins, Billy, "On Turning Ten,"
115–16
communal-social-political
transformation, 103–4,
126–48, 201
compassion, 11, 80, 122, 153, 162,
216; practice and, 193, 195,
200–204

conflict, time of, 2–4
congregation, being part of, 193–96
consciousness-raising, 202–3;
in the church, 139–42
Constantine, 127
consubstantiation, 60*n*.7
contemplation, 198–99
Cover, Robin C., 184*n*.8
Cox, Harvey, 78*n*.8
creation stories, 49–52
credo, 39–40
creed, 39–40, 159
cross, 112–13; being born again and,
112–13; faith in the, 96; political
meaning of, 138
Crossan, John Dominic, 79*n*.15, 132,
133, 147*n*.9, 147*n*.10, 147*n*.14
cultural-linguistic traditions, 213–14

D

daily discipline, 199–200
Dalai Lama, 223
death, 34; of Jesus, 54, 81–83,
91–96, 97, 107–13, 171
debt, 134–35
de Waal, Esther, 163*n*.2
Didache, 134
differences, bridging, 16–18
diversity, religious, 16–17, 208–26
Dossey, Larry, 205*n*.9
doubt, 30
Dozier, Verna, 186*n*.23

E

earlier paradigm, 2–4, 5, 7–12,
17–18; Bible, 7–12, 15, 18,
43–44; God, 61; Jesus, 81–82;

vision of Christian life, 9–12, 18;
vision of Christian tradition, 7–9
Easter, 54–55, 56–57, 82–83, 89, 92,
100n.12, 138, 160
Eck, Diana, 208–9, 225n.1, 225n.2
economy, 140–42, 202; justice and,
144; power, 145
education, 194–95
Edwards, Tilden, 206n.13
Egypt, 129–31, 169, 176–77, 179
Ehrenriech, Barbara, 95–96,
100n.20, 202, 206n.16
emerging paradigm, 2–4, 5–6, 207;
Bible, 13–14, 15, 43–60; faith,
25–42; God, 61–79; Jesus,
80–100; vision of Christian life,
13–14, 149; vision of Christian
tradition, 13–14
Enlightenment, 11, 12, 13, 29, 63,
68, 208, 211
environment, 143–44
Eucharist, 58, 97, 158, 165, 213
evolution, 51
exclusivism, Christian, 3, 4,
111, 220
external forms, 218–19

F
faith, 3, 10, 25–42; as *assensus*,
28–31, 37–39; centrality of, 27–28;
in the cross, 96; emerging paradigm, 25–42; as *fidelitas*, 32–34;
as *fiducia*, 31–32; four meanings
of, 28–37; as *visio*, 34–37; the
way of the heart, 25–42
fidelitas, faith as, 32–34
fidelity, 32–34
fiducia, faith as, 31–32

"flatland" modernity, 214, 225n.8
forgiveness, 168–70
formation, 190–200; of Christian
character, 192; of Christian
identity, 190–92
Foster, Richard J., 125n.25, 206n.12
Fowler, James, 42n.11
Francis, St., 97–98
Freedman, David Noel, 184n.8
friendship, Christian, 200
fundamentalism, 6

G
Gallup, George Jr., 20n.3
Gandhi, Mahatma, 92
Garden of Eden, 49–50, 51, 114,
166, 176
gays and lesbians, 3, 4, 139
Gilkey, Langdon, 184n.7
God, 3, 17, 38, 45, 61–79; character
of, 74–78; concepts of, 65–70;
declining importance in Western
culture, 62–65; earlier paradigm,
61; emerging paradigm, 61–79;
heart of, 80–100; the heart of
reality, 61–79; Jesus as metaphor
and sacrament of, 96–99; justice
and, 126–48; Kingdom of,
126–48; panentheism, 65–70;
paying attention to, 189–90; as
personal, 70–73; "retail," 71, 72;
supernatural theism, 65, 68–70;
"wholesale," 71, 72
Gomes, Peter, 146n.2, 205n.5
Good Friday, 92, 100n.12, 138
gospels, 99n.5, 107–11; dying and
rising in, 107–11; nature of,
84–86; synoptic, 107–9

grace, 11, 76, 95, 220
"great harlot," 137
Green, Garrett, 20*n*.4

H

Hammarskjöld, Dag, 163, 163*n*.9
healer, Jesus as, 90
heart, 26; Bible and, 43–60; closed,
    151–54; faith and, 25–42; God
    and, 61–79, 80–100; home and,
    207–26; Jesus and, 80–100; of
    justice, 126–48; of the matter,
    187–206; meaning of, 1–2;
    metaphor for the self, 149–51;
    new, 103–25; opening the,
    149–63; practice and, 187–206;
    of reality, 61–79; of the
    tradition, 43–60; transforming
    the, 164–86; way of the, 25–42
heaven, 10, 182; salvation as, 171–72
Hebrew Bible, 47, 75, 76, 87, 172,
    175–77, 180, 221; God's passion
    for justice in, 129–31
Herberg, Will, 225*n*.2
Heschel, Abraham, 163*n*.6
Hick, John, 226*n*.16
Hinduism, 209, 210, 217
historical product, Bible as, 13, 43,
    45–46, 48–49
Holocaust, 36, 67, 196
Horsley, Richard, 147*n*.13
Huntington, Samuel, 226*n*.13
hymns, 157–58, 224

I

identity formation, Christian,
    190–92

idolatry, 33
imperial power, use of, 144–45
individualism, 128
individual-spiritual-personal
    transformation, 103–25
intentionality, 119–21
internal core, 218
intervention, divine, 66–67
Islam, 80, 119, 188, 209, 210, 211,
    216, 217, 223
Israel, 45, 46, 47, 49, 75, 129, 130,
    169, 178

J

James, William, 61, 63, 71, 78*n*.1,
    78*n*.11, 117–18, 123, 125*n*.26,
    205*n*.4, 217
Jerusalem, 108–9; temple in, 94, 176
Jesus, 3, 4, 11, 15, 17, 26, 37–38,
    80–100, 105, 131, 177, 221; birth
    of, 52–53, 81; crucifixion,
    112–13; death and rising, 54, 81,
    82–83, 91–96, 97, 107–13, 171;
    earlier paradigm, 81–82;
    emerging paradigm, 80–100;
    faith in the cross, 96; heart of
    God, 80–100; is Lord, 135–36;
    meaning of christological
    language, 86–89; as metaphor
    and sacrament of God, 96–99;
    nature of the gospels, 84–86;
    post-Easter, 82–83; pre-Easter,
    82–83, 89–91; "the way" of, 108–9
Jewish mystic, Jesus as, 89–90
Jones, Alan, 163*n*.1
Joseph, 100*n*.12
Judaism, 80, 88, 89–90, 129, 135,
    188, 208, 210, 211, 217, 223

justice: God of, 75–77; heart of,
126–48; in Hebrew Bible,
129–31; meanings for our time,
138–45; in New Testament,
131–38; practice and, 193, 195,
200–204

K

Kaufman, Gordon, 213, 225n.6
Kavanaugh, Aidan, 41n.3
Keating, Thomas, 69, 116, 125n.24,
199, 205n.11
Keen, Sam, 42n.11
Keillor, Garrison, 51
Kierkegaard, Søren, 31
King, Martin Luther Jr., 92, 206n.12
Kingdom of God, 126–48; New
Testament, 131–35
Knitter, Paul F., 226n.15
Küng, Hans, 20n.4

L

Lamott, Anne, 197, 205n.8
Lane, Belden, 70, 78n.10
Lao Tzu, 70, 119, 216
lecto divina, 198
Lent, 160
Lewis, C. S., 2, 86, 99n.6
life, Christian, 3, 9, 101–226; in age
of pluralism, 207–26; Bible and,
59–60; born-again metaphor,
103–25; earlier paradigm, 9–12,
18; emerging paradigm, 13–14,
149; individual-spiritual-personal
transformation, 103–25; justice
and, 126–48; opening the heart,
149–63; practice, 187–206;

social-political transformation,
103–4, 126–48, 201;
transforming the heart, 164–86
Lindbeck, George, 213, 225n.7
Lindsey, D. Michael, 20n.3
literalism, biblical, 4, 8–9, 12, 15, 16,
43–44, 49–57, 81–82
liturgical words, 158–60
Lord's Prayer, 131, 133–35, 158–59,
165
love, 11, 40, 122–23; God of, 75–77
Luther, Martin, 36–37, 76, 118

M

Mackenzie, Ross, 185n.21
Macquarrie, John, 60n.6
Mann, Thomas, 50, 52
Martos, Joseph, 60n.6
McFague, Sallie, 204
McLaren, Brian, 20n.4
media, Christian, 21–7
meditation, 198
Menninger, Karl, 184n.3
Merton, Thomas, 155, 156
metaphor, 36, 84; Bible as, 49–57,
59, 60; born-again, 103–25; as
bridge, 56–57; in gospels, 84–85;
heart, as metaphor for the self,
149–51; Jesus as metaphor of
God, 96–99; thin places, 149–53;
truth of, 49–56
modernity, 11–12, 212, 214
Moses, 53, 80, 129–30, 169
movement initiator, Jesus as, 91
Muhammad, 80, 119
Muller, Wayne, 206n.13
Murphy, Nancey, 20n.4
music, 157–58, 224

Muslims, 80, 119, 188, 209, 210, 211, 216, 217, 223

N
Nasr, Seyyed Hossein, 226n.11, 226n.12
Native Americans, 51, 156
near-death experiences, 181
Newell, Philip, 163n.2
Nicene Creed, 39, 45
Nicodemus, 105–6, 142
Niebuhr, H. Richard, 34, 36, 41n.9
Niebuhr, Reinhold, 166–67, 184n.5, 185n.10
Nolan, Albert, 83, 99n.4
nonreligious worldview, 63
nourishment, practice as, 192–200
Nouwen, Henri, 100n.21

O
opening the heart, 149–63
ordination of women, 3
orthodoxy, 16, 29

P
Palmer, Parker, 124n.21
Pallis, Marco, 226n.12
panentheism, 65–70
papal infallibility, 7, 12, 21n.6, 212
paradigm change, time of, 5–6
Pascal, Blaise, 117
passion narratives, 97
Paul, 28, 36, 76, 93, 94, 117, 121–22, 123n.12, 135, 155, 173, 174, 178, 183, 201; on dying and rising, 109–11

paying attention to God, 189–90
Peck, M. Scott, 90
personal, God as, 70–73
Peters, Ted, 184n.7
Phillips, Kevin, 140, 148n.21, 148n.22, 148n.23, 148n.24, 148n.25
Pilate, 201
pluralism, religious, 46, 208–11; being Christian in an age of, 207–26
political transformation, 103–4, 126–48, 201
practice, 187–206; communities of, 214–15; compassion and justice, 193, 200–204; formation and nourishment, 190–200; purposes of, 189–93
prayer, 196–99
primordial tradition, 217–18, 221
Protestant Reformation, 4, 27–28, 42n.12, 76, 188, 220
purgatory, 182

Q
Q, 99n.5, 123n.5
Qur'an, 80

R
reality, 61–79; God and, 61–79; heart of, 61–79; worldview and, 62–65
reductionist understanding of religion, 211–12
reincarnation, 182
religious worldview, 63–65
repentance, 179–84

requirements, 10–11; God of, 75

resurrection, and "born again" metaphor, 107–13

Reumann, John, 146n.5

Revelation, book of, 59, 87, 121, 131, 183

Roma, 137–38

Roman Empire, early Christian perceptions of, 136–38

S

sacrament: Bible as, 13, 43, 57–59, 60; Jesus as metaphor and sacrament of God, 96–99

sacramental understanding of religion, 213–15

sacred scripture, Bible as, 47–48

salvation, 76, 171–86; afterlife and, 181–84; as heaven, 171–72; response and, 179; sin, repentance, and, 179–84; social and personal, 178–79; stories of, 175–78; in this life, 172–75

Schmidt, Richard, 206n.12

Scroggs, Robin, 42n.10, 125n.28

Scudder, Vida, 201, 203, 206n.15

self-consciousness, birth of, 114–17

Sellner, Edward C., 163n.2

separated self, birth of, 114–17, 168

similarities, religious, 215–19

sin, 94–95, 164–71, 179–86; definition of, 166–67; salvation, repentance, and, 179–84; thinking about, 164–71

Sjoberg, Leif, 206n.12

slavery, 121, 128–29, 176

Smith, Huston, 63, 64, 78n.2, 78n.4, 214, 217, 219, 223, 226n.14

Smith, James Bryan, 125n.25, 206n.12

Smith, Wilfrid Cantwell, 39, 41n.4, 42n.12, 60n.4

social prophet, Jesus as, 91

social transformation, 103–4, 126–48

Soelle, Dorothee, 187, 205n.1

"Son of God" metaphor, 87–88

Stark, Rodney, 148n.18

Stendahl, Krister, 60n.4, 89, 222

Stone, Lloyd, 226n.17

Streng, Frederick J., 226n.9

Suchocki, Marjorie Hewitt, 205n.10

Sunday school, 194–95

supernatural theism, 65, 68–70

T

Tamminen, K., 124n.22

Taoism, 70, 119, 216

Tao te Ching, 70, 119

Taylor, Barbara Brown, 206n.12

tax policy, 141–42, 203

Ten Commandments, 33, 166

theological diversity, 17

thin places, 149–63; Christian practices and, 157–61

Thompson, Marjorie, 206n.13

Throckmorton, Burton H., 147n.11

Tickle, Phyllis, 148n.17

Tillich, Paul, 69, 166, 167, 184n.6, 185n.10, 206n.12

transformation, 17; communal-social-political, 103–4, 126–48, 201; communities of, 215; individual-spiritual-personal, 103–25

transubstantiation, 60n.7

Trinity, 83

trust, 31–32, 36
Tutu, Desmond, 179

V
verbal prayer, 196–98
Vincent, Ken, 124n.22
violence, 153, 154
visio, faith as, 34–37

W
Wallis, Jim, 205n.4
wealth, 140–42
Weber, Max, 78n.8
wedding at Cana, 84–85

Weil, Simone, 159
Whitehead, A. N., 42n.9
why be Christian?, 220–25
Wiebe, Phillip H., 99n.3
Wink, Walter, 93, 100n.16
wisdom teacher, Jesus as, 90
worldview, 62–65; religious vs.
    nonreligious, 63–65; significance
    of, 62
Wright, N. T., 99n.1, 147n.7

Z
Zen Buddhism, 119